RICK STEVES' SCANDINAVIA

1997

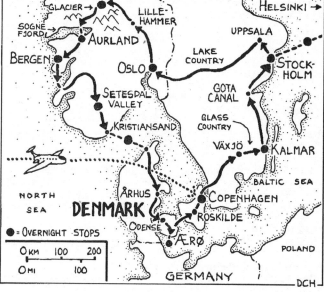

John Muir Publications
Santa Fe, New Mexico

Other JMP travel guidebooks by Rick Steves
   Asia Through the Back Door (with Bob Effertz)
   Europe 101: History and Art for the Traveler
      (with Gene Openshaw)
   Europe Through the Back Door
   Mona Winks: Self-Guided Tours of Europe's Top Museums
      (with Gene Openshaw)
   Rick Steves' Baltics & Russia (with Ian Watson)
   Rick Steves' Europe
   Rick Steves' France, Belgium & the Netherlands (with Steve Smith)
   Rick Steves' Germany, Austria & Switzerland
   Rick Steves' Great Britain &Ireland
   Rick Steves' Italy
   Rick Steves' Spain & Portugal
   Rick Steves' Phrase Books: French, German, Italian,
      Spanish/Portuguese, and French/Italian/German

Thanks to Brian Carr Smith and Jane Klausen for research help and to
my wife, Anne, for making home my favorite travel destination.
Thanks also to Thor, Hanne, Geir, Hege, and Kari-Anne, our Norwegian family. In loving memory of Berit Kristiansen, whose house was
my house for twenty years of Norwegian travel.

John Muir Publications, P.O. Box 613, Santa Fe, NM 87504
Copyright © 1997, 1996, 1995 by Rick Steves
Cover © 1997 by John Muir Publications
All rights reserved

Printed in the United States of America
First printing February 1997

Previously published as *2 to 22 Days in Norway, Sweden, and Denmark*
© 1988, 1989, 1991, 1992, 1994

For the latest on Rick's lectures, guidebooks, tours, and PBS-TV
series, contact Europe Through the Back Door, Box 2009, Edmonds,
WA 98020, tel. 206/771-8303, fax 206/771-0833, online at
ricksteves@aol.com, or on the web at http://www.ricksteves.com.

ISSN 1085-7206
ISBN 1-56261-331-6

Europe Through the Back Door Editor Risa Laib
John Muir Publications Editors Chris Hayhurst, Dianna Delling
Production Marie J.T. Vigil, Nikki Rooker
Maps David C. Hoerlein
Cover Design Cowgirls Design, Kathryn Lloyd-Strongin
Design Linda Braun
Typesetting Lani Bevacqua
Printer Banta Company
Cover Photo Nyhavn, Copenhagen; Leo de Wys Inc./Vladpans

Distributed to the book trade by
Publishers Group West
Emeryville, California

The Best Destinations in Scandinavia

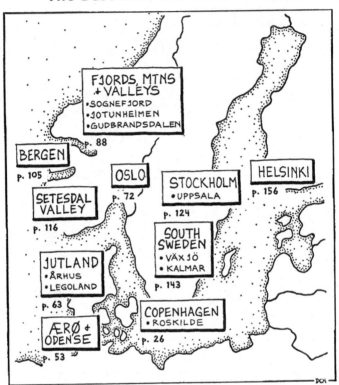

CONTENTS

Introduction **1**

Planning Your Trip 2 • Trip Costs 2 • Exchange Rates 3 • Prices, Times, and Discounts 4 • When to Go 4 • Sightseeing Priorities 5 • Red Tape 5 • Banking 5 • Travel Smart 8 • Tourist Information 8 • Recommended Guidebooks 9 • Rick Steves' Books and Videos 9 • Maps 10 • Transportation 11 • Telephones and Mail 14 • Sleeping 15 • Eating 19 • The Language Barrier 21 • One Region, Different Countries 22 • Stranger in a Strange Land 23 • Back Door Manners 23 • Send Me a Postcard, Drop Me a Line 23 • Back Door Travel Philosophy 24

Denmark
    Copenhagen **26**
    Central Denmark: Ærø and Odense **53**
    Jutland: Legoland and Århus **63**

Norway
    Oslo **72**
    Fjords, Mountains, and Valleys **88**
    Bergen **105**
    South Norway's Setesdal Valley **116**

Sweden
    Stockholm **124**
    South Sweden: Växjö and Kalmar **143**

Finland
    Helsinki **156**

Appendix **173**

Let's Talk Telephones 173 • Public Transportation 174 • Numbers and Stumblers 177 • Metric Conversion 178 • Climate 178 • Road Scholar Feedback Form 179 • Faxing Your Hotel Reservation 181

Index **182**

INTRODUCTION

This book breaks Scandinavia into its top big-city, small-town, and rural destinations. It gives you all the information and opinions necessary to wring the maximum value out of your limited time and money in each of these destinations. If you plan a month or less in Scandinavia and have a normal appetite for information, this lean and mean little book is all you need. Experiencing the culture, people, and natural wonders of Scandinavia economically and hassle-free has been my goal for over 20 years of traveling, tour guiding, and travel writing. With this book, I pass on to you the lessons I've learned, updated for 1997.

Rick Steves' Scandinavia is your smiling Swede, your Nordic navigator, a tour guide in your pocket. This book is balanced to include a comfortable mix of exciting capital cities and cozy small towns. It covers the predictable biggies and mixes in a healthy dose of Back Door intimacy. Along with seeing Tivoli Gardens, Hans Christian Andersen's house, and *The Little Mermaid*, you'll take a bike tour of a sleepy remote Danish isle, dock at a time-passed fjord village, and wander among eerie, prehistoric monoliths in Sweden. To save time, maximize diversity, and avoid tourist burnout, I've been very selective. We won't cruise both the Geirangerfjord and the Sognefjord, just the better of the two—Sognefjord.

The best is, of course, only my opinion. But after more than two busy decades of travel writing, lecturing, and tour guiding, I've developed a sixth sense of what tickles the traveler's fancy.

This Information Is Accurate and Up-to-Date

This book is updated every year. Most publishers of guidebooks that cover a country from top to bottom can afford an update only every two or three years (and even then, it's often by letter). Since this book is selective, covering only the places I think make the top month or so, I'm able to get it updated each year. Even with an annual update, things change. But if you're traveling with the current edition of this book, I guarantee you're using the most up-to-date information available. If you're packing an old book, you'll learn the seriousness of your mistake . . . in Scandinavia. Your trip costs about $10 per waking hour. Your time is valuable. This guidebook saves lots of time.

Planning Your Trip

This book is organized by destinations. Each of these destinations is a mini-vacation on its own, filled with exciting sights and homey, affordable places to stay. In each chapter, you'll find:

Planning Your Time, a suggested schedule with thoughts on how to best use your limited time.

Orientation, including tourist information, city transportation, and an easy-to-read map designed to make the text clear and your arrival smooth.

Sights with ratings: ▲▲▲—Don't miss; ▲▲—Try hard to see; ▲—Worthwhile if you can make it; no rating—Worth knowing about.

Sleeping and **Eating**, with addresses and phone numbers of my favorite budget hotels and restaurants.

Transportation Connections to nearby destinations by train and route tips for drivers.

The **Appendix** is a traveler's tool kit, with telephone tips, a climate chart, and public transportation routes.

Browse through this book, choose your favorite destinations, and link them up. Then have a great trip! You'll travel like a temporary local, getting the absolute most out of every mile, minute, and kroner. You won't waste time on mediocre sights because, unlike other guidebooks, I cover only the best. Since your major financial pitfall is lousy expensive hotels, I've worked hard to assemble the best accommodations values for each stop. And as you travel the route I know and love, I'm happy you'll be meeting some of my favorite Scandinavian people.

Trip Costs

Five components make up the cost of your trip: airfare, surface transportation, room and board, sightseeing, and shopping/entertainment/miscellaneous.

Airfare: Don't try to sort through the mess. Get and use a good travel agent. A basic round-trip U.S.A.-to-Copenhagen flight should cost $800–$1,000, depending on where you fly from and when. Always consider saving time and money in Europe by flying "open jaws" (for instance, flying into Copenhagen and out of Bergen).

Surface Transportation: For a three-week whirlwind trip of all my recommended destinations, allow $500 per person for public transportation (first class, 21-day Scanrail pass and extra boat rides; only $400 if you go second class), or $600 per person (based on two people sharing car and gas) for a three-week car rental, tolls, gas, and insurance. Car rental is usually cheapest if arranged from the U.S.A.

Room and Board: In 1997, you can eat and sleep well in Scandinavia for $60 a day for room and board. A $60-a-day budget allows $10 for lunch, $15 for dinner, and $35 for lodging (based on two people splitting the cost of a $70 double room that includes breakfast). That's basic and alcohol-free, but doable. Students and tightwads do it on $40 ($15–$20 a bed, $20 for meals and snacks). But budget sleeping and eating require the skills and information covered in this book.

Sightseeing: In big cities, figure $5–$10 per major sight, $2 for minor ones, and $25 for splurge experiences (e.g., tours or folk concerts). The major cities have cards giving you a 24-hour free run of the public transit system and entrance to all the sights for about $20. An overall average of $15 per day works for most people. Don't skimp here. After all, this category directly powers most of the experiences all the other expenses are designed to make possible.

Shopping/Entertainment/Miscellaneous: In Scandinavia, this category can brutalize your budget. While Scandinavia is expensive, transportation passes, groceries, alternative accommodations, admissions, and enjoying nature are affordable (about what you'd pay in England or Italy). When things are expensive, remind yourself you're not getting less for your travel dollar. Up here, there simply aren't any lousy or cheap alternatives to classy, cozy, sleek Scandinavia. Electronic eyes flush youth-hostel toilets and breakfasts are all-you-can-eat.

If you take full advantage of this book, you will save a shipload of money and days of headaches. Read it carefully from start to finish. Many of the general skills and tricks used in Copenhagen work in Oslo and Stockholm as well.

Exchange Rates

I've priced things in local currencies throughout the book. While each of the Scandinavian countries' kroner (crowns) have different values, they are close.

> 5.7 Danish kroner = $1
> 6.3 Norwegian kroner = $1
> 6.4 Swedish kroner = $1

Kroner are decimalized: 100 øre = 1 krone. Kroner are not accepted abroad (except at foreign exchange services and banks).

Standard abbreviations are: Danish krone, DKK; Swedish krone, SEK; and Norwegian krone, NOK. I'll keep it simple. For all three countries, I'll use the krone abbreviation, "kr," and "6 kr = $1" as the exchange rate. To translate local Scandinavian prices into U.S. dollars, divide by six (35 kr = about $6).

Finland's markka (FIM or mk) is worth about 20 cents (4.5 mk = $1). To convert to U.S. dollars, divide Finnish prices by five (40 mk = about $8).

Prices, Times, and Discounts

The prices in this book, as well as the hours and telephone numbers, are accurate as of mid-1996. I know you'll understand that this, like any other guidebook, starts to yellow even before it's printed.

In Scandinavia—and in this book—you'll be using the 24-hour clock. After 12:00 noon, keep going—13:00, 14:00, etc. For anything over 12, subtract 12 and add p.m. (14:00 is 2:00 p.m.)

This book lists peak-season hours for sightseeing attractions (July and August). Off-season, roughly October through April, expect shorter hours and fewer activities. Confirm your sightseeing plans locally, especially when traveling between October and May.

I have not listed special age discounts in this book. But in keeping with its social orientation, Scandinavia is Europe's most generous corner when it comes to youth, student, senior, and family discounts. If you are any of the above, always mention it. Students should travel with the ISIC card (International Student Identity Card, normally available at university foreign study offices in North America). Spouses often pay half price when doing things as a couple. Children usually pay half price or less (for example, in hostels).

When to Go

Summer is by far the best. Scandinavia bustles and glistens under the July and August sun. Scandinavian schools get out around June 20, most local industries take July off, and the British and central Europeans tend to visit Scandinavia in August. You'll notice crowds during these times, but it's never as crowded as southern Europe. While you could do the trip without hotel reservations, I compare prices and reserve my favorite places by calling a day or two in advance as I go.

"Shoulder season" travel (in late May, early June, and

September), with minimal crowds, decent weather, and sights and tourist fun spots still open, lacks the vitality of summer (although the big cities tend to be very crowded in early June). Things quiet down when the local kids go back to school (around August 20).

Winter has no tourist crowds for good reason. It's a bad time to explore Scandinavia. Many sights and accommodations are closed or open on a limited schedule. Business travelers drive hotel prices way up. Winter weather can be cold and dreary, and nighttime will draw the shades on your sightseeing well before dinner.

Sightseeing Priorities

Depending on the length of your trip, here are my recommended priorities:

3 days:	Copenhagen, Stockholm, Oslo, connected by night trains
5 days, add:	More time in capitals
7 days, add:	"Norway in a Nutshell" fjord trip, Bergen
10 days, add:	14-hour cruise to Helsinki, and slow down
14 days, add:	Ærø, Odense, Roskilde, Frederiksborg
17 days, add:	Jutland, Kalmar
21 days, add:	Lillehammer, Jotunheimen, Växjö, Setesdal
24 days, add:	Riga, Latvia, and Tallinn, Estonia
30 days, add:	Side trip to St. Petersburg, and slow down

Red Tape

Traveling throughout this region requires only a passport—no shots and no visas. Border crossings between Norway, Sweden, Denmark, and Finland are a wave-through. When you change countries, however, you do change money, postage stamps, and more. Local sales taxes on souvenirs and gifts purchased are refunded when you leave Scandinavia. When purchasing expensive items, ask the local merchant for tax-refund instructions.

Banking

Bring traveler's checks in dollars along with some plastic (ATM, credit, or debit cards). Banking in Scandinavia is straightforward. You'll have almost no loss because of the buy and sell rates (they're within about 2 percent of each other). Exchange rates are nearly standard. The banks make their

Whirlwind Three-Week Tour

money off a stiff 20-kr–40-kr-per-check fee. Bring traveler's checks in large denominations. If you have only small-denomination checks, shop around.

In Norway, some banks charge 1 or 2 percent rather than per check. In many cases, small cash exchanges are cheaper outside of banks, at places that offer worse rates but smaller (or no) fees such as exchange desks on international boats and the handy FOREX windows at the Copenhagen and Stockholm train stations. American Express offices in each capital change AmExCo checks (and sometimes other brands as well) for no extra fee. Even with their worse-than-banks' exchange rates, those changing less than $1,000 usually save by using AmExCo. Post offices (with longer hours, nearly the same rates, and smaller fees) can be a good place to change money.

ATM machines are everywhere, and offer a good exchange rate. To get a cash advance from a bank machine

Scandinavia's Best Three-Week Trip

Days	Plan	Sleep in
1	Arrive in Copenhagen	Copenhagen
2	Copenhagen	Copenhagen
3	Copenhagen	Copenhagen
4	North Zealand, into Sweden	Växjö
5	Växjö, Kalmar, Glass Country	Kalmar
6	Kalmar to Stockholm	Stockholm
7	Stockholm	Stockholm
8	Stockholm	boat
9	Helsinki	boat
10	Uppsala to Oslo	Oslo
11	Oslo	Oslo
12	Oslo	Oslo
13	Lillehammer, Gudbrandsdalen	Jotunheimen/ Sogndal
14	Jotunheimen Country Aurland	Sogndal/
15	Sognefjord, Norway in Nutshell	Bergen
16	Bergen	Bergen
17	Long drive south, Setesdal	boat
18	Jutland, Århus, Legoland	Århus/Billund
19	Jutland to Ærø	Ærøskøbing
20	Ærø	Ærøskøbing
21	Odense, Roskilde	Copenhagen

While this three-week itinerary is designed to be done by car, it can be done by train and bus. Scandinavia in 21 days by train is most efficient with a little reworking: I'd go overnight whenever possible on any train ride six or more hours long. Streamline by doing North Zealand, Odense, and Ærø as a three-day side trip from Copenhagen, skipping the Växjö–Stockholm train (there is no Copenhagen–Kalmar overnight train). The Bergen/Setesdal/Århus/Copenhagen leg is possible on public transit, but Setesdal (between Bergen and Kristiansand) is not worth the trouble if you don't have the freedom a car gives you.

If you really want to see Legos and the Bogman, do Jutland from Copenhagen. A flight home from Bergen is wonderfully efficient. Otherwise, it's about 20 hours by train from Bergen to Copenhagen via Oslo. British Midland has $139 flights from Bergen to London (800/788-0555 in U.S.A.).

you'll need a four-digit PIN (numbers only, no letters) with your bankcard. Before you go, verify with your bank that your card will work, then use it whenever possible.

Visa and MasterCard are more commonly accepted than American Express. Just like at home, credit or debit cards work easily at larger hotels, restaurants, and shops, but smaller businesses prefer payment in hard kroner.

You should use a money belt. Thieves target tourists. A money belt (call 206/771-8303 for our free newsletter/catalog) provides peace of mind. You can carry lots of cash safely in a money belt.

Don't be petty about changing money. The greatest avoidable money-changing expense is having to waste time every few days returning to a bank. Change a week's worth of money, get big bills, stuff them in your money belt, and travel!

Travel Smart

Upon arrival in a new town, lay the groundwork for a smooth departure. Reread this book as you travel and visit local tourist information offices. Buy a phone card and use it for reservations, reconfirmations, and double-checking hours. Enjoy the friendliness of the local people. Ask questions. Most locals are eager to point you in their idea of the right direction. Wear your money belt, learn the local currency, and develop a simple formula to quickly estimate rough prices in dollars. Keep a notepad in your pocket for organizing your thoughts, and practice the virtue of simplicity. Those who expect to travel smart, do.

Plan ahead for banking, laundry, post office chores, and picnics. Mix intense and relaxed periods. Every trip (and every traveler) needs at least a few slack days. Pace yourself. Assume you will return.

Tourist Information

Any town with much tourism has a well-organized, English-speaking tourist information office (which I'll abbreviate as "TI" in this book). The TI should be your first stop in a new city. Prepare. Have a list of questions and a proposed plan to double-check. If you're arriving late, telephone ahead (and try to get a map for your next destination from a TI in the town you're leaving).

While the TIs offer room-finding services, this is a good deal only if you're in search of summer and weekend deals on business hotels. The TIs can help you with small pensions and private homes, but you'll save both yourself and your host money by going direct with the listings in this book.

The **Scandinavian National Tourist Office** in the U.S.A. is a wealth of information (P.O. Box 4649, Grand Central Station, New York, NY 10163, 212/949-2333, fax 212/983-5260). Before your trip, get their free general information booklet about the Scandinavian countries and request any specific information you may want (city maps, calendars of events, and lists of festivals).

Recommended Guidebooks

Especially if you'll be traveling beyond my recommended destinations, you may want some supplemental information. When you consider the improvements they'll make in your $3,000 vacation, $30 for extra maps and books is money well spent. Especially for several people traveling by car, the weight and expense are negligible. One simple budget tip can easily save the price of an extra guidebook.

Lonely Planet's *Scandinavian & Baltic Europe* is thorough, well-researched, and packed with good maps and hotel recommendations for low- to moderate-budget travelers. The hip Rough Guide's *Scandinavia* is thick. *Let's Go: Europe* has only skimpy chapters on Scandinavia. Because of the relatively small market, there just aren't many guidebooks out on Scandinavia. I think of all my European destination guidebooks, this one fills the biggest void.

Rick Steves' Books and Videos

Rick Steves' Europe Through the Back Door (Santa Fe, N.M.: John Muir Publications, 1997) gives you budget travel skills on minimizing jet lag, packing light, planning your itinerary, traveling by car or train, finding budget beds without reservations, changing money, avoiding rip-offs, outsmarting thieves, hurdling the language barrier, staying healthy, taking great photographs, using your bidet, and much more. The book also includes chapters on 40 of my favorite "Back Doors," three of which are in Scandinavia.

Rick Steves' Country Guides are a series of eight guidebooks covering Europe, the Baltics/Russia, Britain/Ireland, France/Belgium/Netherlands, Germany/Austria/Switzerland, Italy, and Spain/Portugal, just as this one covers Scandinavia.

These guidebooks are updated annually and are published each January.

Europe 101: History and Art for the Traveler (co-written with Gene Openshaw; Santa Fe, N.M.: John Muir Publications, 1996) gives you the story of Europe's people, history, and art. Written for smart people who were asleep during their history and art classes before they knew they were going to Europe, *101* helps resurrect the rubble. (Like most European histories, it has little to say about Scandinavia, but it will broaden your knowledge of Europe and give depth to your sightseeing.)

Mona Winks: Self-Guided Tours of Europe's Top Museums (co-written with Gene Openshaw; Santa Fe, N.M.: John Muir Publications, 1996) gives you one- to three-hour self-guided tours through Europe's 20 most exhausting and important museums (but nothing on Scandinavia).

While I've designed a series of four phrase books, there is virtually no language barrier in Scandinavia, so I wouldn't bother with a phrase book for traveling here.

My television series, *Travels in Europe with Rick Steves*, may re-air on your local PBS station. It's also available as a series of information-packed videotapes, along with my two-hour slide-show lecture on Scandinavia (call us at 206/771-8303 for our free newsletter/catalog).

Maps

Train travelers can do fine with a simple rail map (such as the one that comes with your train pass) and with city maps picked up from the TI as you travel. But drivers shouldn't skimp on maps—get one good overall road map for Scandinavia (either the Michelin Scandinavia or the Kummerly and Frey Southern Scandinavia 1:1,000,000 edition). The only detailed map worth considering is the "Southern Norway-North" (Sør Norge-nord, 1:325,000) by Cappelens Kart ($12 in Scandinavian bookstores). Study the key carefully to get the most sightseeing value out of your map. Excellent city and regional maps are available from local TIs, and are usually for free.

The maps in this book, drawn by Dave Hoerlein, are concise and simple. Dave, who is well-traveled in Scandinavia, has designed the maps to help you locate recommended places and the tourist offices, where you'll find more in-depth maps of the necessary cities or regions (cheap or free).

Transportation

Getting to Scandinavia
Copenhagen is the most direct and least expensive Scandinavian capital to fly into from the U.S.A. It is also Europe's gateway to Scandinavia from points south. There are often cheaper flights from the U.S.A. into Frankfurt and Amsterdam than into Copenhagen, but it's a long, rather dull, one-day drive from there (with a two-hour, $60 per car and passenger ferry crossing at Puttgarten, Germany). By train, the trip is effortless—overnight from Amsterdam, Paris, Frankfurt, or Berlin. The $120-trip is free with your Eurailpass (but not with the Scanrail pass).

In Scandinavia: By Car or Train?
While a car gives you the ultimate in mobility and freedom, enables you to search for hotels more easily, and carries your bags for you, the train zips you effortlessly from city to city, usually dropping you in the center and near the tourist office. Cars are great in the countryside but an expensive headache in places like Oslo, Copenhagen, and Bergen. Three or four people travel cheaper by car. With a few exceptions, trains cover my recommended destinations wonderfully.

Trains
The Scanrail pass is one of the great Nordic bargains. There are two types (each with several variations): one sold in the U.S.A. (the best value for most travelers) and one in Scandinavia. The one sold in Scandinavia is purchased easily on the spot at any major train station. Both give you free run of many boats (such as Stockholm to Finland) and all trains in the region (though they do not cover supplements for Sweden's X2000 trains and Norway's Myrdal–Flåm segment). Both passes go easy on the upgrade to first class. Even though Scandinavian second class is like southern European first class, for $7 a day extra, you might consider first class.

A Eurailpass, which costs much more than a comparable Scanrail pass, is a good value only for those coming to Scandinavia from central Europe (a three-week first-class Eurailpass costs about $678).

Scanrail 'n' Drive passes offer a flexible and economical way to mix rail and car rental (handy if you plan to explore

Cost of Public Transportation

SCANRAIL PASS

	1st class	2nd class	2nd class under 26	2nd class over 55	1st class over 55
Any 5 out of 15 days	$222	$176	$132	$153	$195
Any 10 days out of 1 month	346	278	209	242	301
21 consecutive days	400	320	240	278	348
1 month of consecutive days	504	404	303	351	438

Trolls 4-11 half price. 1st class youth and senior passes are available.

SCANRAIL 'N DRIVE PASS

Any 5 rail days and 3 Hertz car days in a 15 day period.

	2 adults 1st	2 adults 2nd	1 adult 1st	1 adult 2nd	extra car days (maximum 5)
A-Economy car	$289	$249	$365	$325	$55
B-Compact car	319	279	425	385	75
C-Intermediate car	329	289	455	415	85

Extra fee for Finland car rental. You cannot buy extra rail days.

NORWAY RAILPASS

	1st class	2nd class
3 days in a month	$190	$135
7 consecutive days	250	190
14 consecutive days	330	255

Prices are about 20% less between October and April.
Kids 5-16 half price, under 4 free.

FINNRAIL PASS

	1st class	2nd class
3 days in a month	$179	$119
5 days in a month	249	169
10 days in a month	339	229

Children 6-17 half, under 6 free.

Scandinavia:
Point-to-point 2nd class rail fares in $US.

Sweden's Glass Country or the Norwegian mountains and fjords).

Reservations are required on the super-fast Danish and Swedish trains and on all long Norwegian trips.

Consider the efficiency of night travel. The *couchette* supplement (a bed in a compartment with two triple bunks) costs $20 beyond your first- or second-class ticket or pass. A "sleeper," giving you the privacy of a double or triple compartment, costs about $50 per bed.

Car Rental

Car rental is usually cheapest when arranged (well in advance) in the U.S. through your travel agent, rather than in Scandinavia. You'll want a weekly rate with unlimited mileage. If you're traveling for more than three weeks, ask about leasing a car. Each major rental agency has an office in the Copenhagen airport. Comparison-shop through your agent and Rafco, a small Danish company near the Copenhagen airport that rents nearly new Seat (Volkswagen) cars at almost troublemaking prices. The manager, Ken, promises my readers a 10 percent discount over his "Money Saver" rates: about $50/day (includes CDW insurance) to rent an economy Seat Ibiza for a minimum of 21 days. Similar deals exist on larger cars and minibuses. Rafco has small motor homes (ideal for families on a budget) for about $750/week (with gear, four–six beds, kitchen, WC, and a 10 percent discount for travelers with this book). For a brochure, contact Rafco, Englandsvej 380, DK-2770 Kastrup, Denmark, tel. 45/32 51 15 00, fax 45/32 51 10 89.

Driving

Except for the dangers posed by the scenic distractions and moose crossings, Scandinavia is a great place to drive. Your American license is accepted. Gas is expensive, over $4 per gallon (gas in Denmark is cheaper than in its northern neighbors); but roads are good (though nerve-wrackingly skinny in western Norway); traffic is generally sparse; drivers are sober and civil; signs and road maps are excellent; local road etiquette is similar to that of the U.S.; and seat belts are required. Use your headlights day and night; it's required in most of Scandinavia. Bikes whiz by close and quiet, so be on guard.

There are plenty of good facilities, gas stations, and scenic rest stops. Snow is a serious problem off-season in the mountains. Parking is a headache only in major cities, where expensive garages are safe and plentiful. Denmark uses a parking windshield-clock disk (free at TIs, post offices, and newsstands; set it when you arrive and be back before your posted time limit is up). Even in the Nordic countries, thieves break into cars. Park carefully, use the trunk, and show no valuables. Never drink and drive. Even one drink can get a driver into serious trouble.

As you navigate, you'll find town signs followed by the letters N, S, Ø, V, or C. These stand for north, south, east, west, and center, respectively, and understanding them will save you lots of wrong exits. Due to recent changes, many maps have the wrong road numbers. It's safest to navigate by town names.

Telephones and Mail

Smart travelers use the telephone every day: for making hotel reservations, calling tourist information offices, and phoning home. The key to dialing long distance is understanding area codes and having a phone card.

Scandinavia's phone cards aren't credit cards, just handy cards you insert in the phone instead of coins. Each country sells a card (usually in denominations of about $5 and $10) good for use only in that country. You can buy phone cards at post offices, newsstands, and tobacco shops.

Dialing Direct: Norway and Denmark do not use area codes. Just dial local numbers direct from anywhere in the country. Sweden and Finland do have area codes. When making calls within Sweden or Finland, include the entire area code (which starts with a zero).

Calling internationally, you'll need to:

1. Dial the international access code of the country you're calling from.

2. Then dial the country code of the country you're calling.

3. If the country uses area codes, dial the area code next, *omitting the initial zero*. If the country does not use area codes, skip this step.

4. Then dial the local number.

To call one of my favorite B&Bs in Copenhagen from anywhere in Denmark, just dial its local number directly (32 95 96 22). To call the Copenhagen B&B from the U.S., dial 011 (the U.S.'s international access code), 45 (Denmark's country code), then 32 95 96 22.

To call Stockholm's hostel-in-a-ship from anywhere in Sweden, dial 08 (Stockholm's area code), then the local number: 679-5015. To call the Stockholm hostel from the U.S., dial 011 (our international access code), 46 (Sweden's country code), 8 (Stockholm's area code without the zero), then 679-5015. To call my office from Sweden, dial 009 (Sweden's international access code), 1 (the U.S.'s country code),

206/771-8303. For a listing of international access codes and country codes, see the Appendix.

Hotel-room phones are a terrible rip-off for calls to the U.S.A. Never call home from your hotel room unless your hotel allows toll-free access to your USA Direct Service (many don't).

USA Direct Services: Calling the U.S.A. from any kind of phone is easy if you have an AT&T, MCI, or Sprint calling card. Each card company has a toll-free number in each European country that puts you in touch with an English-speaking operator who will take your card number and the number you want to call, put you through, and bill your home phone number for the call (at the cheaper U.S.A. rate of about $1 a minute plus a $2.50 service charge). You'll save money on calls of three minutes or more. Hanging up when you hear an answering machine is an expensive mistake—talk! Better yet, first use a coin or a Scandinavian phone card to call home for five seconds—long enough to say "call me," or to make sure an answering machine is off so you can call back, using your USA Direct number, to connect with a person. European time is six/nine hours ahead of the east/west coast of the U.S.A. For a list of AT&T, MCI, and Sprint calling-card operators, see the Appendix. Avoid using USA Direct for calls between European countries; it's much cheaper to call direct using coins or a Scandinavian phone card.

Mail: If you must have mail stops, consider a few pre-reserved hotels along your route or use American Express Mail Services. Most American Express offices will hold mail for one month. (They mail out a free listing of addresses.) This service is free to anyone using an AmExCo card or traveler's checks (and available for a small fee to others). Allow ten days for U.S.-to-Scandinavia mail delivery. Federal Express makes two-day deliveries, for a price. Phoning is so easy that I've dispensed with mail stops altogether.

Sleeping

Accommodations expenses will make or break your budget. Vagabonds sleep happily everywhere for $15 per night. An overall average of $60 per night per double is possible using this book's listings. Unless noted, the accommodations I've listed will hold a room with a phone call until 18:00 with no deposit, and the proprietors speak English. I like small, central, clean, traditional, friendly places that aren't listed in other guidebooks. Most places listed meet five of these six virtues.

In the interest of smart use of your time, I favor hotels and restaurants handy to your sightseeing activities and public transportation. Rather than list hotels scattered throughout a city, I choose a convenient, colorful neighborhood and recommend its best accommodations values, from $10 bunk beds to $140 doubles.

Tourist information offices' room-finding services, if you have no place in mind, can be worth the 30-kr fee. Be very clear about what you want. (Say "cheap," and mention that you have sheets or a sleeping bag, and whether you will take a twin or double, if you require a shower, and so on.) They know the hotel quirks and private-room scene better than anybody. Official price listings are often misleading, since they omit cheaper oddball rooms and special clearance deals.

To sleep cheap, bring your own sheet or sleeping bag and offer to provide it in low-priced establishments. This can save $10 per person per night, especially in rural areas. Families can get a price break; normally a child can sleep very cheaply in mom and dad's room. To get the most sleep for your dollar, pull the dark shades to keep out the very early morning sun.

Sleep Code

To save space while giving more specific information for people with special concerns, I've described my recommended hotels with a standard code. When there is a range of prices in one category, the price will fluctuate with the season, size of room, or length of stay. Prices listed are for the room, not per person (unless otherwise noted).

S = Single room or price for one person using a double.

D = Double or twin room. Double beds are usually big enough for non-romantic couples.

T = Three-person room (often a double bed with a single bed moved in).

Q = Four-adult room (extra child's bed is usually less).

b = Private bathroom with toilet and shower or tub. (Rooms without a "b" have access to a shower and toilet down the hall.)

CC = Accepts credit cards (**V** = Visa, **M** = MasterCard, **A** =American Express). If CC isn't mentioned, assume you'll need to pay cash.

If a hotel is listed in this book as "D-360 kr, Db-450 kr, CC:V," the hotel charges 360 kr (about $60) for a double room without a private bathroom, 450 kr (about $75) for a double with bathroom, and accepts Visa or hard kroner in payment.

Hotels

Hotels are expensive ($80–$150 doubles) with some exceptions. Business-class hotels dump prices to attract tourists with "summer" and "weekend" rates (Friday, Saturday, and sometimes Sunday). The much-advertised hotel discount cards or clubs offer nothing more than these rates, which are available to everyone anyway. To sleep in a fancy hotel, it's cheapest to arrive without a reservation and let the local tourist office book you a room. Hotels are expensive, but when a classy, modern $200 place has a $100 summer special that includes two $10 buffet breakfasts, the dumpy $60 hotel room without breakfast becomes less exciting.

There are actually several tiers of rates, including tourist office, weekend, summer, summer weekend, and walk-in. "Walk-ins" at the end of a quiet day can often get a room even below the summer rate. Many modern hotels have "combi" rooms (singles with a sofa that makes into a perfectly good double), which are cheaper than a full double. Also, many places have low-grade older rooms, considered unacceptable for the general public and often used by workers on weekdays outside of summer. If you're on a budget, ask for cheaper rooms with no windows or no water. And if a hotel is not full, any day can become a summer day.

Hostels

Scandinavian hostels, Europe's finest, are open to travelers of all ages. They offer classy facilities, members' kitchens, cheap hot meals (often breakfast buffets), plenty of doubles (for a few extra kroner), and great people experiences. Receptionists speak English and will hold a room if you promise to arrive by 18:00. Many close in the off-season. Buy a membership card before you leave home. Those without cards are admitted for a $5-per-night guest membership fee. Bring bedsheets from home or plan on renting them for about $5 per stay. You'll find lots of Volvos in hostel parking lots, as Scandinavians know hostels provide the best (and usually only) $15 beds in town. Hosteling is ideal for the two-bunk family (four-bed rooms, kitchens, washing machines, discount family memberships). Pick up each country's free hostel directory at any hostel or TI.

Making Reservations

During most of the year (except, for instance, in the capitals during conventions—early June is packed in Oslo and Stockholm), you can do this entire trip easily without reservations or by making reservations a day in advance as you travel.

Still, given the high stakes, erratic accommodations values, and the quality of the gems I've found for this book, I'd highly recommend calling ahead for rooms a day or two in advance as you travel. If tourist crowds are down, you might make a habit of calling between 9:00 and 10:00 on the day you plan to arrive, when the hotel knows who'll be checking out and just which rooms will be available. I've taken great pains to list telephone numbers with long-distance instructions (see Telephone and Mail, above, and the Appendix). Use the telephone and the convenient telephone cards.

Most hotels listed are accustomed to English-only speakers. A hotel receptionist will trust you and hold a room until 17:00 (5:00 p.m.) without a deposit, though some will ask for a credit-card number. Honor (or cancel by phone) your reservations. Long distance is cheap and easy from public phone booths. Don't let these people down—I promised you'd call and cancel if for some reason you won't show up. Don't needlessly confirm rooms through the tourist office; they'll take a commission.

If you know which dates you need and want a particular place, reserve a room before you leave home. To reserve from home, call, fax, or write the hotel. Phone and fax costs are reasonable, and simple English is fine. To fax, use the form in the Appendix. If you're writing, add the zip code and confirm the need and method for a deposit. In Europe, dates appear as day/month/ year, so a two-night stay in August would be "2 nights, 16/8/97 to 18/8/97"—European hotel jargon uses your day of departure. You'll often receive a letter back from the hotel requesting one night's deposit. A credit card will usually be accepted as a deposit, though you may need to send a signed traveler's check or a bank draft in the local currency. If you provide your credit card number as the deposit, you can pay with your card or with cash when you arrive; if you don't show up, you'll be billed for one night. Reconfirm your reservations a day in advance for safety.

Private Rooms
Throughout Scandinavia, people rent out rooms in their homes to travelers for around $40 per double. Prices are so cheap because it's a "taxation optional" form of income in Europe's most highly taxed corner. While some put out a "Værelse," "Rom," "Rum," or "Hus Rum" sign, most operate solely through the local TI (which occasionally keeps these B&Bs a secret until all hotel rooms are taken). You'll get your own key to a lived-in, clean, and comfortable (but usually simple) private room with free access to the family shower and WC. Booking direct saves both you and your host the cut the TI takes. (The TIs are very protective of their lists. If you enjoy a big-city private home that would like to be listed in this book, I'd love to hear from you.)

Camping
Scandinavian campgrounds are practical, comfortable, and cheap ($5 per person with camping card, available on the spot). The national tourist office has a fine brochure/map listing all their campgrounds. This is the middle-class Scandinavian family way to travel: safe, great social fun, and no reservation problems.

Huts
Most campgrounds provide huts *(hytter)* for wannabe campers with no gear. Huts normally sleep four to six in bunk beds, come with blankets and a kitchenette, and charge one fee (around $40), plus extra if you need sheets. Since locals typically move in for a week or two, many campground huts are booked for summer long in advance. If you're driving late with no place to stay, find a campground and grab a hut.

Eating
The smartest budget travelers do as most Scandinavians do—avoid restaurants. Prepared food is heavily taxed, and the local cuisine isn't worth trip bankruptcy. Especially outside Denmark, alcohol will floor your budget. Of course, you'll want to take an occasional splurge into each culture's high cuisine, but the "high" refers mostly to the price tag. Why not think of eating on the road as eating at home without your kitchen? Get creative with cold food and picnics. I eat well on a budget in Scandinavia using the following tips.

Breakfast

Hotel breakfasts are a huge and filling buffet, about an $8–$10 option. This includes cereal or porridge, *let* (lowfat) or *sød* (whole) milk, various kinds of drinkable yogurt (pour the yogurt in the bowl and sprinkle the cereal over it), bread, crackers, cheese (the brown stuff is goat's cheese—your trip will go better when you develop a taste for it), cold cuts, jam, fruit, juice, and coffee or tea. Coffee addicts can buy a thermos and get it filled in most hotels and hostels for $3 or $4.

I bring a baggie to breakfast and leave with a light lunch—sandwich and apple or a can of yogurt. Yes, I know, this is almost stealing, but here's how I rationalize it: Throughout my trip, I'm paying lots of taxes to support a social system that my host (but not me) will enjoy; I could have eaten what I take at that all-you-can-eat sitting, but choose to finish breakfast elsewhere . . . later. And the Vikings did much worse things. After a big breakfast, a light baggie lunch fits nicely into a busy sightseeing day.

If you skip your hotel's breakfast, you can visit a bakery to get a sandwich and cup of coffee. Bakeries have wonderful inexpensive pastries. The only cheap breakfast is one you make yourself. Many simple accommodations provide kitchenettes, or at least hot pads and coffee pots.

Lunch

Scandinavians aren't big on lunch, often just grabbing a sandwich *(smørrebrød)* and a cup of coffee at their work desk. Follow suit with a quick picnic or a light meal at a sandwich shop or snack bar.

Picnics

Scandinavia has colorful markets and economical supermarkets. Picnic-friendly mini-markets at gas and train stations are open late. Some shopping tips: Wasa cracker bread (Sport is my favorite; Ideal *flatbrød* is ideal for munchies), prepackaged meat and cheese, goat cheese (*geitost; ekte* means pure and stronger), yogurt (drink it out of the carton), freshly cooked fish in markets, fresh fruit and vegetables, lingonberries, mustard and sandwich spreads (shrimp, caviar) in a squeeze tube, boxes of juice, milk, *pytt i panna* (Swedish hash), and rye bread. Grocery stores sell a cheap, light breakfast: a handy yogurt with cereal and a spoon. If you're lazy, most places offer cheap ready-made sandwiches. If you're bored, most have hot chicken, salads by the portion, fresh and cheap liver pâté, and other ways to picnic without sandwiches.

Dinner

The large meal of the Nordic day is an early dinner. Alternate between cheap, forgettable, but filling cafeteria or fast-food dinners ($12), and atmospheric, carefully chosen restaurants popular with locals ($20). Look for the *dagens rett*, an affordable one-plate daily special. One main course and two salads or soups fill up two travelers without emptying their pocketbooks. The cheap eateries close early—in Scandinavia, a normal, practical, fill-the-tank dinner is usually eaten around 18:00. Anyone eating out later is "dining," will linger longer, and can expect to pay much more. A $15 Scandinavian meal is not that much more than a $10 American meal, since tax and tip are included in the menu price.

In most Scandinavian restaurants, you can ask for more potatoes or vegetables, so a restaurant entrée is basically an all-you-can-eat deal. First servings are often small, so take advantage of this. Fast-food joints, pizzerias, Chinese food, and salad bars are inexpensive. Booze will break you. A small beer costs $5 in Oslo. Drink water (served free with an understanding smile at most restaurants). Waitresses and waiters are well paid, and tips are normally included, although it's polite to round up the bill.

Most Scandinavian nations have one inedible dish that is cherished with a perverse but patriotic sentimentality. These dishes often originate with a famine and are kept in use to remind the young of their foremothers' and forefathers' suffering. Norway's penitential food, lutefisk (dried cod marinated for several days in potash and water), is used for Christmas and jokes.

The Language Barrier

Of course, it would be great to speak the local language, but in Scandinavia, English is all you need. They say a Scandinavian can speak any language that will separate a tourist from his money. Whatever the motive, especially among the young, English is Scandinavia's foreign language of choice. Learn the polite words and a few very basic phrases, and you'll have absolutely no problems.

A few words you'll see a lot are: *gamla* (old), *lille* (small), *stor* (big), *takk* (thanks), *slot* (castle or palace), *fart* (trip, comes in many varieties), *time* (hour), *centrum* (center), *gate* (street), *øl* (beer), *forbudt* (not allowed), and *udsalg* or *salg* (sale).

Even though today's small children enjoy cartoons in English, each country does have its own language. Except for Finnish, they are closely related and very similar to English (a cousin of the Nordic tongues), but with a few letters we don't have (Æ, Ø, Å). While tourists can usually ignore pronunciation fine points with no problem, these letters do affect alphabetizing. Whenever I can't find something (such as Århus town in a map index), I look after "Z," where they store special Nordic-alphabet letters.

One Region, Different Countries

Scandinavia is western Europe's least populated, most literate, most prosperous, most demographically homogenous, least churchgoing, most highly taxed, and most socialistic corner.

While Finland and Iceland are odd ducks in northern Europe, Denmark, Norway, and Sweden are pretty similar. They each have distinct but closely related languages (so close that they can laugh at each other's TV comedies). While the state religion is Lutheran, and 90 percent of the people are registered as Lutherans, only a small percentage actually attend church other than at Easter or Christmas.

Each country is a constitutional monarchy with a royal family who knows how to stay out of the tabloids and work with the parliaments. Scandinavia is the home of cradle-to-grave security, and consequently, the most highly taxed corner of Europe. Schools must be good, because illiteracy is nearly unknown, and almost everybody speaks English. Blessed with a pristine nature and sparse populations, the Scandinavians are environmentalists (except for the Norwegian appetite for whaling). The region is also a leader in progressive lifestyles and social experiments. More than half the young married couples in Denmark are "married" only because they've lived together for so long and have children.

Denmark, packing 5 million fun-loving Danes into a flat and gentle land the size of Switzerland, is the most densely populated. Sweden, the size of California, has 8.5 million (mostly blondes). And 4.2 million Norwegians stretch out in long and skinny Norway. Oslo is as far from the north tip of Norway as it is from Rome.

Stranger in a Strange Land

We travel all the way to Scandinavia to enjoy differences—to become temporary locals. One of the beauties of travel (especially in Scandinavia) is the opportunity to see that there are logical, civil, and even better alternatives to "truths" we always considered God-given and self-evident. While the fast and materialistic culture of the United States is sneaking into these countries in many ways, simplicity has yet to become subversive.

Scandinavians are into "sustainable affluence." They have experimented aggressively in the area of social welfare—with mixed results. Travel in Scandinavia can rattle a Republican. Fit in, don't look for things American on the other side of the Atlantic, and you're sure to enjoy a full dose of Scandinavian hospitality.

If there is a negative aspect to the Scandinavian image of Americans, it is that we are big, loud, aggressive, impolite, rich, and a bit naive. While Scandinavians look bemusedly at some of our Yankee excesses—and worriedly at others—they nearly always afford us individual travelers all the warmth we deserve.

Back Door Manners

While updating this book, I heard over and over again that my readers are considerate and fun to have as guests. Thank you for traveling as temporary locals who are sensitive to the culture. It's fun to follow you in my travels.

Send Me a Postcard, Drop Me a Line

If you enjoy a successful trip with the help of this book and would like to share your discoveries, please send any tips, recommendations, criticisms, or corrections to me at Europe Through the Back Door, Box 2009, Edmonds, WA 98020. I personally read and value all feedback. Tips actually used may get you a first-class railpass in heaven.

For our latest travel information, tap into our Web site: http://www.ricksteves.com, or find us on America Online (key word: Rick Steves). Our E-mail address is ricksteves@aol.com. Anyone is welcome to request a free issue of our Back Door quarterly newsletter (it's free anyway).

Judging from all the positive feedback and happy postcards I receive from travelers who have used this book, it's safe to assume you're on your way to a great Scandinavian vacation. Thanks, and happy travels!

BACK DOOR TRAVEL PHILOSOPHY
As Taught in Rick Steves' *Europe Through the Back Door*

Travel is intensified living—maximum thrills per minute and one of the last great sources of legal adventure. Travel is freedom. It's recess, and we need it.

Experiencing the real Europe requires catching it by surprise, going casual . . . "Through the Back Door."

Affording travel is a matter of priorities. (Make do with the old car.) You can travel—simply, safely, and comfortably—anywhere in Europe for $60 a day plus transportation costs. In many ways, spending more money only builds a thicker wall between you and what you came to see. Europe is a cultural carnival, and time after time, you'll find that its best acts are free and the best seats are the cheap ones.

A tight budget forces you to travel close to the ground, meeting and communicating with the people, not relying on service with a purchased smile. Never sacrifice sleep, nutrition, safety, or cleanliness in the name of budget. Simply enjoy the local-style alternatives to expensive hotels and restaurants.

Extroverts have more fun. If your trip is low on magic moments, kick yourself and make things happen. If you don't enjoy a place, maybe you don't know enough about it. Seek the truth. Recognize tourist traps. Give a culture the benefit of your open mind. See things as different but not better or worse. Any culture has much to share.

Of course, travel, like the world, is a series of hills and valleys. Be fanatically positive and militantly optimistic. If something's not to your liking, change your liking. Travel is addicting. It can make you a happier American, as well as a citizen of the world. Our Earth is home to nearly 6 billion equally important people. It's humbling to travel and find that people don't envy Americans. They like us but, with all due respect, they wouldn't trade passports.

Globetrotting destroys ethnocentricity. It helps you understand and appreciate different cultures. Travel changes people. It broadens perspectives and teaches new ways to measure quality of life. Many travelers toss aside their hometown blinders. Their prized souvenirs are the strands of different cultures they decide to knit into their own character. The world is a cultural yarn shop. And Back Door Travelers are weaving the ultimate tapestry. Come on, join in!

DENMARK

COPENHAGEN

Copenhagen (København) is Scandinavia's largest city. With about a million people, it's home to more than a quarter of all Danes. A busy day cruising the canals, wandering through its palace, taking a historic walk, and strolling the Strøget (Europe's greatest pedestrian shopping mall) will get you oriented, and you'll feel right at home. Copenhagen is Scandinavia's cheapest and most fun-loving capital, so live it up.

Planning Your Time

A first visit deserves two days.

Day 1: Get set up around 9:00. If staying there, browse Christianshavn, Copenhagen's "Little Amsterdam." At 10:00 explore the subterranean Christiansborg Castle ruins under today's palace. At 11:00 take the 50-minute guided tour of Denmark's royal Christiansborg Palace. At 12:00 catch the harbor tour boat for a relaxing cruise out to the *Mermaid.* Have a 13:30 buffet lunch at Riz-Raz. Visit the Use It information center. Tour the Rosenborg Castle and see the crown jewels. Siesta in the park. Take the "Heart and Soul" walk described below as you shop and stroll along the Strøget pedestrian mall.

Day 2: Catch the 10:30 city walking tour or tour the Ny Carlsberg Glyptotek art gallery. Smørrebrød lunch. Trace Denmark's cultural roots in the National Museum. The afternoon is free, with many options, including a brewery tour, Nazi Resistance museum (free tour often at 14:00), Thorvaldsen's Museum, or the Amalienborg Palace square. Evening at Tivoli Gardens before catching a night train out.

With a third day, side-trip out to Roskilde and Frederiksborg. Remember the efficiency of sleeping in-and-out by train. If flying in, most flights from the States arrive in the morning. After that, head for Stockholm and Oslo. Kamikaze sightseers see Copenhagen as a Scandinavian bottleneck. They sleep in-and-out heading north and in-and-out heading south, with two days and no nights in the city. Considering the joy of Oslo and Stockholm, this isn't that crazy if you have limited time. You can check your bag at the station and take a 10-kr shower in the Interail Center.

You can set yourself up in my best rooms for your entire Scandinavian tour with a quick trip to the Telecom telephone center in the train station.

Orientation

Nearly all of your sightseeing is in Copenhagen's compact old town. By doing things on foot you'll stumble into some surprisingly cozy corners, one of the charms of Copenhagen that many miss. Study the map. The medieval walls are now roads that define the center: Vestervoldgade (literally, "western wall street"), Nørrevoldgade, and Østervoldgade. The fourth side is the harbor and the island of Slotsholmen where *København havn* ("merchants' harbor") was born in 1167. The next of the city's islands is Amager, where you'll find the local "Little Amsterdam" district of Christianshavn. What was Copenhagen's moat is now a string of pleasant lakes and parks, including Tivoli Gardens. To the north is the old "new town," where the Amalienborg Palace is surrounded by streets on a grid plan, and *The Little Mermaid* poses relentlessly, waiting for her sailor to return and the tourists to leave.

The core of the town, as far as most visitors are concerned, is the axis formed by the train station, Tivoli Gardens, the Rådhus (city hall) square, and the Strøget pedestrian street. It's a great walking town, bubbling with street life and colorful pedestrian zones.

Tourist Information

The tourist office is now run by a for-profit consortium called "Wonderful Copenhagen." This colors the advice and information it provides. Still, it's worth a quick stop for the top-notch freebies it provides, such as a city map and *Copenhagen This Week* (a free, handy, and misnamed monthly guide to the

city, worth reading for its good maps, museum hours with telephone numbers, sightseeing tour ideas, shopping ideas, and
calendar of events, including free English tours and concerts).
The TI is across from the train station, near the corner of
Vesterbrogade and Bernstorffsgade, next to the Tivoli entrance
(daily May, June, and first half of September 9:00–18:00; daily
July and August 8:00–20:00; mid-September to April weekdays
9:00–17:00, Saturday 9:00–14:00, closed Sunday; tel. 33 11 13
25). Corporate dictates prohibit the TI from freely offering
other brochures (walking tour schedules and brochures on any
sights of special interest), but ask and you shall receive. Thinking ahead, get information and ferry schedules for your entire
trip in Denmark (Frederiksborg Castle, Louisiana Museum,
Kronborg Castle, Roskilde, Odense, Ærø, Århus, and
Legoland). The TI's room-finding service charges you and the
hotel a fee and cannot give hard opinions. Do not use it. Get
on the phone and call direct (everyone speaks English).

Use It is a much better information service. This "branch"
of Huset, a hip, city government–sponsored, student-run cluster
of cafés, theaters, and galleries, caters to Copenhagen's young
but welcomes travelers of any age. It's a friendly, driven-to-help,
energetic, no-nonsense source of budget travel information, with
a free room-finding service, ride-finding board, cheap transportation deals, free luggage storage, pen-pals-wanted scrapbook,
free condoms, lockers, and Copenhagen's best free city maps.
Their free *Playtime* publication is full of Back Door–style travel
articles on Copenhagen and the Danish culture, special budget
tips, and events. They have brochures on just about everything,
including self-guided tours for bikers, walkers, and those riding
scenic bus #6. They have a list of private rooms (200-kr doubles
without breakfast). Use It is a ten-minute walk from the station,
down Strøget, right on Rådhustræde for 3 blocks to #13 (daily
9:00–19:00, June through September; weekdays 10:00–16:00 the
rest of the year, tel. 33 15 65 18, fax 33 15 75 18). After hours,
their night board lists the cheapest rooms available in town.

The **Copenhagen Card** covers the public transportation
system and admissions to nearly all the sights in greater Copenhagen, which stretches from Helsingør to Roskilde. It covers virtually all the city sights, Tivoli, and the bus in from the airport.
Available at any tourist office (including the airport's) and the
central station: 24 hours, 140 kr; 48 hours, 230 kr; 72 hours, 295
kr. It's hard to break even, unless you're planning to side-trip on

the included (and otherwise expensive) rail service. It comes with a handy book explaining the 57 included sights, such as: Christiansborg Palace (normally 30 kr), Castle Ruins (20 kr), National Museum (30 kr), Ny Carlsberg Glyptotek (15 kr), Rosenborg Castle (40 kr), Tivoli (44 kr), Frederiksborg Castle (30 kr), and Roskilde Viking Ships (30 kr), plus round-trip train rides to Roskilde (70 kr) and Frederiksborg Castle (70 kr).

Arrival in Copenhagen

By Train: The main train station, Hovedbanegården (HOETH-ban-gorn; learn that word—you'll need to recognize it), is a temple of travel and a hive of travel-related activity. You'll find lockers (25 kr/day), a *garderobe* (35 kr/day per rucksack), a post office, a modern telecommunications center (above the post office, daily 8:00–22:00, Saturday and Sunday 9:00–21:00; easy, fair long-distance phone booths and rentable office services), a grocery store (daily 8:00–24:00), 24-hour thievery, and bike rentals. The Interail Center, a service the station offers to mostly young travelers (but anyone with a Eurailpass, Scanrail, student BIGE or Transalpino ticket, or Interail pass is welcome) is a very pleasant lounge with 10-kr showers, free (if risky) luggage storage, city maps, snacks, information, and other young travelers (June–September 6:30–24:00). If you just need the map and *Playtime*, a visit here is quicker than going to the TI. Train info tel. 33 14 17 01.

Most travelers arrive in Copenhagen after an overnight train ride. The station has two long-hours money exchange desks. Den Danske Bank (7:00–22:00 daily) is fair (charging the standard 40-kr minimum or 20-kr per-check fee for traveler's checks). FOREX (8:00–21:00 daily), with a worse rate but charging only 10 kr per traveler's check with no minimum, is better for small exchanges. On a $100 exchange, I saved 22 kr at FOREX. (Even better is the American Express office, off Strøget; see Helpful Hints, below). While you're in the station, reserve your overnight train seat or couchette out (at *Rejsebureau*). Long rides require reservations. Bus #8 (in front of the station on the station side of Bernstorffsgade) goes to Christianshavn B&Bs. Note the time the bus departs. The TI is across the street on the left; pick up the free Copenhagen city map, which shows bus routes.

By Plane: Copenhagen's International Airport is a traveler's dream, with a tourist office, bank (standard rates), post office, telephone center, shopping mall, grocery store, and bakery. You can use American cash at the airport and get change back in kroner. (Airport info tel. 31 54 17 01, flight info tel. 31 54 17 01, SAS hotline tel. 32 32 68 00, British Air tel. 31 51 30 17.) If you need to kill a night at the airport, try the fetal rest cabins, the *hvilekabiner* (Sb-265 kr, Db-395 kr, rented by the eight-hour period; reception open 6:00–22:00; reservations same day only, CC:VMA, tel. 32 31 32 31, fax 32 31 31 09).

Getting Downtown from the Airport: Taxis are fast and easy, accept credit cards, and, at about 140 kr to the town center, are a good deal for foursomes. The SAS **shuttle bus** zips between the central train station and airport in 20 minutes for 35 kr. **City bus** #250s gets you downtown (City Hall Square, TI) in 30 minutes for 15 kr (12/hour, across the street and to the right as you exit the airport). If you're going from the airport to Christianshavn, ride #9 just past Christianshavn Torv to the last stop before Knippels Bridge.

Helpful Hints

Ferries: Book any ferries you plan to use in Scandinavia now. Any travel agent can book the boat rides you plan to take later on your trip, such as the Denmark–Norway ferry (ask for special discounts on this crossing) or the Stockholm–Helsinki–Stockholm cruise (the Silja Line office is directly across from the station at Vesterbrogade 6D, open Monday–Friday 9:00–16:30, tel. 33 14 40 80). Drivers heading to Sweden via Helsingør should get a reservation for the ferry (tel. 33 14 88 80, and wait through the Danish recording).

Festivals: Upon arrival, call the local festival/exhibit/ activity hotline at 33 77 96 96. Expect extra fun and crowds in Copenhagen during its festival times—Carnival in late May, the Roskilde Rock Festival in early July, and the Copenhagen Jazz Festival for ten days starting the first Friday in July.

Telephones: Use the telephone liberally. Phone booths are everywhere, calls are 1 kr, everyone speaks English, and *This Week* and this book list phone numbers for everything you'll be doing. All telephone numbers in Denmark are eight digits, and there are no area codes. Calls anywhere in Denmark are cheap; calls to Norway and Sweden cost 6 kr per minute from a booth (half of that from a home). Get a phone card (from newsstands, starting at 20 kr).

E-mail: The Hard 'n' Soft computer store, which offers

Copenhagen

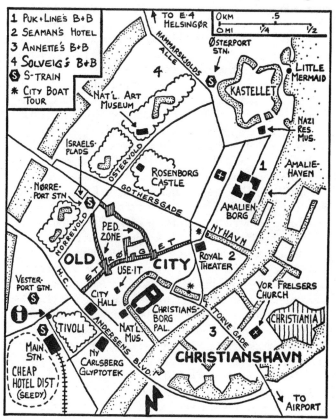

1 PUK + LINE'S B+B
2 SEAMAN'S HOTEL
3 ANNETTE'S B+B
4 SOLVEIG'S B+B
Ⓢ S-TRAIN
✳ CITY BOAT TOUR

hourly computer rentals, has an ISDN Internet connection (Gothersgade 103, near the Hotel KFUM Soldaterhjem).

Traveler's Checks: The American Express Company (Strøget at Amagertorv 18, Monday–Friday 9:00–17:00, Saturday 9:00–14:00, tel. 33 12 23 01) does not charge any fee on their checks (and only 15 kr on any other checks and cash).

Getting Around Copenhagen

By Bus and Subway: Take advantage of the fine bus (tel. 36 45 45 45) and subway system called S-tog (Eurail valid on S-tog, tel. 33 14 17 01). A joint fare system covers greater Copenhagen. You pay 10 kr as you board for an hour's travel within two zones, or buy a blue two-zone *klippekort* from the driver (75 kr for ten one-hour "rides"). A 24-hour pass costs 65 kr. Don't worry much about "zones." Assume you'll be within the middle two zones. Board at the front, tell the driver where you're going, and he'll sell you the appropriate ticket. Drivers are patient, have change, and speak English. City maps list bus and subway routes. Locals are friendly and helpful.

By HT Sightseeing Bus: This route visits nine Copenhagen sights (2/hour, 10:00–16:30, mid-June to August, 20 kr for 24-hour ticket). From the Carlsberg Brewery, bus #6 stops at Tivoli, town hall, national museum, palace, Nyhavn, Amalienborg castle, the Kastellet, and the *Mermaid* (10 kr for one stop-and-go hour), all clearly described in a free, Use It brochure.

By Taxi: Taxis are plentiful and easy to flag down (22-kr drop charge, then 9 kr per km). For a short ride, four people can travel cheaper by taxi than by bus (e.g., 45 kr from train station to Christianshavn B&Bs). Taxis accept all major credit cards.

By Bike: Copenhagen is a joy on a rental bike. Use It has a great biking guide brochure and information about city bike tours (two hours, 50 kr including bike, grunge approach). You can rent bikes at Central Station's Cykelcenter (50 kr/day, weekdays 8:00–18:00, Saturday 9:00–13:00, summer Sundays 10:00–13:00, closed Sunday off-season, tel. 33 33 86 13) and Dan Wheel (2 blocks from the station at 3 Colbjørnsensgade, on the corner of Vesterbrogade, open 9:00–17:30, Saturday and Sunday 9:00–14:00, 35 kr/day, 60 kr/2 days, tel. 31 21 22 27). The best and newest "rentals" are actually free. There are 125 special bike stands scattered around town. Deposit 20 kr in the handlebar lock system of one of the bikes and take the bike where you like. When finished, drop it at any stand to get your deposit back.

Do-It-Yourself Orientation Walk: "Copenhagen's Heart and Soul"

Start from Rådhuspladsen (City Hall Square), the bustling heart of Copenhagen, dominated by the city hall spire. This used to be the fortified west end of town. The king cleverly quelled a French Revolution–type thirst for democracy by giving his people Europe's first great public amusement park. Tivoli was built just outside the city walls in 1843. When the train lines came, the station was placed just beyond Tivoli. The golden girls high up on the building on the square opposite the Strøget's entrance tell the weather: on a bike (fair) or with an umbrella.

Old Hans Christian Andersen sits to the right of the city hall, almost begging to be in another photo (as he did in real life). On a pedestal left of the city hall, note the Lur-Blowers sculpture. The *lur* is a horn that was used 3,500 years ago. The ancient originals (which still play) are displayed in the National Museum and depicted on some tiny butter tubs.

From the less ancient Burger King stretches Copenhagen's main—and Europe's first—pedestrian street, Strøget (stroy-et), actually a series of colorful streets and lively squares that bunny-hop through the old town, connecting the City Hall Square with Kongens Nytorv (the King's New Square), a 15-minute walk away.

The most historic bits and pieces of old Copenhagen are just off this commercial can-can. At the end of the first segment, Frederiksberggade, you'll hit Gammel Torv and Nytorv (Old Square and New Square). This was the old town center. The Oriental-looking kiosk was one of the city's first community telephone centers, before phones were privately owned. The very old fountain was so offensive to people from the Victorian age that the pedestal was added, raising it—they hoped—out of view. The brick church at the start of Amager Torv is the oldest building you'll see here.

The final stretch of Strøget leads past the American Express office and major department stores to Kongens Nytorv, where you'll find the Royal Theater and Nyhavn, a recently gentrified sailors' quarter. This formerly sleazy harbor is an interesting mix of tattoo parlors, taverns, and trendy (mostly expensive) cafés lining a canal filled with glamorous old sailboats of all sizes. Any historic sloop is welcome to moor here in Copenhagen's ever-changing boat museum. Hans Christian Andersen lived and wrote his first stories here.

Continuing north, along the harborside, you'll pass a huge ship that sails to Oslo every evening. Follow the water to the modern fountain of Amaliehave Park. The nearby Amalienborg Palace and Square is a good example of orderly Baroque planning. Queen Margrethe II and her family live in the palace to your immediate left as you enter the square from the harbor side. Her son and heir to the throne, Frederik, recently moved into the palace directly opposite his mother's. While the guards change with royal fanfare at noon only when the queen is in residence, they shower every morning.

Leave the square on Amaliegade, heading north to Kastellet (Citadel) Park and a small museum about Denmark's World
War II resistance efforts. A short stroll, past the Gefion fountain (showing the mythological story of the carving of Denmark out of Sweden) and a church made of flint and along the
water, brings you to the overrated and over-photographed
symbol of Copenhagen, *Den Lille Havfrue—The Little Mermaid.*

You can get back downtown on foot, by taxi, or on bus #1,
#6, or #9 from Store Kongensgade on the other side of Kastel-
let Park (a special bus may run from the *Mermaid* in summer).

Sights—Copenhagen
▲**Copenhagen's Town Hall (Rådhus)**—This city landmark,
between the station/Tivoli/TI and Strøget pedestrian mall,
offers private tours and trips up its 350-foot-high tower. The
city hall is open to the public (free, Monday–Friday, 10:00–
15:00). Tours are given in English and get you into otherwise-
closed rooms (20 kr, 45 minutes, daily 15:00, Saturday 10:00).
Tourists are allowed to romp up the tower's 300 steps for the
best aerial view of Copenhagen (10 kr, Monday–Friday 10:00,
12:00, and 14:00; Saturday 12:00; off-season Monday–Saturday
12:00, tel. 33 66 25 82).

▲**Christiansborg Palace**—This modern *slot*, or palace, built
on the ruins of the original 12th-century castle, houses the parliament, supreme court, prime minister's headquarters, and
royal reception rooms. Guided 40-minute English tours of the
queen's reception rooms let you slip-slide on protect-the-floor
slippers through 22 rooms and gain a good feel for Danish history, royalty, and politics in this 100-year-old, still-functioning
palace (30 kr, June–August, Tuesday–Sunday at 11:00, 13:00,
15:00; off-season Tuesday, Thursday, and Sunday 11:00 and
15:00; tel. 33 92 64 92). For a rundown on contemporary government, you can also tour the parliament building. From the
equestrian statue in front, go through the wooden door, past
the entrance to the Christiansborg Castle ruins, into the courtyard, and up the stairs on the right.

▲**Christiansborg Castle ruins**—An exhibit in the scant
remains of the first castle built by Bishop Absalon—the 12th-
century founder of Copenhagen—lies under the palace (20
kr, daily 9:30–15:30, closed off-season Monday and Saturday,
good 1-kr guide). Early birds note that this sight opens 30
minutes before other nearby sights.

Central Copenhagen

▲▲▲**National Museum**—Focus on the excellent and curiously enjoyable Danish collection, which traces this civilization from its ancient beginnings, laid out chronologically on the ground floor, starting with the "prehistory" section. Very good English explanations make highlights such as the passage graves, mummified Viking bodies with their armor and weapons, the 2,000-year-old Gunderstrup Cauldron, original ancient lur horns, Viking gear, and mead drinking horns particularly interesting (30 kr, enter from Ny Vestergade 10, open 10:00–17:00, closed Monday, tel. 33 13 44 11; occasional free English tours in the summer, call first).

▲**Ny Carlsberg Glyptotek**—Scandinavia's top art gallery, with especially intoxicating Egyptian, Greek, and Etruscan collections, the best of Danish Golden Age (early 19th century) painting, and a heady, if small, exhibit of 19th-century French paintings (Géricault, Delacroix, Manet, Impressionists, Gauguin before and after Tahiti) is an impressive example of what beer money can do. Linger under the palm leaves and glass

dome of the very soothing conservatory. One of the original
Rodin *Thinker*s can be seen for free (wondering how to scale
the Tivoli fence?) in the museum's backyard. This is particularly important if you've not seen the great galleries of central
Europe (15 kr, free on Wednesday and Sunday, behind Tivoli,
open Tuesday–Sunday 10:00–16:00, off-season 12:00–15:00,
tel. 33 41 81 41).

▲▲▲**Tivoli Gardens**—One of the world's most famous
amusement parks, it's 150 years old. It is 20 acres, 110,000
lanterns, and countless ice-cream cones of fun. You pay one
38-kr admission price and find yourself lost in a Hans Christian Andersen wonderland of rides, restaurants, games, march-
ing bands, roulette wheels, and funny mirrors. Tivoli is
wonderfully Danish. It doesn't try to be Disney (open
10:00–24:00, late April to mid-September, closed off-season,
44-kr entry until 13:00, all children's amusements in full swing
11:30–22:00; all amusements open 13:30; events on the half-
hour 18:30–23:00; 19:30 concert in the concert hall can be free
or cost up to 500 kr, depending on the performer; tel. 33 15 10
01). Go in with a full stomach or a discreet picnic (the food
inside is costly). **Søcafeen,** by the lake, allows picnics if you
buy a drink. If you must eat inside, there are cheap *pølser*
(sausage) stands. **Færgekroen** is a good lakeside place for a
beer or some typical Danish food. The Yugoslavian restaurant,
Hercegovina, is a decent value (110-kr buffet). For a reasonable cake and coffee, try the **Viften** café.

Pick up a map and schedule as you enter and locate a bill-
board schedule of events (British flag for English). Free concerts, mime, ballet, acrobats, puppets, and other shows pop up
all over the park, and a well-organized visitor can enjoy an
exciting evening of entertainment without spending a single
krone (though occasionally the schedule is a bit sparse). If the
Tivoli Symphony is playing, it's worth paying for. Rides are
reasonable, but the all-day pass for 138 kr is probably best for
those who may have been whirling dervishes in a previous life.
On Wednesday and Saturday the place closes down (at 23:45)
with a fireworks show. If you're taking an overnight train out
of Copenhagen, Tivoli (just across from the station) is the
place to spend your last Copenhagen hours.

▲▲**Rosenborg Castle**—This impressively furnished
Renaissance-style castle houses the Danish crown jewels and
500 years of royal knickknacks. It's musty with history. Pick up

and follow the 1-kr guide page. The castle is surrounded by the royal gardens, a rare plant collection, and on sunny days, a minefield of sunbathing Danish beauties and picnickers (40 kr, daily June–August 10:00–16:00; May, September, and October 11:00–15:00; there's no electricity inside, so visit at a bright time, S-train: Nørreport, tel. 33 15 32 86). There is a daily changing of the guard mini-parade from Rosenborg Castle (at 11:30) to Amalienborg Castle (at 12:00).

▲**Denmark's Resistance Museum (Frihedsmuseet)**—The fascinating story of a heroic Nazi resistance struggle is explained in English (free, between the Queen's Palace and the *Mermaid*, daily May to mid-September 10:00–16:00, closed Monday; off-season 11:00–15:00, bus #1, #6, or #9, tel. 33 13 77 14).

▲▲▲**Strøget**—Copenhagen's 25-year-old experimental, tremendously successful, and most-copied pedestrian shopping mall is a string of serendipitous streets and lovely squares from the city hall to Nyhavn. Spend some time browsing, people-watching, and exploring both here and along adjacent pedestrian-only streets. The commercial focus of an historic street like Strøget drives up the land value, which generally tears down the old buildings. While Strøget has become quite hamburgerized, charm lurks in many adjacent areas, such as nearby Gråbrødretorv (Grey Brothers' Square). Strædet ("the small street") is Copenhagen's newly pedestrianized street running parallel to Strøget on the water side. (For more on Strøget, see the Orientation Walk, above.) Strøget is not an actual street but the popular name for a series of individually named streets. Many of the best night spots are just off Strøget. The best department stores (Illum and Magasin, see below) are also on Strøget.

▲**Copenhagen Walking Tour**—Once upon a time, American Richard Karpen visited Copenhagen and fell in love with the city (and one of its women). He gives daily two-hour walking tours of his adopted hometown covering its people, history, and contemporary scene. His entertaining single-language walks (there are three covering different parts of the city center) leave daily at 10:30 Monday–Saturday, May through September, from in front of the TI (40 kr, pick up schedule at the TI or Use It, tel. 32 97 14 40). Richard and local historian Helge (Jack) Jacobsen (tel. 31 51 25 90) give reasonably priced private walks and tours. Use It also offers walking tours (40 kr, 15:30 on Wednesday).

▲▲**Harbor Cruise and Canal Tours**—Two companies offer basically the same live, four-language, 60-minute tours through the city canals (2/hour, 10:00–17:00, later in July; May to mid-September). They cruise around the palace and Christianshavn area, into the wide-open harbor, and out to the *Mermaid*. Both leave from near Christiansborg Palace. It's a pleasant way to see the *Mermaid* and take a load off those weary feet. Dress warmly; boats are open-top.

The low-overhead 20-kr Netto-Bådene Tour boats (tel. 31 54 41 02) leave from Holmens Kirke across from the Borsen (stock exchange), just over Knippels Bridge. The competition, a 35-kr harbor tour with a cheaper unguided ride, leaves from Gammel Strand near Christiansborg Palace and the National Museum, and lets you get off the boat at any stop and catch another boat later that day (tel. 33 13 31 05). Don't be confused. If you don't plan to get off the boat, go with Netto. There's no reason to pay double. Boats can also be boarded at Nyhavn.

▲**Vor Frelsers (Our Savior's) Church**—The church's bright Baroque interior is worth a look (free, daily June–August 9:00–16:30, Sunday 12:00–15:30; closes an hour early in spring and fall; off-season 10:00–13:30, tel. 31 57 27 98, bus #8). The unique spiral spire that you'll admire from afar can be climbed for a great city view and a good aerial view of the Christiania commune below. It's 311 feet high, claims to have 400 steps, and costs 20 kr.

Christiania—This is a unique on-again, off-again social experiment, a countercultural utopian attempt that is, to many, disillusioning. An ultra-human mishmash of 1,000 idealists, anarchists, hippies, dope fiends, non-materialists, and people who dream only of being a Danish bicycle seat has established squatters' rights in a former military barracks (follow the beer bottles and guitars down Prinsessegade behind Vor Frelsers' spiral church spire in Christianshavn). This communal cornucopia of dogs, dirt, drugs, and dazed people—or haven of peace, freedom, and no taxes, depending on your perspective—is a political hot potato. No one in the establishment wants it—or has the nerve to mash it. While hard drugs are out, hash and pot are sold openly (with senior discounts) and smoked happily.

Past the souvenir and hash-vendor entry, you'll find a fascinating ramshackle world of moats and ramparts, alternative housing, unappetizing falafel stands, crispy hash browns, a good restaurant (Spiseloppen), handicraft shops, and filth. If you visit, make a point of getting off the main "pusher street."

Christiania's most motley inhabitants are low-life vagabonds from other countries who hang out here in the summer. Now that Christiania is no longer a teenager, it's making an effort to connect better with the rest of society. The community is paying its utilities and even offering daily walking tours. Its free English/Dansk visitor's magazine, *Nitten* (available at Use It), is good reading, offering a serious explanation about how this unique community works/survives. It suggests several do-it-yourself walking tours. Guided tours leave from the front entrance at 15:00 from June through August (20 kr).

Carlsberg Brewery Tour—Denmark's beloved source of legal intoxicants, Carlsberg, provides free one-hour brewery tours followed by 30-minute "tasting sessions" (Monday–Friday 11:00 and 14:00; bus #6 to 140 Ny Carlsberg Vej, tel. 33 27 13 14).

Museum of Erotica—This museum offers a chance to visit a porno shop and call it a museum. It took some digging, but they've documented a history of sex from Pompeii to present day. Visitors get a peep into the world of 19th-century Copenhagen prostitutes; a chance to read up on the sex lives of Martin Luther, Queen Elizabeth, Charlie Chaplin, Casanova, and others; and the arguably artistic experience of watching the "electric *tabernakel*," 12 busy but silent screens of porn to the accompaniment of classical music. (Not worth the 49-kr entry fee but better than the Amsterdam equivalents, just past Tivoli at Vesterbrogade 31, daily 10:00–23:00 May–September; 11:00–20:00 the rest of the year, tel. 33 12 03 11). For the real thing—and free—wander Copenhagen's dreary little red-light district along Istedgade behind the train station.

Hovedbanegården—The great Copenhagen train station is a fascinating mesh of Scandinanity and transportation efficiency. Even if you're not a train traveler, check it out (fuller description in Orientation, above).

Nightlife—For the latest on Copenhagen's hopping jazz scene, pick up the *Copenhagen Jazz Guide* at the TI or the more "alternative" *Playtime* magazine at Use It.

More Sights—Copenhagen

Thorvaldsen's Museum features the early 18th-century work of Denmark's greatest sculptor (free, next to Christiansborg Palace, 10:00–17:00, closed Monday). The noontime **changing**

of the guard at the Amalienborg Palace is boring: all they change is places. **Nyhavn,** with its fine old ships, tattoo shops (pop into Tattoo Ole at #17—fun photos, very traditional), and jazz clubs, is a wonderful place to hang out. Copenhagen's **Open Air Folk Museum** is a park filled with traditional Danish architecture and folk culture (30 kr, open April–October 10:00–17:00, closed Monday; shorter hours off-season, outside of town in the suburb of Lyngby, S-train to Sorgenfri, then bus #184, tel. 42 85 02 92).

Organized **bus tour**s of the city leave from the Town Hall Square in front of the Palace Hotel at 9:30 and 13:00 (160 kr, 1.5 to three hours). Danes gather at Copenhagen's other great amusement park, **Bakken** (free, daily April–August 14:00–24:00, 30 minutes by S-train to Klampenborg, then walk through the woods, tel. 39 63 73 00).

If you don't have time to get to the idyllic island of Ærø (see chapter on Central Denmark), consider a trip to the tiny fishing village of **Dragør** (30 minutes on bus #30 or #33 from Copenhagen's City Hall Square).

Shopping

Copenhagen's colorful **flea market** is small but feisty and surprisingly cheap (summer Saturdays 8:00–14:00 at Israels Plads). An antique market enlivens Nybrogade (near the palace) every Friday and Saturday. Other flea markets are listed in *Copenhagen This Week*. The city's top department stores (Illum at 52 Østergade, tel. 33 14 40 02, and Magasin at 13 Kongens Nytorv, tel. 33 11 44 33) offer a good, if expensive, look at today's Denmark. Both are on Strøget and have fine cafeterias on their top floors.

Danes shop cheaper at Daells Varehus (corner of Krystalgade and Fiolstræde). At UFF on Kultorvet you can buy nearly new clothes for peanuts and support charity. Just across Vesterbrogade from Tivoli, Scala is a new glitzy mishmash of 45 shops, lots of eateries, and entertainment. Survey Scala from its bubble elevator. Shops are open Monday–Friday 10:00–19:00; Saturday 9:00–16:00.

The department stores and the Politiken Bookstore on the Rådhus Square have a good selection of maps and English travel guides. If you buy more than 300 kr ($50) worth of stuff, you can get the 25 percent VAT (MOMS in Danish) back if you buy from a shop displaying the Danish Tax-Free Shopping emblem. If you have your purchase mailed, the tax can be deducted from your bill. Call 32 52 55 66, see the shopping-oriented *Copenhagen This Week*, or ask a merchant for specifics.

Sleeping in Copenhagen
(6 kr = about $1)
Sleep Code: **S** = Single, **D** = Double/Twin, **T** = Triple, **Q** = Quad, **b** = bathroom, **CC** = Credit Card (Visa, MasterCard, Amex).

I've listed the best budget hotels in the center (with doubles for 400 kr–600 kr with breakfast), rooms in private homes an easy bus ride or 15-minute walk from the station (around 330 kr per double with breakfast), and dormitory options (100 kr per person with breakfast). Unless noted, breakfast is included in the price.

Hotel Sankt Jørgen has big, friendly-feeling rooms with plain old wooden furnishings. Brigitte and Susan offer a warm welcome and a great value (S-350 kr, D-450 kr, third person-125 kr extra, 10 percent less in winter, breakfast served in your room, elevator, a 12-minute walk from the station or catch bus #13 to the first stop after the lake; Julius Thomsensgade 22, DK-1632 Copenhagen V, tel. 35 37 15 11, fax 35 37 11 97).

Ibsen's Hotel is a rare, simple, bath-down-the-hall, cheery, and central budget hotel, run by three women who treat you like you're paying top dollar (S-450 kr, Sb-650 kr, D-600 kr, Db-950 kr, third person-150 kr, no elevator, lots of stairs; CC:VMA, Vendersgade 23, DK-1363 Copenhagen, bus #5, #7E, #16, or #40 from the station, or S-train: Nørreport, tel. 33 13 19 13, fax 33 13 19 16).

Hotel KFUM Soldaterhjem, originally for soldiers, is on the fifth floor, with no elevators (S-215 kr, S plus hideabed-315 kr, D-340 kr without breakfast; Gothersgade 115, Copenhagen K, tel. 33 15 40 44). The reception is on the first floor up (open 8:30–23:00, weekends 15:00–23:00) next to a budget cafeteria.

Cab-Inn Copenhagen is a radical innovation: 86 identical, tiny but luxurious, cruise ship-type staterooms, all bright and shiny with TV, video player, coffeepot, shower, and toilet. Each room has a single bed that expands into a comfortable double with one or two fold-down bunks on the walls. The staff will hardly give you the time of day, but it's tough to argue with this efficiency (S-395 kr, D-495 kr, T-595 kr,

Q-695 kr, breakfast-40 kr, easy parking-30 kr, CC:VMA; Danasvej 32-34, 1910 Frederiksberg C; five minutes on bus #29 to center; tel. 31 21 04 00, fax 31 21 74 09). **Cab-Inn Scandinavia** is its twin, 400 meters away (tel. 35 36 11 11).

Hotel 9 Små Hjem is also good. Reservations are necessary (Db-485 kr, CC:VMA, Classensgade 40, DK-2100 Copenhagen Ø; 12 minutes on bus #40 from the station; tel. 35 26 16 47, fax 35 43 17 84).

The Excelsior Hotel is a big, mod, tour-group hotel a block behind the station (Db-770 kr, 4 Colbjørnsensgade, DK-1652 Copenhagen, tel. 31 24 50 85, fax 31 24 50 87). Some people like it.

Sleeping in Rooms in Private Homes

Following are a few leads for Copenhagen's best accommodations values. Most are in the lively Christianshavn neighborhood. While each TI has its own list of B&Bs, by booking direct you'll save yourself and your host the tourist-office fee. *Always* call ahead; they book in advance. Each family speaks English.

In Christianshavn: This area is a never-a-dull-moment hodgepodge of the chic, artistic, hippie, and hobo, with beer-drinking Greenlanders littering streets in the shadow of fancy government ministries. Colorful with lots of shops, cafés, and canals, it's an easy ten-minute walk to the center, and has good bus connections to the airport and downtown.

Annette and Rudy Hollender enjoy sharing their 300-year-old home with my readers. Even with sinkless rooms and three rooms sharing one toilet/shower, it's a comfortable and cheery place to call home (S-225 kr, D-300 kr, T-400 kr, breakfast-40 kr; Wildersgade 19, 1408 Copenhagen K, tel. 32 95 96 22, fax 31 57 24 86). Take bus #9 from the airport, bus #8 from the station, or bus #2 from the city hall. From downtown, push the button immediately after crossing Knippels Bridge, and turn left off Torvegade down Wildersgade. If Annette's place is full, she runs a network of about 20 rooms, all at the same price in this charming locale.

Morten Frederiksen, a laid-back, ponytailed sort of guy, rents five rooms in a mod-funky-pleasant loft. It's a clean, comfy, good look at today's hip Danish lifestyle and has a great location right on Christianshavn's main drag (D-250 kr, T-350 kr, Q-450 kr, two minutes from Annette's, Torvegade 36, tel. 32 95 32 73).

Solveig Diderichsen rents three rooms from her comfortable home (S-225 kr, D-300 kr, T-400 kr). She serves no breakfast but offers kitchen facilities, and there's a good bakery around the corner. Her high-ceilinged, ground-floor apartment is in a quiet embassy neighborhood behind the Østre Anlæg park (three stops on the subway from the central station, to Østerport, then a three-minute walk, or bus #6 or #1 from Vesterbrogade near the station, or bus #9 direct from the airport, Upsalagade 26, 2100 Copenhagen Ø, tel. 35 43 22 70, fax 35 43 39 58). If her place is full, she can find you a room in one of her friends' B&Bs.

Annette Haugballe rents four modern, comfortable rooms in the quiet, green, and residential Frederiksberg area (D-300 kr, easy parking, Hoffmeyersvej 33, 2000 Frederiksberg; on bus line #1 from station or City Hall Square, and near Peter Bangsvej S subway station; tel. 38 74 87 87). Her parents and her friends also rent rooms.

Near the Amalienborg Palace: This is a stately embassy neighborhood—no stress but a bit bland and up lots of stairs. It's very safe, and you can look out your window to see the queen's place (and the guards changing). It's a ten-minute walk north of Nyhavn and Strøget. **Puk** (pook) **De La Cour** rents two rooms in her mod, bright, and easygoing house (D-275 kr with no breakfast but tea, coffee, and a kitchen/family room available, Amaliegade 34, fourth floor, tel. 33 12 04 68). Puk's friend **Line Voutsinos** offers a similar deal (Amaliegade 34, third floor, tel. 33 14 71 42).

Outside the City Center: Friendly **Gitte Kongstad** rents two apartments with kitchenettes and a little garden, ideal for families (Badensgade 2, 2300 Copenhagen, tel./fax 32 97 71 97). Contact her directly for prices and directions.

Sleeping in Flats for Hire

Many Copenhagen residents head for their country bungalows during summer and hire an agency to rent out their homes for a minimum of three nights. These places are mostly in the center of town, completely furnished with a kitchen and the lived-in works (TV, stereo, washer and dryer, and so on), and are a particularly good deal for families or small groups who would trade away the B&B friendliness for the privacy of this less personal alternative. **H.A.Y.4U** takes drop-ins but recommends that you reserve a month in advance (near Strøget at Kronprinsensgade

10, 1114 Copenhagen K, tel. 33 33 08 05, fax 33 32 08 04).
Rates vary from 350 kr/day for one-bedroom places to 550
kr/day for four-person places.

Sleeping in Hostels

Copenhagen energetically accommodates the young
vagabond on a shoestring. The Use It office is your best
source of information. Each of these places charges about 100
kr per person for bed and breakfast. Some don't allow sleeping bags, and if you don't have your own hostel bedsheet,
you'll normally have to rent one for around 30 kr. IYHF hostels require a membership card but will normally sell you a
"guest pass" for 22 kr.

The modern **Copenhagen Hostel** (IYHF) is huge, with
60 170-kr doubles, five-bed dorms at 70 kr/bed, no curfew,
excellent facilities, cheap meals, and a self-serve laundry.
Unfortunately, it's on the edge of town: bus #10 from the station to Mozartplads, then #37; afternoons look for bus #46
direct from the station (Vejlands Alle 200, 2300 Copenhagen
S, tel. 32 52 29 08, fax 32 52 27 08).

The grungy **City Public Hostel**, with big rooms and beds
for 100 kr, open to all from mid-May through August, has only
one advantage: it's a short walk from the station (Absalonsgade
8, tel. 31 31 20 70).

The Danish **YMCA/YWCA**, at Valdemarsgade 15, is a
ten-minute walk from the train station or a short ride on bus
#6 (dorm bed-65 kr, breakfast-25 kr, tel. 31 31 15 74). It's only
open in July and August.

The Sleep-In is popular with the desperate or adventur-
ous (July–August, four-bed cubicles in a huge 452-bed co-ed
room, no curfew, pretty wild, lockers, always has room; Bleg-
damsvej 132; bus #1, tel. 35 26 50 59). Free condoms. In the
summer, **Jørgensens Hotel** rents beds to backpackers in small
dorms (100 kr/bed, extra for sheets, near Nørreport, Rømers-
gade 11, tel. 33 13 81 86, fax 33 15 51 05).

Eating in Copenhagen

Copenhagen's many good restaurants are well listed by category in *Copenhagen This Week*. Since restaurant prices include
25 percent tax, your budget may require alternatives. These
survival ideas for the hungry budget traveler in Copenhagen
will save lots of money.

Picnics

Irma (in arcade on Vesterbrogade next to Tivoli) and **Brugsen** are the two largest supermarket chains. **Netto** is a cut-rate outfit with the cheapest prices. The little grocery store in the central station is expensive but handy (daily 8:00–24:00).

Viktualiehandler (small delis) and bakeries, found on nearly every corner, sell fresh bread, tasty pastries (a *wienerbrød* is what we call a "Danish"), juice, milk, cheese, and yogurt (drinkable, in tall liter boxes). Liver paste (*leverpostej*) is cheap and a little better than it sounds.

Smørrebrød

Denmark's famous open-face sandwiches cost a fortune in restaurants, but the many smørrebrød shops sell them for 8 kr–30 kr. Drop into one of these often no-name, family-run budget savers, and get several elegant OFSs to go. The tradition calls for three sandwich courses: herring first, then meat, then cheese. It makes for a classy—and cheap—picnic. Downtown you'll find these handy local alternatives to Yankee fast-food chains: **Centrum** (Vesterbrogade 6 C, long hours, across from station), **City Smørrebrød** (Gothersgade 12, open 8:00–14:00, closed Saturday and Sunday, near Kongens Nytorv), **Domhusets Smørrebrød** (Kattesundet 18, Monday–Friday 7:00–14:30), **Sorgenfri** (just off the Strøget, Brolæggerstræde 8, Monday–Friday 11:00–14:00), one in a basement at Kompagnistræde 31, 30 meters from Riz-Raz, and one at the corner of Magstræde and Rådhusstræde (next to Huset/Use It, Monday–Friday, 7:00–14:30). There is one in Nyhavn, on the corner of Holbergsgade and Peder Skrams Gade.

The Pølse

The famous Danish hot dog, sold in *pølsevogn* (sausage wagons) throughout the city, is one of the few typically Danish institutions to resist the onslaught of our global fast-food culture. They are fast, cheap, tasty, easy to order ("hot dog" is a Danish word for weenie, study the photo menu for variations), and almost worthless nutritionally. Even so, the local "dead man's finger" is the dog kids love to bite.

By hanging around a pølsevogn you can study this institution. It's a form of social care: only difficult-to-employ people, such as the handicapped, are licensed to run these wiener-mobiles. As they gain seniority they are promoted to work at more central locations. Danes like to gather here for munchies and *pølsesnak* ("sausage talk"), the local slang for empty chatter.

Inexpensive Restaurants

Riz-Raz, around the corner from Use It at Kompagnistræde 20, serves a healthy, all-you-can-eat, 49-kr Mediterranean buffet lunch (daily 11:00–17:00), and an even bigger 69-kr dinner buffet (until 23:00), which has to be the best deal in town. And they're happy to serve free water with your meal. Department stores serve cheery, reasonable meals (especially the top floor of **Illum**, an elegant circus of reasonable food under a glass dome, just past the Amex office; **Magasin**; or **Daells Varehus**, at Nørregade 12). At **El Porron**, you'll find delicious Spanish tapas (Vendersgade 10, one block from Ibsen's Hotel).

Fast-food joints are everywhere. Look for all-you-can-eat pizza and salad bars. **Det Lille Apotek** is a reasonable, candle-lit place popular with locals (just off Strøget, between the Frue Church and the Round Tower at Lille Kannikestræde). **Peppe's Pizza** serves "Real American Pizza." If the weather's good, get a pie to go and picnic in the nearby Rosenborg Park.

Koldt Bord

For a fun, affordable way to explore your way through a world of traditional Danish food, try a Danish *koldt bord* (an all-you-can-eat buffet). The handiest is the famous koldt bord at the central station's **Bistro Restaurant** (134-kr dinner, served daily 11:30–21:30, tel. 33 14 12 32). As their ad brags, "There are more specialties than you can overcome." Use a new plate with each course. The food is laid out chronologically. Start opposite the desserts and work your way through pickled herring, cold cuts, soup, hot meat and vegetables, cheese, and dessert. They serve free tap water.

Good Eating in Christianshavn

Café Wilder serves creative and hearty dinner salads by candle-light to a trendy local clientele (corner of Wildersgade and Skt. Annæ Gade, a block off Torvegade). To avoid having to choose just one of their interesting salads, try their three-salad plate (55 kr with bread). They also feature a budget dinner plate for around 70 kr and are happy to serve free water. Across the street, the **Luna Café** is also good and serves a slower-paced meal. Choose one of three good dinner salads and bread for 40 kr. The beer is 18 kr.

Locals like the **La Novo** Italian restaurant, where the 50-kr lasagna is a meal in itself (Torvegade 49). The **Cibi E Vini** deli serves take-out sandwiches and pastas (Torvegade 28, near the bridge, daily 10:00–18:00, Saturday 10:00–14:00). Right on the community square, you'll find a huge grocery store, fruit stands under the Greenlanders monument, and a great bakery (at the bus stop, Torvegade 45). The **Ravelin Restaurant** serves good traditional Danish-style food at reasonable prices to happy local crowds on a lovely lakeside terrace (only on sunny days, Torvegade 79).

Eating Downtown

Parnas (Lille Kongensgade 16, almost every night at 20:30–03:00, live piano sing-song, tel. 33 11 49 10) and **Skindbuksen** (Lille Kongensgade 4, tel. 33 12 90 37) are both cozy, atmospheric, dark, reasonable, popular with locals, and just off Strøget. **Vin and Ølgod** is the place to go for old-time singing, dancing, eating, and drinking rowdiness (Skindergade 45, 19:00–02:00, closed Sunday and Monday, tel. 33 13 26 25). For an idyllic wooded break from the city, in the city, find **Roberta's Café** for hearty pita salads (Nørre Farimagsgade 6, in the northeast corner of Ørsteds Park).

Transportation Connections—Copenhagen

By train to: Hillerød/Frederiksborg (40/day, 30 min), **Louisiana Museum** (Helsingør train to Humlebæk, 40/day, 30 min), **Roskilde** (16/day, 30 min), **Odense** (16/day, 3 hrs), **Helsingør** (ferry to Sweden, 40/day, 50 min), **Stockholm** (8/day, 8 hrs), **Oslo** (4/day, 10 hrs), **Växjö** (via Alvesta, 6/day, 5 hrs), **Kalmar** (6/day, via Alvesta and Växjö, 7 hrs), **Berlin** (via Gedser, 2/day, 9 hrs), **Amsterdam** (2/day, 11 hrs), **Frankfurt/Rhine** (4/day, 10 hrs).

Cheaper **bus trips** are listed at Use It. All Norway- and Sweden-bound trains go right onto the Helsingør–Helsingborg ferry. The crossing and reservation are included in any train ticket. There are convenient overnight trains from Copenhagen directly to Stockholm, Oslo, Berlin, Amsterdam, and Frankfurt.

A quickie cruise from Copenhagen to Oslo: A luxurious cruise ship leaves daily from Copenhagen (departs 17:00, returns 9:15 two days later; 16 hours sailing each way and seven hours in Norway's capital). Special packages give you a bed in a double cabin, a fine dinner, and two smørgåsbord breakfasts for around $200 in summer. Call DFDS Scandinavian Seaways (tel. 33 42 33 42). It's easy to make a reservation in the U.S.A. (tel. 800/5DF-DS55).

NEAR COPENHAGEN: ROSKILDE, HILLERØD, FREDERIKSBORG CASTLE, LOUISIANA, HELSINGØR, KRONBORG CASTLE

Copenhagen's the star, but there are several worthwhile sights nearby, and the public transportation system makes side-tripping a joy. Visit Roskilde's great Viking ships and royal cathedral. Tour Frederiksborg, Denmark's most spectacular castle, and ponder the cutting edge at Louisiana, a superb art museum with a coastal setting as striking as its art. At Helsingør, do the dungeons of Kronborg Castle before heading on to Sweden.

Planning Your Time

Roskilde's Viking ships and the Frederiksborg Palace are the area's essential sights. Each (an easy 30-minute commute from Copenhagen followed by a 15-minute walk) can be done in half a day. You'll find fewer tour-bus crowds in the afternoon. While you're in Roskilde, pay your respects to the tombs of the Danish royalty. By car, you can see these sights on your way in or out of Copenhagen. By train, do day trips from Copenhagen—then sleep to and from Copenhagen to heavyweight sights eight or ten hours away.

Consider getting a Copenhagen Card (see Copenhagen Orientation, above), which covers your transportation and admission to all major sights.

Roskilde

Denmark's roots, both Viking and royal, are on display in Roskilde, a pleasant town 20 miles west of Copenhagen. Five hundred years ago, Roskilde was Denmark's leading city. Today, the town that introduced Christianity to Denmark in A.D. 980 is most famous for hosting northern Europe's biggest annual rock/jazz/folk festival (four days in early July). Wednesday and Saturday are flea/flower/produce market days. Its TI, next to the cathedral, is helpful (tel. 42 35 27 00). Roskilde is an easy side-trip from Copenhagen by train (30 minutes, several per hour).

Greater Copenhagen

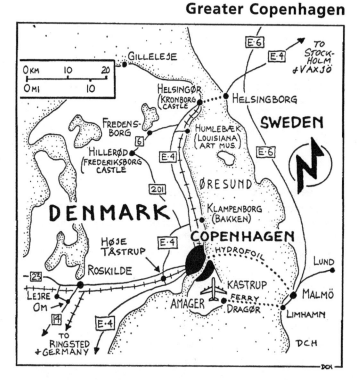

Sights—Roskilde
▲▲**Roskilde Cathedral**—Roskilde's imposing 12th-century, twin-spired cathedral houses the tombs of 38 Danish kings and queens. It's a stately, modern-looking old church with great marble work, paintings (notice the impressive 3-D painting with Christian IV looking like a pirate, in the room behind the small pipe organ), wood carvings in and around the altar, and the silly little glockenspiel (that plays high above the entrance at the top of every hour). The 20-kr guidebook is very good. (10-kr admission, open April–September 9:00–16:45; off-season 10:00–15:00, Saturday 9:00–12:00, Sunday 12:30–15:45.) It's a pleasant walk through a park down to the harbor and Viking ships.

▲▲▲**Viking Ship Museum (Vikingeskibshallen)**—Roskilde's award-winning museum displays five different Viking ships—one is like the boat Leif Erikson sailed to America 1,000 years ago; another is like those depicted in the Bayeux Tapestry. The

descriptions are excellent—and in English. It's the kind of
museum where you want to read everything. As you enter, buy
the 15-kr guide booklet and request the 15-minute English
movie introduction. These ships were deliberately sunk 1,000
years ago to block a nearby harbor and were only recently exca-
vated, preserved, and pieced together. The ships aren't as intact
as those in Oslo, but the museum does a better job of explaining
shipbuilding. The museum cafeteria serves a traditional smørrebrød—great after a hard day of pillage, plunder, or sightseeing.
(30-kr entry, open April–October 9:00–17:00, November–March
10:00–16:00, tel. 46 35 65 55.)

Hillerød and Frederiksborg Castle
The traffic-free center of this Danishly cute town (just outside
the gates of the mighty Frederiksborg Castle, past the Tourist
Information office) is worth a wander. The TI can book rooms
in private homes for 125 kr per person and 30 kr per breakfast
(tel. 42 26 28 52).

▲▲**Frederiksborg Castle**—This grandest castle in Scandinavia is often called the Danish Versailles. Frederiksborg (built
1602–1620) is the castle of Christian IV, Denmark's great
builder king. You can almost hear the cackle of royal hoofbeats
as you walk over the moat through the stately cobbled courtyard, past the Dutch Renaissance brick facade and into the lavish interior. Much of the castle was reconstructed in 1860, with
the normal Victorian flair. The English guidebook is unnecessary, since many rooms have a handy English information
sheet and there are often tours on which to freeload. Listen for
hymns on the old carillon at the top of each hour. The many
historic paintings are a fascinating scrapbook of Danish history. Savor the courtyard. Picnic in the moat park, or enjoy the
elegant Slotsherrens Kro cafeteria at the moat's edge (30 kr,
daily summer 10:00–17:00; April and October 10:00–16:00;
November–March 11:00–15:00). Easy parking. From Copenhagen, take the S-train to Hillerød and then enjoy a pleasant
15-minute walk, or catch bus #701 or #702 (free with S-tog
ticket or train pass) from the train station (tel. 42 26 04 39).

Louisiana
This is Scandinavia's most raved-about modern art museum.
Located in the town of Humlebæk, beautifully situated on the
coast 20 miles north of Copenhagen, Louisiana is a holistic

place—masterfully mixing its art, architecture, and landscape. Wander from famous Chagalls and Picassos to more obscure art. Poets spend days here nourishing their creative souls with new angles, ideas, and perspectives. The views over one of the busiest passages in the nautical world are nearly as inspiring as the art. The cafeteria (indoor/outdoor) is reasonable and welcomes picnickers who buy a drink (49-kr admission or included in a special round-trip tour's ticket, daily 10:00–17:00, Wednesday until 22:00, tel. 49 19 07 19).

Take the train from Copenhagen toward Helsingør, and get off (in 36 minutes) at Humlebæk. Then it's a free bus (#388) connection or a ten-minute walk through the woods. From Frederiksborg, there are rare Humlebæk buses, but most will have to connect via Helsingør.

Helsingør and Kronborg Castle

Often confused with its Swedish sister, Helsingborg, just 2 miles across the channel, Helsingør is a small, pleasant Danish town with a medieval center, Kronborg Castle, and lots of Swedes who come over for lower-priced alcohol. There's a fine beachfront hostel, **Vandrerhjem Villa Moltke** (dorm bed-65 kr, S-148 kr, D-222 kr, T-280 kr, tel. 49 21 16 40), a mile north of the castle. I've met people who prefer small towns and small prices touring Copenhagen with this hostel as their base (two 50-min trains/hour to Copenhagen). Helsingør TI: tel. 49 70 47 47.

▲▲**Kronborg Castle**—Helsingør's Kronborg Castle (also called Elsinore) is famous for its questionable (but profitable) ties to Shakespeare. Most of the "Hamlet" castle you'll see today, darling of every big bus tour and travelogue, was built long after Hamlet died, and Shakespeare never saw the place. But there was a castle here in Hamlet's day, and a troupe of English actors worked here in Shakespeare's time (Shakespeare may have known them or even been one of them). "To see or not to see?" It's most impressive from the outside.

If you're heading to Sweden, Kalmar Castle (see the chapter on South Sweden) is a better medieval castle. But you're here, and if you like castles, see Kronborg. Don't miss the 20-minute dungeon tours that leave on the half-hour. In the basement, notice the statue of Holger Danske, a mythical Viking hero revered by Danish children. The story goes that this Danish superman will awake if the nation is ever in danger and will restore peace and security to the land.

The royal apartments include English explanations (30 kr, daily May–September 10:30–17:00; April and October 11:00–16:00; November and March 11:00–15:00; closed Monday off-season, tel. 49 21 30 78). The free grounds between walls and sea are great for picnics, with a pleasant view of the strait between Denmark and Sweden. If you're rushed, the view from the ferry will suffice.

Route Tips for Drivers
Copenhagen to Hillerød (45 min) to Helsingør (30 minutes) to Växjö, Sweden (3.5 hours including ferry): Just follow the town name signs. Leave Copenhagen, following signs for E-4 and Helsingør. The freeway is great. Hillerød signs lead to the Frederiksborg Castle (not to be confused with the nearby Fredensborg slot, or palace) in the pleasant town of Hillerød. Follow signs to Hillerød C (for "center"), then "slot" (for "castle"). While the E-4 freeway is the fastest, the "Strandvejen" coastal road (152) is pleasant, going past some of Denmark's finest mansions (including that of Danish writer Karen Blixen, a.k.a. Isak Dinesen of *Out of Africa* fame, in Rungstedlund, which is now a museum, 30 kr, daily May–September, 10:00–17:00, tel. 42 57 10 57).

The freeway leads right onto the ferry to Sweden (follow the signs to Helsingborg, Sweden). Boats leave every 20 minutes. Buy your ticket as you roll on board (305 kr one-way for car, driver, and up to five passengers; round-trip gives you the return at less than half price). Reservations are free and smart (tel. 49 26 26 81 and wait out the obnoxious tune). If you arrive before your time, you can probably drive onto any ferry.

The 30-minute Helsingør–Helsingborg ferry ride gives you just enough time to enjoy the view of the Kronborg "Hamlet" castle, be impressed by how narrow this very strategic channel is, and change money. The ferry exchange desk's rate is a tad below the banks', but its 5-kr-per-check fee beats Sweden's standard 40-kr minimum fee for traveler's checks. In Helsingborg, follow signs for E-4 and Stockholm. The road's good, traffic's light, and towns are all clearly signposted. You can change money at the post office in the pleasant town of Markaryd's (just off the road, open late). At Ljungby, road 25 takes you to Växjö and Kalmar. Entering Växjö, skip the first Växjö exit and follow the freeway into "*centrum*," where it ends. It's about a six-hour drive from Copenhagen to Kalmar.

CENTRAL DENMARK: ÆRØ AND ODENSE

The sleepy isle of Ærø is the cuddle after the climax. It's the perfect time-passed world in which to wind down, enjoy the seagulls, and take a day off. Get Ærø-dynamic and pedal a rented bike into the essence of Denmark. Stop for lunch in a traditional *kro* (country inn). Settle into a cobbled world of sailors, who, after someone connected a steam engine to a propeller, decided that maybe building ships in bottles was more their style.

On your way to (or from) Ærø, drop by the bustling city of Odense, home of Hans Christian Andersen and a fine open-air folk museum.

Planning Your Time
Odense is a transportation hub, the center of the island of Funen. It is an easy stop, worth half a day on the way to or from Ærø. More out of the way, Ærø is a well-worthwhile headache to get to. Once there, you'll want two nights and a day to properly enjoy it.

ISLAND OF ÆRØ
This small (22-by-6-mile) island on the south edge of Denmark is salty and sleepy as can be. Tombstones here say things like, "Here lies Christian Hansen at anchor with his wife. He'll not weigh until he stands before God." It's the kind of island where baskets of new potatoes sit in front of houses—for sale on the honor system. Being about 10 miles across the water from Germany, you'll see plenty of smug Germans who return regularly to this peaceful retreat.

Central Denmark

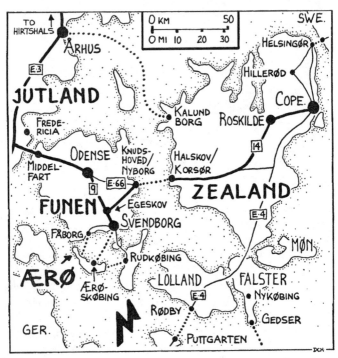

Ærøskøbing

Ærøskøbing is Ærø's town in a bottle. The government, recognizing the value of this amazingly preserved little town, prohibits modern building anywhere in the center. It's the only town in Denmark protected in this way. Drop into the 1680s, when Ærøskøbing was the wealthy home port of more than 100 windjammers. The many Danes who come here for the tranquillity—washing up the cobbled main drag in waves with the landing of each boat—call it the fairy-tale town. The Danish word for "cozy" is *hyggelig* (hew-glee), and that describes Ærøskøbing well.

Ærøskøbing is just a pleasant place to wander. Stubby little porthole-type houses lean on each other like drunk, sleeping sailors, and cast-iron gaslights still shine each evening. The harbor now caters to holiday yachts, and on midnight low tides you can almost hear the crabs playing cards. Snoop around town. It's OK. Notice all the "snooping

Ærøskøbing

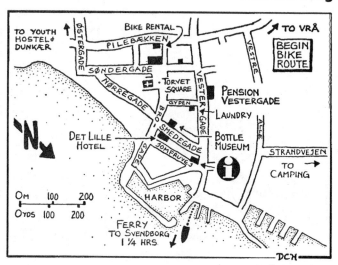

mirrors" on the houses. Antique locals are following your every move.

The town economy, once rich with the windjammer trade, hit the rocks in the 20th century. Outside of tourism, there are few jobs. Kids 15 to 18 years old go to a boarding school in Svendborg; few return. It's an interesting discussion: Do the island folk pickle their culture in tourism or forget about the cuteness and get modern?

Orientation

The town of Ærøskøbing is tiny. Everything is just a few cobbles from the ferry landing.

Tourist Information: The TI is straight ahead as you get off the ferry (Monday–Friday 10:00–15:00, shorter hours off-season, tel. 62 52 13 00, fax 62 52 14 36). They can find you a 220-kr double in a private home.

Ferries: If you're driving, plan ahead. When you arrive in Ærø, reserve a spot on the ferry for your departure (office hours: Monday–Friday 8:00–16:00, tel. 62 52 40 00).

Sights—Ærøskøbing

▲**The "Bottle Peter" Museum**—This is a fascinating house of 750 different bottled ships. Old Peter Jacobsen bragged that

Ærø Island Bike Route

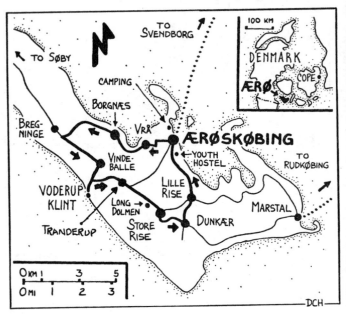

he drank the contents of each bottle, except those containing milk. He died in 1960 (most likely buried in a glass bottle), leaving a lifetime of tedious little creations for visitors to marvel at (15 kr, daily 10:00–17:00 May–September; off-season Monday–Thursday 13:00–17:00, Sunday 10:00–13:00; on Smedegade).

▲**The Hammerich House**—These 12 funky rooms in three houses are filled with 200- to 300-year-old junk (15 kr, summer 11:00–15:00, closed off-season). The third sight in town, the Ærø Museum, is nowhere near as interesting as the Hammerich House.

▲▲▲**The Ærø Island Bike Ride (or Car Tour)**—This 18-mile trip will show you the best of this windmill-covered island's charms. While the highest point on the island is only 180 feet, the wind can be strong, and the hills seem long. This ride is good exercise. If your hotel can't loan you a bike (ask), rent one from the Energi Station (Monday–Friday 8:00–17:30, Saturday 9:00–14:00, Sunday 10:00–14:00, go through the door at the Søndergade end of the Torvet, past the garden to the next road; ask for their 15-kr *"cykel* map," 40 kr for three-speeds, Pile-

bækken 7, tel. 62 52 11 10). The youth hostel and the campground also rent bikes. On Ærø there are no deposits and few
locks. Ready to go? May the wind be always at your back.

Leave Ærøskøbing to the west on the road to Vrå. You'll
see the first of many U-shaped farms, typical of Denmark. The
three sides block the wind and are used for storing cows, hay,
and people. *Gaard* (farm) shows up on many local names. Until
the old generation's gone, you'll see only sturdy old women
behind the wheelbarrows. Bike along the coast in the protection
of the dike that made the once-salty swampland to your left
farmable. You'll see a sleek modern windmill, and soon, a pleasant cluster of mostly modern summer cottages called Borgnæs.
(At this point, wimps can take a shortcut directly to Vindeballe.)

Keep to the right, toward Ø. Bregninge Mark, pass
another Vindeballe turnoff, go along a secluded beach, and
then climb uphill over the island's 180-foot summit to Bregninge. Unless you're tired of thatched and half-timbered cottages, turn right and roll through Denmark's "second longest
village" to the church. Take a peek inside. (Great pulpit for
frustrated preachers and photo hams, public WC in the church
yard.) Then roll back through Bregninge past many more
U-shaped gaards, heading about a mile down the main road
towards Vindeballe, taking the Vodrup turnoff to the right.

A straight road leads you downhill (with a jog to the right)
to a rugged bluff called Vodrup Klint. If I were a pagan, I'd wor-
ship here—the sea, the wind, the chilling view. Notice how the
land slipped in long chunks to make terraces stepping down to
the sea. Hike down to the foamy beach. While the wind can
drag a kite-flier at the top, the beach can be ideal for sunbathing.

Then it's on to Tranderup. You'll roll past the old farm
full of cows, a lovely pond, and right past a row of wind-bent
stumps. (Care to guess the direction of the prevailing wind?)
Follow the sign to Tranderup, stay parallel to the big road
through the town, past a lovely farm that does bed and breakfast, the potato stand, and finally to the main road. Turn right.
At the Ærøskøbing turnoff, just before the tiny little white
house, turn left to the big stone (commemorating the return of
the island to Denmark from Germany in 1750). Seattle-ites
should be sure to visit Claus Clausen's rock (in the picnic area),
a memorial to an extremely obscure Washington state pioneer.

Return to the big road, pass the little white house, and
head toward Store Rise, the next church spire in the distance.

Just after the Stokkeby turnoff, follow the very rough tree-lined path on your right to the Langdysse (Long Dolmen) Tingstedet, just behind the church spire. Here you'll see a 5,000-year-old early Neolithic burial place, often guarded by the megalithic lamb. Ærø had more than 100 of these prehistoric tombs, but few survived.

Carry on down the lane to the Store Rise church. Inside, notice the little ships hanging in the nave, the fine altarpiece, and Martin Luther keeping his Protestant hand on the rudder in the stern. Can you find anyone buried in the graveyard whose name doesn't end in *sen*? Continue down the main road with the impressive—and hopeful—forest of modern windmills on your right, until you get to Dunkær.

For the home stretch, take the small road, signed "Lille Rise," past the topless windmill. Except for the Lille Rise, it's all downhill from here, as you coast past great sea views back home to Ærøskøbing.

Still rolling? Bike out past the campground, along the *strand* (beach) to poke into the coziest little beach houses you'll never see back in the "big is beautiful" U.S.A. This is Europe, where the concept of sustainability is neither new nor subversive.

Sleeping in Ærøskøbing
(6 kr = about $1)
Sleep Code: **S** = Single, **D** = Double/Twin, **T** = Triple, **Q** = Quad, **b** = bathroom, **CC** = Credit Card (Visa, MasterCard, Amex).

Pension Vestergade is a pleasantly quirky old place (built for a sea-captain's daughter in 1784) located right on the main street in the town center. Phyliss Packness takes very good care of her guests, with a homey TV room and a library with Ærø guidebooks you can use (S-175 kr, D-300 kr, D-425 kr with a kitchen, no breakfast, good discount for three-night stays, Vestergade 44, 5970 Ærøskøbing, tel. 62 52 22 98). Loft rooms have great views; climb upstairs to snoop around. This is your ideal home on Ærø. Picnic in the backyard or upstairs. Phyllis' pension fills up early, so call well in advance and reconfirm a day or two ahead of arrival.

Det Lille Hotel, a former 19th-century captain's home, is warm, tidy, and modern, like a sailboat. A room includes a huge breakfast. Just one street off the harbor, next to the cutest house in town (S-310 kr, D-450 kr, 130 kr per extra bed, CC:VM, Smedegade 33, 5970 Ærøskøbing, tel. and fax 62 52 23 00).

For a budget room in a private home in town, try **Margit Kruse** (ten-minute walk from ferry, tel. 62 52 24 70, English spoken) or the **Hoffmann home** (tel. 62 52 12 31, no English spoken). There are several very peaceful bed and breakfasts in the countryside. **Julie and Aksel Hansen's Graasten B&B** is a kid-friendly dairy farm 300 meters from the sea (D-230 kr, 35-kr for breakfast, 75-kr evening meals, 45-kr bike rentals, kitchenette for guests, Østermarksvej 20, 7 km from Ærøskøbing toward Marstal, tel. and fax 62 52 24 25, English spoken).

The **Ærøskøbing Youth Hostel** is a glorious place, equipped with a fine living room, a members' kitchen, and family rooms with two or four beds (80 kr each, D-200 kr, T-270 kr). The place is usually full mid-June to mid-August and closed October–March. It's 500 yards out of town (Smedevejen 13, tel. 62 52 10 44, fax 62 52 16 44).

The three-star **campground,** on a fine beach, offers a lodge with fireplace, windsurfing, and four-person cottages from 285–325 kr, some with kitchenettes (sheets and blankets rent for 10 kr per day). Open May–September, it always has room for campers, 40 kr each (face the water, follow waterfront to the left, a short walk from the center; tel. 62 52 18 54).

Eating in Ærøskøbing

OK, the truth is that without tourism, this island has no economy. The eateries are touristic. Only picnicking is cheap. But good values do hide out. My favorite places are on or near the top of Vestergade (near Pension Vestergade). **Pilegården** (top of Vestergade) and **Lille Claus Café** (across from ferry, 60-kr specials) serve good, reasonably priced food. **Det Lille Hotel** serves a good and reasonable *dagens rett.* **MUMM's** candlelit ambience is occasionally blown out by the German yachting crowd, but the food is fine—if pricey (Søndergade 12). A $5 dinner? The **bakery** serves homemade bread, cheese, a tin of liver paste, and a liter of drinkable yogurt. The homemade waffle cones in the pink Vaffelbageriet shop across the street from the Vestergade Pension are stomping good.

Transportation Connections—Ærøskøbing

Ærøskøbing is accessible by ferry from **Svendborg**. It's a pleasant 70-minute crossing (345-kr round-trip per car and driver, 105-kr round-trip per person; you can leave the island via any of the three different Ærø ferry crossings).

From Svendborg, there are six boats a day (7:30, 10:30, 13:30, 16:30, 19:30, and 22:30, Saturday and Sunday morning departures about an hour later, but double-check), and while walk-ons always make it on board, cars need reservations (tel. 62 52 40 00). A special ferry/bus combo ticket gives you the whole island with stopovers.

ODENSE

Founded in 988, named after Odin (the Nordic Zeus), Odense is famous today primarily for its hometown storyteller, Hans Christian Andersen. He once said, "Perhaps Odense will one day become famous because of me, and perhaps people from many countries will travel to Odense because of me." Today Odense (OH-then-za) is one of Denmark's most visited towns. Denmark's third-largest city, with 183,000 people, it is big and industrial. But its old center retains some of the fairy-tale charm it had in the days of H.C.A., and has plenty to offer.

Tourist Information: The TI, in the town hall right downtown, runs city bus tours and a *Meet the Danes* program (open daily summer 9:30–16:30, Sunday 11:00–19:00; off-season Monday–Friday 9:00–17:00, Saturday 10:00–13:00, tel. 66 12 75 20). For a quick visit, all you need is the free map/guide from the Hans Christian Andersen Hus. (Note: The Danes call him "Hoe See," for "H.C." Andersen.)

Sights—Odense

▲**Den Fynske Landsby Open-Air Museum**—This sleepy gathering of 24 old buildings preserves the 18th-century culture of this region. There are no explanations in the buildings, because the many school groups who visit play guessing games. Pick up the 15-kr guidebook. (25-kr admission, open daily June–August 10:00–19:00; April–May and September–October 10:00–16:00, tel. 66 13 13 72.) From mid-July to mid-August, there are H. C. Andersen plays in the theater at 16:00 every afternoon. The 50-kr play ticket includes admission 90 minutes early (not before 14:30) to see the museum.

▲▲**Hans Christian Andersen Hus**—This museum is packed with mementos from the popular writer's life, his many letters and books, and hordes of children and tourists. It's fun if you like his tales (25 kr, open daily summer 9:00–18:00, shorter hours off-season, Hans Jensens Stræde 37, tel. 66 13 13 72 ext. 4662). Things are explained well in English, so the guidebook is unnecessary (but pick up the free city guide). The garden fairy-tale parade, with kid-pleasing H.C.A. play vignettes, thrills kids daily (late June through early August) in the museum garden at 11:00, 13:00, and 15:00. Across the street is a popular shop full of imaginative mobiles and Danish arts and crafts. Just around the corner is Flensted Uromagerens Hus (the mobile-maker's house).

▲**Møntergarden Urban History Museum**—Very close to the H.C.A. Hus and the H.C.A. Hotel, this fun little museum (15 kr, daily 10:00–16:00) offers three stories of Odense history, early photos, a great coin collection, and the cheapest coffee in Denmark.

Sleeping in Odense
(6 kr = about $1)
The **H.C.A. Hotel** has a special July to mid-August deal for those who'd like to spend the night (650 kr doubles, with breakfast, tel. 66 14 78 00, fax 66 14 78 90).

Transportation Connections—Odense
By train to: Copenhagen (hrly, 3 hrs, train goes right onto the ferry), **Århus** (hrly, 2 hrs), **Svendborg** (hrly, 1 hr, to Ærø ferry), **Roskilde** (hrly, 2.5 hrs).

Route Tips for Drivers
Århus or Billund to Ærø: The freeway takes you over a suspension bridge on the island of Fyn (Funen in English). At Odense take Highway 9 south to Svendborg. Ideally, call the day before to confirm ferry times. If you're taking your car, get a reservation. Figure about two hours to drive from Billund to Svendborg.

Leave your car in Svendborg (at the easy long-term parking lot 2 blocks from the ferry dock) and sail for the castaway isle of Ærø. The Svendborg–Ærøskøbing ferry is an easy 70-minute crossing (345-kr round-trip per car and driver, 105-kr round-trip per person). There are only six boats a day (7:30, 10:30, 13:30, 16:30, 19:30, and 22:30; Saturday and Sunday morning departures about an hour later, but double-check; cars need reservations; call 62 52 40 00). A special ferry/bus combo ticket gives you the whole island with stopovers.

Ærø to Copenhagen via Odense: Catch the 6:00 ferry back to Svendborg (7:00 Saturday and Sunday). Call 62 52 40 00 for information. Reservations for walk-ons are never necessary. On Saturday and Sunday, there are normally no early trips. By 7:40, you'll be driving north on Highway 9; follow signs first to Fåborg, past the Egeskov castle to Odense. If you're doing the folk museum, leave Route 9 just south of town at Højby, turning left toward Dalum and the Odense Campground (on Odensevej). Look for "Den Fynske Landsby" signs (near the train tracks, south edge of town). If you're going directly to fairy-tale land, drive into town and follow the signs to H. C. Andersen Hus. Parking is simple on the street near the H. C. Andersen Hotel (set your window clock, one-hour limit). Drop into the hotel to get the free, excellent Odense map/guide (you can also get it at the H.C.A. Hus). Everything's dead until 9:00. There's coffee in the hotel, or buy your picnic on Øvergade street.

It's a 30-minute drive from Odense to the ferry (following signs for Nyborg, E-20, and Knudshoved). The freeway passes Nyborg and butts right up to the Knudshoved–Halsskov ferry. Call 53 57 15 77 or 65 31 40 54 for a free reservation (advisable during the summer, rarely necessary otherwise). Tickets cost 270 kr for a car, driver, and up to four passengers each way. Boats leave about twice an hour for the one-hour crossing. In 1998, the bridge that you see next to the ferry will be finished (though the ferries will continue to run). It will end halfway across the Bælt strait with a tunnel that spirals straight down and does the rest of the crossing underground. On Zealand, head for København (Copenhagen). At Ringsted, signs will take you to Roskilde. Set your sights on the twin church spires and then follow signs to Vikingskibene, the Viking ships.

Copenhagen is just 30 minutes from Roskilde. If you're returning your car to the airport, stay on E-20 to the bitter end, following signs to København C, and then to Dragør/Kastrup Airport.

JUTLAND: LEGOLAND AND ÅRHUS

Jutland, the part of Denmark that juts up from Germany, is a land of sand dunes, Lego toys, moated manor houses, and fortified old towns. Make a pilgrimage to the most famous land in all of Jutland: the pint-sized kid's paradise, Legoland. In Århus, the lively capital of Jutland, wander the pedestrian street of this busy port, tour its boggy prehistory, and visit centuries-old Danish town life in its open-air museum.

Planning Your Time

Jutland (Jylland in Danish) is worth two days on a three-week trip through Scandinavia. On a quick trip, drivers coming in from Norway might take the overnight boat from Kristiansand to Hirtshals. By noon you'll be in Århus. Den Gamle By (Old Town museum) is worth an afternoon. Spend the next morning at Legoland, on the way to Funen and Ærø. Speedier travelers could make Århus an afternoon stop only and drive to Legoland that evening (which is free if you enter late).

LEGOLAND

Legoland is Scandinavia's top kids' sight. If you have a child (or think you might be one), it's a fun stop. This huge park is a happy combination of rides, restaurants, trees, smiles, and 33 million Lego bricks creatively arranged into such wonders as Mt. Rushmore, the Parthenon, "Mad" Ludwig's castle, and the Statue of Liberty. It's a Lego world here, as everything is cleverly related to this very popular toy. Surprisingly, however, the restaurants don't serve Legolamb.

The indoor "museum" features the history of the company, high-tech Lego creations, a great doll collection, and a toy museum full of mechanical wonders from the early 1900s, many ready to jump into action as soon as you push the button. There's a Lego playroom for hands-on fun—and a campground across the street if your kids refuse to move on. (110-kr entry, 100 kr for kids ages 3–13, 70 kr for kids over 60; gets you on all the rides if you arrive after 18:00, 19:00 July and early August, open daily April 1–October 31, 10:00 to 20:00; until 21:00 in July; closed off-season, tel. 75 33 13 33). The gates are unguarded but don't worry, Legoland doesn't charge in the evening. Some rides close down a little early, but it's basically the same place after dinner as during the day—with fewer tour groups.

Legoland is located in the otherwise unremarkable town of Billund. The local tourist office (in Legoland, tel. 75 33 19 26) can arrange rooms for about 300 kr for a double. (See Sleeping, below.)

Sights—Near Legoland

Jelling—I know you've always wanted to see the hometown of the ancient Danish kings, Gorm the Old and Harald Bluetooth. And this is your chance. Jelling is a small village (12 miles from Legoland, just off the highway near Vejle) with a small church that has Denmark's oldest frescoes and two old runic stones in its courtyard—often called "Denmark's birth certificate."

▲**Ribe**—A Viking port 1,000 years ago, Ribe is the oldest, and possibly loveliest, town in Denmark. It's an entertaining mix of cobbled lanes and leaning old houses, with a fine church (5 kr, bright modern paintings under old Romanesque arches). A smoky, low-ceilinged, very atmospheric inn, the Weis' Stue, rents a few rooms and serves good meals across the street from the church (tel. 75 42 07 00). Drop by the TI for its handy walking-tour brochure, or better yet, catch one of the guided town walks (20 kr, daily 11:30, Torvet 3, tel. 75 42 15 00).

Sleeping near Legoland, in Billund
(6 kr = about $1)
Sleep Code: **S** = Single, **D** = Double/Twin, **T** = Triple, **Q** = Quad, **b** = bathroom, **CC** = Credit Card (Visa, MasterCard, Amex).

Jutland: Legoland and Århus

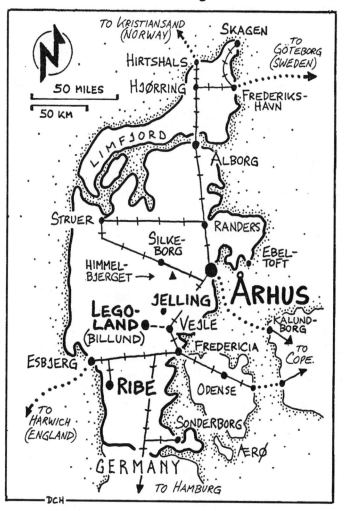

The **Legoland Hotel** adjoins Legoland (925 kr for a family-of-four room including discounted admission to the park, tel. 75 33 12 44, fax 75 35 38 10). The **Hotel Svanen** is nearby in Billund (Sb-595 kr, Db-695 kr, extra bed-125 kr to 140 kr, Nordmarksvej 8, tel. 75 33 28 33, fax 75 35 35 15).

Private rooms are the key to a budget visit here. The following place is great, with about four doubles. **Mary Sort** has a great setup in a forest just outside of town. Her guests enjoy a huge living room, a kitchen, lots of Lego toys, and a kid-friendly yard (D-280 kr including breakfast, discounts for kids; leave Billund on the Grindsted road, turn right on Stilbjergvej after the Shell station, about a half-mile down the road on the right at Stilbjergvej 4, tel. 75 33 23 27).

Billund Youth Hostel is brand new, with 85-kr dorm beds and D-285 kr (Ellehammers Alle 2, 7190 Billund; bus #912/44 from Vejle stops nearby; tel. 75 33 27 77, fax 75 33 28 77).

ÅRHUS

Denmark's second-largest city, with a population of 280,000, Århus (OAR-hoos) is Jutland's capital and cultural hub. Its Viking founders, ever conscious of aesthetics, chose a lovely wooded where-the-river-hits-the-sea setting. Today it bustles with a lively port and an important university. It's well worth a stop.

Tourist Information: Visit the TI in the town hall to get the helpful Århus brochure and map (open Monday–Friday 9:30–18:00, Saturday 9:30–17:00, Sunday 9:30–13:00 mid-June to mid-September; shorter hours off-season and closed Sunday; tel. 86 12 16 00, fax 86 12 95 90). They run a fine city introductory bus tour (daily in summer from the TI at 10:00 for 2.5 hours; 45 kr, which also gives you 24 hours of unlimited city bus travel). For a longer visit, consider getting the two-day Århus Passet (110 kr), which covers all sights, the city bus introductory tour, and transportation.

Getting Around Århus: City buses easily connect the center and train station with the open-air and prehistory museums.

Sights—Århus

▲▲▲**Den Gamle By**—The Old Town open-air folk museum puts Århus on the touristic map. This is a unique gathering of 70 half-timbered houses and crafts shops, all wonderfully furnished just as they were back in Hans Christian Andersen's day. The Mayor's House (from 1597) is the nucleus and reason enough to visit. Unlike other Scandinavian open-air museums that focus on rural folk life, Den Gamle By re-creates old Danish town life. (50-kr entry, open daily June–August 9:00–18:00; May and September 9:00–17:00; shorter hours off-season; there are some English descriptions inside; take bus #3 or walk 15 minutes from

Århus

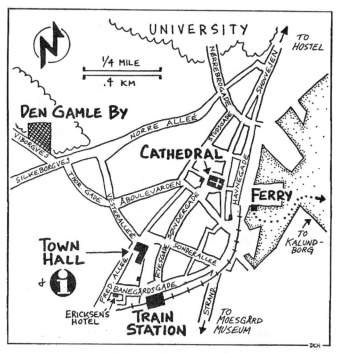

the train station to Viborgvej 2, tel. 86 12 31 88.) Ask about walking tours, often at 13:00 and 16:00, and pick up the schedule of tours. After hours, the buildings are locked but the peaceful park is open. There's a fine botanical garden next door.

▲**Forhistorisk Museum Moesgård**—This prehistory museum at Moesgård, just south of Århus, is famous for its incredibly well-preserved Grauballe Man. This 2,000-year-old "bog man" looks like a fellow half his age. You'll see his skin, nails, hair, and even the slit in his throat given him at the sacrificial banquet. The museum has fine Stone, Bronze, Iron, and Viking Age exhibits (30 kr, open daily 10:00–17:00; off-season 10:00–16:00, closed Monday, Moesgård Allé 20, tel. 89 42 11 00). Take bus #6 from the Århus station to the last stop. Behind the museum, a prehistoric open-air museum ("trackway," good 10-kr guide booklet) stretches 2 miles down to a fine beach from which, in the summer, bus #19 takes you back downtown. The museum cafeteria sells picnics-to-go if you're in the mood.

Århus Cathedral—This late Gothic (from 1479) church is Denmark's biggest—over 300 feet long and tall (open daily except Sunday 9:30–16:00; off-season 10:00–15:00).

Other Århus Attractions—Århus has a great pedestrian street that stretches at least two ice-cream cones from the cathedral to the train station (Søndergade/Clements Torv). There's lots more to see and do in Århus, including an art museum (Århus Kunstmuseum, 30 kr, 10:00–17:00, closed Monday, shorter hours off-season, bus #1 and #6 from train station, tel. 86 13 52 55), a Viking museum (free, in a bank basement across from the cathedral), and a "Tivoli" amusement park.

Sleeping in Århus
(6 kr = about $1)

All accommodations are centrally located near the train station and TI. Sleep Code: **S** = Single, **D** = Double/Twin, **T** = Triple, **Q** = Quad, **b** = bathroom, **CC** = Credit Card (Visa, MasterCard, Amex).

Eriksen's Hotel is a shipshape, friendly, creative little place with showers down the hall and cheap meals (S-315 kr, D-460 kr, includes breakfast, CC:VM, Banegårdsgade 6-8, tel. 86 13 62 96, fax 86 13 76 76).

Hotel Windsor is another budget alternative (S-375 kr, D-515 kr, includes breakfast, Skolebakken 17, tel. 86 12 23 00, fax 86 13 64 00).

The **Århus Sleep In** is an alternative culture center offering 75-kr dorm beds, D-180 kr, Db-280 kr, cheap meals, and rental blankets (open 24 hours a day, mid-June to mid-September, Havnegade 20, tel. 86 19 20 55).

The TI can set you up in a private home for 125 kr per person in a double. They also have summer deals on ritzy hotels that can match the prices of the two hotel listings above. The local **youth hostel** is a good one, with 70-kr beds and plenty of family rooms, situated near the water 2 miles out of town (Marienlundsvej 10; bus #1, #6, #9, or #16 to the end and follow the signs; tel. 86 16 72 98).

Eating in Århus

The pizza at **Restaurant Italia** is popular and reasonable (corner of Mindebrogade and Åboulevarden). **Munkestuen** has good 120-kr meals (Klostertorvet 5, tel. 86 12 95 67). At popular **Dee Dee's Sandwiches & Salads**, nothing costs more than 40 kr (just across from the train station). Try the brunch at cozy **Café Jorden** (11:00–14:00, Badstuegade 3). The area around Klostertorvet/Klostergade is great for cafés, restaurants, and people-watching. The park in front of Musikhuset concert hall is good for picnics.

Transportation Connections—Århus
By train to: Hirtshals (16/day, 2.5 hrs), **Odense** (16/day, 2 hr), **Copenhagen** (hrly, 4.5 hrs), **Hamburg** (3/day, 5.5 hrs).

Ferries: Day and night, ferries sail between Hirtshals, Denmark, and Kristiansand, Norway. On board, you'll find a decent smørgåsbord, music, duty-free shopping, and a bank (no fee). The crossing takes just four hours (overnight, six) and the cost ranges wildly from 98 kr to 360 kr (July and weekends are priciest). The charge for a car is 180 kr to 500 kr; a "car package" deal lets five in a car travel for 1,390 kr (summer, Monday–Thursday). On the overnight crossing, you can sleep in varying levels of comfort and privacy (40 kr for a reclining seat, 65 kr for a simple curtains-for-privacy couchette, 110 kr to 130 kr for a bed in a four-berth room, or 130 kr to 260 kr for a bed in a private double with shower). Call Color Line for information, schedules, and reservations (8:00–22:00, Sunday 8:00–21:00, tel. 99 56 19 77 in Denmark; in the U.S.A. tel. 212/319-1300, fax 212/319-1390). You can phone in a reservation (advisable if you've got a car or want to rent a room) and pay when you arrive at the dock.

Route Tips for Drivers
Ferry dock at Hirtshals to Århus to Billund: From the dock in Hirtshals, drive E-45 south (signs to Hjørring, Ålborg). It's about a two-hour drive even if you take the more scenic road 507 from Ålborg (signs to Hadsund). E-45 brings you right into central Århus. Those skipping Århus will skirt the center, turning right on Nordre Ringgade to follow E-45 south. To get to the Århus commercial center, follow signs to the center, then Domkirke. There's a handy pay parking lot right across from the cathedral. You'll see signs all over town directing you to the open-air folk museum, Den Gamle By.

From Århus, continue south on E-45 (leave on the Skanderborg road; signs to Vejle, Kolding). For Legoland, take the Vejle S (after the Vejle N) exit sign Billund. Billund is a non-threatening Lego-sized town.

NORWAY

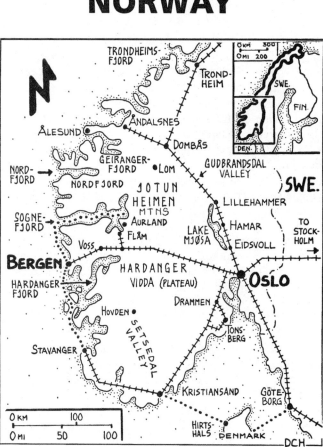

OSLO

Oslo is the smallest and least earthshaking of the Nordic capitals, but this brisk little city offers more sightseeing thrills than you might expect. Sights of the Viking spirit—past and present—tell an exciting story. Prowl through the remains of ancient Viking ships and marvel at more peaceful but equally gutsy modern boats like the *Kon Tiki*, *Ra*, and *Fram*. Dive into the country's folk culture at the open-air folk museum and get stirred up by Norway's heroic spirit at the Nazi resistance museum.

For a look at modern Oslo, browse through the new yuppie-style harbor shopping complex, tour the striking city hall, take a peek at sculptor Vigeland's people pillars, and climb the towering, knee-shaking Holmenkollen ski jump.

Situated at the head of a 60-mile-long fjord, surrounded by forests, and populated by 500,000 people, Oslo is Norway's cultural hub and an all-you-can-see smørgåsbord of historic sights, trees, art, and Nordic fun.

Planning Your Time

Oslo offers an exciting two-day slate of sightseeing thrills. Ideally, sleep on the train in from Stockholm, spend two days, and leave on the night train to Copenhagen, or on the scenic train to Bergen the third morning. Spend the two days like this:

Day 1: Set up. Visit the TI. Tour the Akershus Castle and Nazi resistance museum. Take a picnic on the ferry to Bygdøy and enjoy a view of the city harbor. Tour the *Fram*, *Kon Tiki*, and Viking ships. Finish the afternoon at the Norwegian Open

Air Folk Museum. Boat home. For evening culture, consider the Norwegian Masters' performance (18:00) and the folk music and dance show (21:00 Monday and Thursday).

Day 2: At 10:00 catch the city hall tour, then browse through the National Gallery. Spend the afternoon at Vigeland Park and at the Holmenkollen ski jump and museum. Browse Karl Johans Gate (all the way to the station) and Aker Brygge harbor in the early evening for the Norwegian *paseo*. Consider munching a fast-food dinner on the harbor mini-cruise.

Orientation

Oslo is easy to manage, with nearly all its sights clustered around the central "barbell" street (Karl Johans Gate, with the Royal Palace on one end and the train station on the other), or in the Bygdøy district, a ten-minute ferry ride across the harbor.

Tourist Information

The **Norwegian Information Center** displays Norway as if it were a giant booth at a trade show (on the waterfront between the city hall and Aker Brygge, daily 9:00–20:00, shorter hours off-season, tel. 22 83 00 50). Stock up on brochures for Oslo and all of your Norwegian destinations, especially the *Bergen Guide*. Pick up the free Oslo map, Sporveiskart transit map, *What's on in Oslo* monthly (for the most accurate listing of museum hours and special events), *Streetwise* magazine (hip and fun to read, telling you how to definitely not be one of those tourists), and the free annual *Oslo Guide*. Consider buying the Oslo Card (unless your hotel provides it for free, see below). The info center has a rack of free pages on contemporary Norwegian issues and life (near the door); a 30-minute "multi-vision" slide show taking you around Norway (free, top of the hour, in theater in the back); a 30-minute video called *Look to Norway* that runs all day; and rooms showcasing various crafts and ways you can spend your money here. The tourist information window in the central station (daily 8:00–23:00, less off-season) is much simpler but can handle your needs just as well.

Use It is a hard-working youth information center, providing lots of solid, money-saving, experience-enhancing information to young, student, and vagabond travelers (summer only 7:30–18:00, Saturday 9:00–14:00, closed Sunday, Møllergata 3, tel. 22 41 51 32). They have telephones, E-mail, and free coffee and tea. Read their free *Streetwise* magazine for ideas on eating and sleeping cheap, good night spots, best beaches, and so on.

The **Oslo Card** (24 hours-130 kr, 48 hours-200 kr, or 72 hours-240 kr) gives you free use of all city public transit, and boats, free entry to all sights, a free harbor mini-cruise tour, free parking, and many more discounts—and is also a handy handbook. As admissions go up, this card becomes an increasingly better deal. Almost any two-day visit to Oslo will be cheaper with the Oslo Card (which costs less than three Bygdøy museum admissions, the ski jump, and one city bus ride). The TI's special Oslo Package hotel deal (described under Sleeping, below) includes this card with your discounted hotel room.

Arrival in Oslo

Oslo S, the modern central train station, is slick and helpful, with a late-hours TI, room-finding service, late-hours bank (fair rates, normal fee), supermarket (weekdays 7:00–23:00, shorter hours on Saturday, closed Sunday), and an **Interrail Center** that offers any traveler with a train pass 15-kr showers, free rucksack storage racks, a bright and clean lounge, cheap snacks, a bulletin board for cheap sleeping deals, and an information center (open 7:00–23:00, mid-June to September). Pick up information leaflets on the Flåm and Bergen Railway. Train info: tel. 81 50 08 88 (06:30–23:30).

Getting Around Oslo

By Public Transit: Oslo's transit system is made up of buses, trams, ferries, and a subway. Tickets cost 18 kr and are good for one hour of use on any combination of the above. (Flexicards give eight rides for 100 kr, buy tickets as you board, bus info tel. 177; note: you can dial 177 throughout Norway to get local bus and train information.) **Trafikanten,** the public transit information center, is under the ugly tower immediately in front of the station. Their free "Sporveiskart for Oslo" transit map is the best city map around and makes the transit system quite inviting. The similar but smaller "Visitor's Map Oslo" is easier to use and also free. The **Dagskort Tourist Ticket** is a 40-kr, 24-hour transit pass that pays for itself on the third ride. The Oslo Card (see Tourist Information, above) gives you free run of the entire transit system. Note how gracefully the

Oslo Center

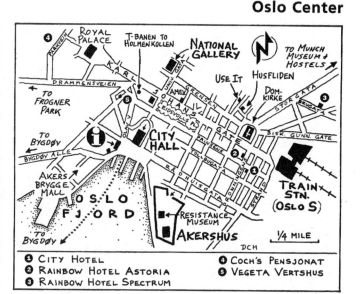

● CITY HOTEL	❹ COCH'S PENSJONAT
● RAINBOW HOTEL ASTORIA	❺ VEGETA VERTSHUS
● RAINBOW HOTEL SPECTRUM	

subway lines fan out after huddling at Stortinget. Take advantage of the way they run like clockwork, with schedules clearly posted and followed.

By Bike: Oslo is a good biking town, especially if you'd like to get out into the woods or ride a tram uphill out of town and coast for miles back. *Den Rustne Eike*, "the rusty spoke," organizes tours and rents bikes (three hours/60 kr–95 kr, six hours/85 kr–135 kr depending on bike, 30 percent less on weekends; daily May–September 10:00–18:30, closes at 17:30 off-season; on the harbor next to the Norway Information Center; tel. 22 83 72 31).

Sights—Downtown Oslo

Note: Because of Norway's passion for minor differences in opening times from month to month, I've generally listed only the peak-season hours. Assume opening hours shorten as the days do. The high season in Oslo is mid-June to mid-August. (I'll call that "summer" in this chapter.)

▲▲**City Hall**—Construction on Oslo's richly decorated Rådhuset began in 1931. Finished in 1950 to celebrate the city's 900th birthday, Norway's leading artists (including Edvard Munch) all contributed to what was an avant-garde thrill in its day. The interior's 2,000 square yards of bold and colorful murals (which take you on a voyage through the collective psyche of Norway, from its simple rural beginnings through the scar tissue of the Nazi occupation and beyond) are meaningful only with the excellent, free guided tours (15 kr, 10:00, 12:00, and 14:00 Tuesday–Friday, entry on the Karl Johans side; open 9:00–17:00, Sunday 12:00–17:00, tel. 22 86 16 00).

▲Akershus Castle—One of the oldest buildings in town, this castle overlooking Oslo's harbor is mediocre by European standards but worth a look if you're there for the tour. Its grounds make a pleasant park with grassy ramparts, pigeon-roost cannons, and great picnic spots with city views (20 kr for castle entry, open daily 10:00–16:00, Sunday 12:30–16:00, July to mid-September, open Sunday through end of September; closed in winter; free 50-minute English tours daily in summer at 11:00, 13:00, and 15:00, Sunday 13:00 and 15:00 only; tel. 22 41 25 21).

▲▲Norwegian Resistance Museum (Norges Hjemmefront-museum)—A stirring story about the Nazi invasion and occupation is told with wonderful English descriptions. This is the best look in Europe at how national spirit endured total German occupation (in the Akershus Castle, 15 kr, daily summer 10:00–17:00, Sunday 11:00–17:00, closes one hour earlier off-season).

▲National Gallery—Located downtown (Universitets Gata 13), this easy-to-handle museum gives you an effortless tour back in time and through Norway's most beautiful valleys, mountains, and villages, with the help of its romantic painters (especially Dahl). The gallery also has several Picassos, a noteworthy Impressionist collection, some Vigeland statues, and a representative roomful of Munch paintings, including the famous version of *The Scream*. His paintings here make a trip to the Munch museum unnecessary for most. For an entertaining survey of 2,500 years of sculpture, go through the museum gift shop and down the stairs to the right for a room filled with plaster copies of famous works (free, Monday, Wednesday, Friday, and Saturday 10:00–16:00; Thursday 10:00–20:00; Sunday 11:00–15:00, closed Tuesday, tel. 22 20 04 04).

▲▲Browsing—Oslo's pulse is best felt along and near the central Karl Johans Gate (from station to palace) and in the trendy new harborside Aker Brygge Festival Market Mall (a glass-and-chrome collection of sharp cafés and polished produce stalls just west of the city hall). The buskers are among the best in Europe.

▲▲▲**Vigeland Sculptures in Frogner Park and the Vigeland Museum**—The 75-acre park contains a lifetime of work by Norway's greatest sculptor, Gustav Vigeland. From 1924 through 1942, he sculpted 175 bronze and granite statues. The statues—all nude, each unique—surround Vigeland's 60-foot-high tangled tower of 121 bodies called "the monolith of life." Pick up the free map from the box on the kiosk wall as you enter. The park is more than great art. It's a city at play. Enjoy its urban Norwegian ambience. Then visit the Vigeland Museum to see the models for the statues and more in the artist's studio. Don't miss the photos on the wall showing the construction of the monolith (20 kr for museum, open 10:00–18:00, Sunday 12:00–19:00, closed Monday; open 12:00–16:00 and free off-season, tel. 22 44 11 36). The park is always open and free. Take T-bane #2, bus #20 or #45, or tram #12 or #15 to Frogner Plass.

Oslo City Museum—Located in the Frogner Manor farm in the Frogner Park, this museum tells the story of Oslo since 1909. A helpful free English brochure guides you through the exhibits (20 kr, open 10:00–18:00, Saturday and Sunday 11:00–17:00, closed Monday; shorter hours off-season, tel. 22 43 06 45).

▲▲**Edvard Munch Museum**—The only Norwegian painter to have a serious impact on European art, Munch (monk) is a surprise to many who visit this fine museum. The emotional, disturbing, and powerfully expressionist work of this strange and perplexing man is arranged chronologically. You'll see paintings, drawings, lithographs, and photographs. Don't miss *The Scream*, which captures the fright many feel as the human "race" does just that (40 kr, 10:00–18:00, Sunday 12:00–18:00, off-season closes as early as 16:00 and all day Monday; take T-bane to "Munch" stop; tel. 22 67 37 74). If the price or location is a problem, you can see a roomful of Munch paintings in the free National Gallery downtown.

Sights—Oslo's Bygdøy Neighborhood

▲▲▲**Bygdøy**—This exciting cluster of sights is on a park-like peninsula just across the harbor from downtown (18 kr, free with transit pass or Oslo Card; accessible by bus #30 from the station and National Theater or by ferry, departing from city hall three times an hour, 8:30–21:00). The Folk Museum and Viking ships are a ten-minute walk from the first stop, Dronningen. The other museums are at the second stop, Bygdøynes.

Greater Oslo

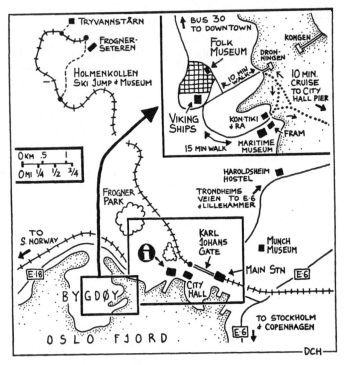

(See inset on the Greater Oslo map.) Otherwise, all Bygdøy
sights are within a 15-minute walk of each other.

▲▲**Norwegian Folk Museum**—Brought from all corners of
Norway, 140 buildings are reassembled on these 35 acres.
While Stockholm's Skansen was the first to open to the public,
this museum is a bit older, starting in 1885 as the king's private
collection. You'll find craftspeople doing their traditional
things; security guards disguised in cute, colorful, and traditional local costumes; endless creative ways to make do in a
primitive log-cabin-and-goats-on-the-roof age; a 12th-century
stave church; and a museum filled with toys and fine folk costumes. The place hops in the summer but is dead off-season.
Catch the free one-hour guided walks at 10:00, 12:00, and
14:00 (call to confirm schedule). Otherwise, glean information
from the 10-kr guidebooks and the informative attendants who
look like Rebecca Boone's Norwegian pen pals (50 kr, daily
June–August 9:00–18:00; off-season 10:00–17:00). For folk

dance performances, tour, and crafts demonstration schedules, call 22 12 37 00.

▲▲**Viking Ships**—Three great ninth-century Viking ships are surrounded by artifacts from the days of rape, pillage, and—ya sure, yu betcha—plunder. There are no museum tours, but everything is well described in English, and it's hard not to hear the English-speaking bus tour guides. There was a time when much of a frightened Europe closed every prayer with "and deliver us from the Vikings, Amen." Gazing up at the prow of one of these sleek time-stained vessels, you can almost hear the screams and smell the armpits of those red-heads on the rampage (30 kr, daily summer 9:00–18:00, off-season 11:00–15:00). To miss the tour-group crowds, come early, late, or at lunchtime.

▲▲**The *Fram***—This great ship took modern-day Vikings Amundsen and Nansen deep into the Arctic and Antarctic, far-ther north and south than any ship before. For three years the *Fram* was part of an arctic ice drift. The exhibit is fascinating. Read the ground-floor displays, then explore the boat (20 kr, daily summer 9:00–17:45, shorter hours off-season). You can step into the lobby and see the ship's hull for free. Dry-docked by the waterfront is the boat Amundsen used to "discover" the Northwest Passage (*Fram* ticket gets you aboard).

▲▲**The *Kon-Tiki* Museum**—Next to the *Fram* are the *Kon-Tiki* and the *Ra II*, the boats Thor Heyerdahl built and sailed 4,000 and 3,000 miles, respectively, to prove that early South Americans could have sailed to Polynesia and Africans could have populated Barbados. He made enough money from his adventures to also prove that rich Norwegians can stay that way only by moving to low-tax Monaco (25 kr, daily 9:30–17:45, off-season 10:30–16:45).

▲**Norwegian Maritime Museum**—If you like the sea, this museum is a salt lick, providing a fine look at Norway's mari-time heritage (25 kr, 50 kr for a family, daily 10:00–19:00, off-season 10:30–16:00 and sometimes later).

Other Oslo Sights and Activities

▲**Henie-Onstad Art Center**—Norway's best private mod-ern art collection, donated by the famous Norwegian Olympic skater/movie star, Sonja Henie (and her husband), combines modern art, a stunning building, a beautiful fjord-side setting, and the great café/restaurant Pirouetten. Don't miss her glittering trophy room near the entrance of the center (40 kr, Monday 11:00–17:00, Tuesday–Friday 9:00–21:00, weekends 11:00– 19:00, tel. 67 54 30 50). It's in Høvikodden, 8 miles SW of Oslo; catch bus #151, #152, #251, or #261 from the Oslo train station or from Universitets Plass by the National Theater.

▲▲**Holmenkollen Ski Jump and Ski Museum**—Overlooking Oslo is a tremendous ski jump with a unique museum of skiing. The T-bane #1 gets you out of the city and into the hills and forests that surround Oslo. After touring the history of skiing in the museum, ride the elevator and climb the 100-step stairway to the thrilling top of the jump for the best possible view of Oslo—and a chance to look down the long and frightening ramp that has sent so many tumbling into the agony of defeat. The ski museum is a must for skiers—tracing the evolution of the sport from 4,000-year-old rock paintings, to crude l,500-year-old skis, to the slick and quickly evolving skis of our century. (50 kr, ski jump and museum open daily 9:00–20:00 in June, 9:00–22:00 in July and August, closes earlier off-season.)

For a special thrill, step into the **Simulator** and fly down the French Alps in a Disneyland-style downhill ski-race simulator. My legs were exhausted after the four-minute terror. This stimulator, parked in front of the ski museum, costs 35 kr. (Japanese tourists, who wig out over this one, are usually given a free ride after paying for four.)

To get to the ski jump, ride the T-bane line #1 to the Holmenkollen stop and hike up the road ten minutes. For a longer but easier walk, ride to the end of the line and walk down past the Frognerseteren Hovedrestaurant. This classy, traditional old place, with a terrace that offers a commanding view of the city, is a popular stop for apple cake and coffee or a splurge dinner (open until 22:00, tel. 22 14 37 36). From the restaurant it's a 30-minute walk downhill through the woods on a gravel path that runs generally parallel to Holmenkollenveien.

The nearby Tryvannstårnet observatory tower offers a lofty 360-degree view of Oslo in the distance, the fjord, and endless forests, lakes, and soft hills. It's impressive but not necessary if you climbed the ski jump, which gives you a much better view of the town (open 10:00–19:00 in June, 9:00–22:00 in July, and 9:00–20:00 in August, tel. 22 14 67 11).

Forests, Lakes, and Beaches—Oslo is surrounded by a vast forest dotted with idyllic little lakes, huts, joggers, bikers, and sun-worshipers. Mountain-bike riding possibilities are endless (as you'll discover if you go exploring without a guide or good map). For a quick ride, you can take the T-bane (with your bike; it needs a ticket too) to the end of line #1 (Frogner-seteren, 30 minutes from Nationaltheatret, gaining you the most altitude possible) and follow the gravelly roads (mostly downhill but with some climbing) past several dreamy lakes to Sognsvann at the end of T-bane line #3 (a one-hour ride, not counting time lost). Farther east, from Maridalsvannet, a bike path follows the Aker River all the way back into town. For plenty of trees and none of the exercise, ride the T-bane #3 to Sognsvann (with a beach towel rather than a bike) and join in the lakeside scene. Other popular beaches (such as Bygdøy Huk and others on islands in the harbor) are described in Use It's *Streetwise* magazine.

Harbor and Fjord Tours—Several tour boats leave regularly from Pier 3 in front of the city hall. A relaxing and scenic 50-minute mini-cruise with a boring three-language commentary departs hourly and costs only 70 kr (or free with Oslo Card, daily 11:00–20:00, tel. 22 20 07 15). They won't scream if you bring something to Munch. The cheapest way to enjoy the scenic Oslo fjord is to simply ride the ferries that regularly connect the nearby islands with downtown (free with the city transport pass).

▲▲▲**Folk Entertainment**—A group of amateur musicians and dancers (Leikarringen, Bondeungdomslaget) gives a short, sweet, caring, and vibrant one-hour show at the Oslo Concert Hall (140 kr to 180 kr, Monday and Thursday in July and August at 20:30; tel. 22 83 45 10; look for the big, brown, glassy overpass on Munkedamsveien; the recommended Vegata Vertshus restaurant is just up the street). For their off-season concert schedule (different locales, usually once a week), call 22 41 40 70.

Parks, Pools, and Wet Fun—The Tusenfryd Amusement Park offers more than 50 rides, plenty of entertainment, family fun, and restaurants. A free, regularly scheduled coach shuttles fun-seekers 20 minutes to the park from the Oslo City Hall (60 kr, 70 kr in July, free with Oslo Card, open 10:30–20:00). Kids love the adjacent new attraction, Viking Land (90 kr, 55 kr for kids under 4'7"). The Viking Voyage is frighteningly realistic.

Oslo offers lots of water fun for about 35 kr (kids half price). In Frogner Park, the Frognerbadet has a sauna, outdoor pools, lots of young families, a cafeteria, and high dives (free with Oslo Card, open mid-May to August, Middelthunsgate 28, tel. 22 44 74 29). Toyenbadet is a modern indoor pool complex with mini-golf and a 100-yard-long water slide (free with Oslo Card, open at odd hours throughout the year, Helgengate 90, a ten-minute walk from Munch Museum, tel. 22 68 24 23). Oslo's botanical gardens (free) are nearby. (For more ideas on swimming, pick up *Streetwise* magazine.)

Nightlife—They used to tell people who asked about nightlife in Oslo that Copenhagen was only an hour away by airplane. Now Oslo has sprouted a nightlife of its own. The scene is always changing. The tourist office has information on Oslo's many cafés, discos, and jazz clubs. Use It is the best source of information for local hot spots.

Shopping—For a great selection (but high prices) in sweaters and other Norwegian crafts, shop at Husfliden, the retail center for the Norwegian Association of Home Arts and Crafts (daily 9:00–17:00, Friday until 18:00, Saturday until 14:00, Den Norske Husflidsforening, Møllergata 4 behind the cathedral, tel. 22 42 10 75). Shops are generally open 10:00–18:00. Many stay open until 20:00 on Thursday and close early on Saturday and all day Sunday.

Sleeping in Oslo
(6 kr = about $1)
Sleep Code: **S** = Single, **D** = Double/Twin, **T** = Triple, **Q** = Quad, **b** = bathroom, **CC** = Credit Card (Visa, MasterCard, Amex).

Yes, Oslo is expensive. In Oslo, the season dictates the best deals. In low season (July to mid-August, and Friday, Saturday, and Sunday the rest of the year), fancy hotels are the best value for softies, with 600 kr for a double with breakfast. In high season (business days outside of summer), your affordable choices are dumpy-for-Scandinavia (but still nice by European standards) doubles for around 500 kr in hotels and 350 kr in private homes. For experience and economy (but not convenience), go for a private home. Oslo's hostels are far from the center, expensive (150 kr per bed), and usually full. Summer vagabonds sleep cheap (100 kr) at the downtown sleep-in.

Like those in its sister Scandinavian capitals, Oslo's hotels are designed for business travelers. Expensive in high season (but full in May and June for conventions; get reservations), empty otherwise. Only the TI can sort through all the confusing hotel "specials" and get you the best deal possible on a fancy hotel—push-list rooms at about half price. Half price is still 600 kr–700 kr, but that includes a huge breakfast and a lot of extra comfort for a few extra kroner over the cost of a cheap hotel. Cheap hotels, whose rates are the same throughout the year, are a bad value in summer but offer real savings in low season.

The TI's **Oslo Package** advertises 600-kr discounted doubles in business-class (normally priced at 1,200-kr) rooms and includes a free Oslo Card (worth 130 kr/day). The Oslo Package is a good deal for couples and an incredible deal for families with children under 16 who are traveling in the summer or on weekends. Two kids under 16 sleep free, breakfast included, and up to four family members get Oslo Cards, covering free admission to sights and all public transportation. The clincher is that the cards are valid for four days, even if you only stay at the hotel for one night (technically, you should stay two nights, but this is not enforced).

Use the TI only for these push-list deals, not for cheap hotels or private homes. Some of the cheaper hotels (my listings) tell the TI (which gets a 10 percent fee) they're full when they're not. Go direct. A hotel getting 100 percent of your payment is more likely to have a room. July and early August are easy, but early June and September can be tight.

Sleeping in Hotels near the Train Station

Each of these places is within a two-minute walk of the station, in a neighborhood your mom probably wouldn't want you hanging around in at night. The hotels themselves, however, are secure and comfortable. Leave nothing in your car. The Paleet parking garage is handy but not cheap—120 kr per 24 hours.

City Hotel, clean, basic, very homey, and with a wonderful lounge, originated 100 years ago as a cheap place for Norwegians to sleep while they waited to sail to their new homes in America. It now serves the opposite purpose (D-550 kr, Db-680 kr, with breakfast, CC:VMA, Skippergata 19, enter from Prinsens Gate, tel. 22 41 36 10, fax 22 42 24 29).

Rainbow Hotel Astoria is a comfortable, modern place, and part of the quickly growing Rainbow Hotel chain that understands what comforts are worth paying for. There are smoke-free floors, an included buffet breakfast; umbrellas, televisions, telephones, and full modern bathrooms in each room.

Ice machines! Most "twins" are actually "combi" rooms with a regular bed and a foldout sofa bed (Sb-395 kr–585 kr, Twin/b-520 kr–685 kr, Db-620 kr–785 kr, with buffet breakfast, rates vary with season, CC:VMA, 3 blocks in front of the station, 50 yards off Karl Johans Gate, Dronningensgate 21, 0154 Oslo, tel. 22 42 00 10, fax 22 42 57 65).

The newest Oslo Rainbow Hotel, **Rainbow Hotel Spectrum**, is also conveniently located and a good value ("combi" Twin/b-560 kr–685 kr, full doubles 100 kr more, nonsmoking rooms available, 3 blocks to the right as you leave the station on Lilletorget, Brugata 7, 0186 Oslo, tel. 22 17 60 30, fax 22 17 60 80). Ask for their brochure on Rainbow Hotels (with similar prices) in other Norwegian cities.

Sleeping in the West End

Ellingsen's Pensjonat, run by friendly Mrs. Wecking (Viking), is a textbook example of a good accommodations value, with no lounge or breakfasts, dreary halls but fine rooms, fluffy down comforters, and a great residential location 4 blocks behind the Royal Palace (a lot of S-230 kr, D-360 kr, Db-450 kr, call well in advance for doubles, Holtegata 25, 0355 Oslo 3, tel. 22 60 03 59, fax 22 60 99 21). Located on Holtegata near the Uranienborg church, it's #25 on the east side of the street (T-bane #19 from the station).

Cochs Pensjonat has 65 plain rooms (plus nine remodeled doubles) and a stale wet-noodle atmosphere, but it's right behind the palace (D-400 kr, Db-510 kr to 560 kr, all Dbs have kitchenettes, no breakfast, CC:VM, tram #11 to Parkveien 25, tel. 22 60 48 36, fax 22 46 54 02).

Frogner Hotel has clean, comfortable rooms with TVs and telephones (D-465 kr, Db-585 kr, CC:VMA, off Bygdøy Allé at Fredrik Stangsgate 33, a 15-minute walk from the center, tel. 22 44 19 35, fax 22 44 43 67). The buffet breakfast tastes best in the garden patio.

Sleeping in Rooms in Private Homes

Mr. Naess offers big, homey old rooms overlooking a park, and the use of a fully equipped kitchen. More urban, this is a flat in a big old building, with workaday shops and eateries nearby (S-150 kr, D-250 kr, T-375 kr, 40 kr extra per person for one night, no breakfast, at Toftegate 45, tel./fax 22 37 58 94). Walk 20 minutes from the station, or take bus #27 from tower in front of station to Olaf Ryes Plass (five stops). Three people (or two with lots of luggage) should take a taxi.

The **Caspari family** rents four comfortable rooms (at variable prices) in their home. Loosely run, it's in a peaceful suburb behind Frogner Park, a quick T-bane ride (get off at Borgen and walk 100 yards more on the right-hand side of the tracks; Heggelbakken 1; tel. 22 14 57 70).

Marius Meisfjord, a retired professor deeply interested in imparting Norse culture, rents rooms on the west side. Beds are 145 kr per person in a house stuffed with ancient furniture and pictures of European royalty (take tram #12 or #15 to Elisensbergveien, walk 2 blocks to Thomas Heftes Gate 46, tel. 22 55 38 46). There is a "possibility of breakfast" for sociable guests.

Sleeping in Youth Hostels

Haraldsheim Youth Hostel (IYHF), a huge, modern hostel, is open all year, situated far from the center on a hill with a grand view, laundry, and self-service kitchen. Its 270 beds (four per room) are often completely booked. Beds in the new fancy quads with private showers and toilets are 165 kr per person, including buffet breakfast. (Beds in simple quads cost 145 kr, with breakfast, sheets 35 kr, guest membership 25 kr; tram #10, #11, or #17 from station to Sinsen, 4 km out of town, five-minute uphill hike; Haraldsheimveien 4; tel. 22 15 50 43, fax 22 22 29 65.) Eurailers can train (2/hour, to Gressen) to the hostel for free.

Holtekilen Sommerhotel is a comfortable university dorm a bit out of town (mid-May to mid-August, D-390 kr with breakfast, 145 kr dorm beds with breakfast, sheets 35 kr, non-members 25 kr extra; Michelets vei 55, Stabbek/Oslo 1320, train to Stabbek and walk ten minutes, or bus #151 or #251 to Kveldsroveien and walk three minutes; ideal for drivers, go west 9 km from center, exit E-18 at Strand, tel. 67 53 38 53).

YMCA Sleep-In Oslo, located near the train station, offers the cheapest mattresses in town in three large rooms with 15–30 mattresses each, plus a left luggage room, kitchen, and piano lounge (earplugs for sale). It's as pleasant as a sleep-in can be (100 kr, no bedding provided, you must bring a sleeping bag or sheets, open 8:00–11:00, 17:00–24:00 July to mid-August, Møllergata 1, entry from Grubbegata, 1 block beyond the cathedral, tel. 22 20 83 97). They take no reservations, but call to see if there's a place.

Sleeping on the Train

Norway's trains offer 100-kr beds in triple compartments, 250-kr beds in doubles. Eurailers who sleep well to the rhythm of the rails have several very scenic overnight trips to choose from (it's light until midnight for much of the early summer at Oslo's latitude).

Eating in Oslo

The thought of a simple open-face sandwich (which looks and tastes like half of something I can make, with an inedible garnish added) for $5, and a beer for nearly as much, ruins my appetite. Nevertheless, one can't continue to sightsee on postcards and train tickets alone.

My strategy is to splurge for a hotel that includes breakfast. A 50-kr Norwegian breakfast is fit for a Viking. Have a picnic for lunch or dinner, using one of the many grocery stores. Basements of big department stores have huge first-class supermarkets with lots of picnic dinner-quality alternatives to sandwiches. Most of the little yogurt tubs with cereal come with a collapsible spoon. The train station has a late-hours grocery.

Since most Norwegians eat early, between 16:00–19:00, the cheapest places close by 19:00. Some cafés serve later, but generally dinners after 19:00 are elegant and quite expensive. Pizzerias and salad bars are the trend. Many pizzerias have all-you-can-eat specials. Chinese and ethnic places are everywhere and reasonably priced. Ask your receptionist for advice.

When you tire of herring, meatballs, and lutefisk, go Oriental at **Thai Orchid** (Peder Claussøns Gate 4, a five-minute walk from the National Gallery, 100–150-kr meals).

Assemble a picnic feast at **Rema 1000**, a supermarket on Holmes Gate, 1 block off the harbor. **Peppe's Pizza** has pleasing pies and a filling lasagna/salad special for 84 kr. **Caroline Café** in the train station is an easy place to grab a bite on your way into or out of town.

Café Sjakk Matt, at Håkon VII Gate 5 near Vegeta Vertshus, has good 80-kr dishes in a hip modern setting.

The **Aker Brygge** (harborfront mall) development isn't cheap, but it has some cheery cafés, classy delis, open-'til-22:00 restaurants, and markets. The **Cruise Café** has reasonable light meals.

Oslo's **Kaffistova** cafeteria is alcohol-free and clean (check out the revolving toilet seats), serving simple, hearty, and typically Norwegian (read "bland") meals for the best price around. You'll get your choice of an entrée and all the salad, cooked vegetables, and "flat bread" you want (or, at least, need) for around 80 kr (open 12:00–21:00, until 17:00 Saturday and 18:00 Sunday in summer, closes earlier off-season, 8 Rosenkrantzgate). The **Norrøna Cafeteria** is another traditional budget-saver (65-kr *dagens rett*, central at 19 Grensen, closes at 17:00, 19:00 off-season). Other cafeterias are found in department stores.

Vegeta Vertshus, which has been keeping Oslo vegetarians fat, happy, and low on the food chain for 60 years, serves a huge selection of hearty vegetarian food that would satisfy even a hungry Viking. Fill your plate once (medium plate-69 kr, large plate-79 kr) or eternally for 108 kr. How's your balance? One plate did me fine (daily 11:00–23:00, no smoking, no meat, Munkedamsveien 3B, near top of Stortingsgata between palace and city hall, tel. 22 83 42 32).

Transportation Connections—Oslo

By train to Bergen: Oslo and Bergen are linked by a spectacularly scenic seven-hour train ride. Reservations are required. Departures are at about 7:40, 10:45, 14:45, 16:05, and 23:00 daily in both directions (480 kr, or 380 kr if you buy a day early and don't travel on Friday or Sunday). For more info, see The Oslo–Bergen Train section in Fjords, Mountains, and Valleys chapter.

By boat to Copenhagen: Consider the cheap quickie cruise that leaves daily from Copenhagen (departs 17:00, returns 9:15 two days later; 16 hrs sailing each way and seven hours in Norway's capital). See Copenhagen chapter for specifics.

FJORDS, MOUNTAINS, AND VALLEYS

While Oslo and Bergen are the big touristic draws, Norway is essentially a land of natural beauty. While there is a certain mystique about the "land of the midnight sun," you'll get the most scenic travel thrills per mile, minute, and dollar by going west rather than north.

Leave Oslo and meander across the center of the country along an arc of tradition-steeped valleys, myth-inspiring mountains, and troll-thrilling fjords. This chapter describes two ways to cover Norway's greatest natural charms:

1. A series of dramatic train, boat, and bus rides called "Norway in a Nutshell," which takes a day from or between Oslo and Bergen.

2. For those with a car and more time, the powerfully scenic arc up Gudbrandsdalen Valley, over the Jotunheimen mountains, and down Norway's greatest fjord, Sognefjord.

Both routes cover the great Aurlandsfjord branch of Sognefjord.

FJORD COUNTRY AND "NORWAY IN A NUTSHELL"

Norway's greatest claims to scenic fame are her deep, lush fjords. A series of well-organized and spectacular bus, train, and ferry connections, appropriately called "Norway in a Nutshell," lays Norway's beautiful fjord country spread-eagle on a scenic platter. This is the seductive Sognefjord—tiny but tough ferries, towering canyons, and isolated farms and villages marinated in the mist of countless waterfalls. You're an eager Lilliputian on the Norwegian Gulliver of nature.

Fjords, Mountains, and Valleys

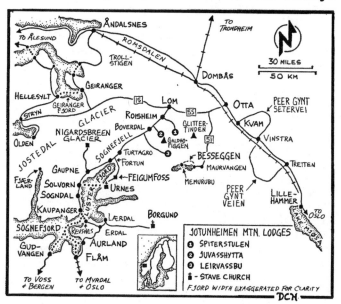

Today the region enjoys very mild weather for its latitude, thanks to the warm Gulf Stream. But 3 million years ago, an ice age made this land as inhabitable as the center of Greenland. Like the hairline on Dick Clark, the ice slowly receded. As the last glaciers of the Ice Age cut their way to the sea, they grooved out long troughs—today's fjords. Since the ice was thicker inland and only a relatively thin lip at the coast, the gouging was deeper inland. The average fjord is 4,000 feet deep far inland and only around 600 feet deep where it reaches the open sea.

The entire west coast is slashed by stunning fjords, but the Sognefjord, Norway's longest (120 miles) and deepest (over a mile), is tops. Anything but Sognefjord is, at best, foreplay. This is it, the ultimate natural thrill Norway has to offer. Aurland is a good home base for your exploration. Aurlandsfjord, a remote, scenic, and accessible arm of the Sognefjord, is possibly the juiciest bite in the scenic pomegranate of Norway. The local weather is actually decent, with about 24 inches of rain per year, compared to over 6 feet annually in nearby Bergen.

Planning Your Time

Even the blitz tourist needs a day for the "Norway in a Nutshell" trip. This is easily done as a long day trip from Oslo or Bergen. (All connections are designed for tourists, explained in English, and convenient and easy.) Ideally, break the trip with an overnight in Flåm or Aurland, carry on into Bergen, and enjoy a day there before sleeping on the night train (past all the scenery you saw westbound) back to Oslo. Those with a car and only one day should take the train from Oslo. With more time, drivers can improve on the "nutshell" by following the more time-consuming and thorough version of this scenic smørgåsbord explained in the second half of this chapter.

Sights—"Norway in a Nutshell"

The most exciting single day trip you could make from Oslo or Bergen is this circular train/boat/bus/train jaunt through this spectacular chunk of fjord country. Rushed travelers zip in and out by train from Oslo or Bergen. Those with more time do the Nutshell segments at their leisure. It's famous, everybody does it, and if you're looking for the scenic grandeur of Norway, so should you.

The all-day trip starts by train every morning from Oslo and Bergen. Tourist offices have brochures with exact times. It's a good side trip or an exciting way to connect the two cities. Here's the route in a nutshell: ride the Oslo–Bergen train to Myrdal (MIUR-doll); take the scenic Myrdal–Flåm train; hop on the Flåm–Gudvangen cruise; and then take the Gudvangen–Voss bus. (It's easy. Just follow the crowds.) At Voss, jump on the Oslo–Bergen train, and head west for Bergen or east for Oslo. The Nutshell trip is possible all year. Some say it's most beautiful in winter. The sights and segments are described below.

▲▲**The Oslo–Bergen Train**—This is simply the most spectacular train ride in northern Europe. You'll hang out the window with your camera smoking as you roar over Norway's mountainous spine. The barren, windswept heaths, glaciers, deep forests, countless lakes, and a few rugged ski resorts create a harsh beauty. The railway, an amazing engineering feat completed in 1909, is 300 miles long, peaks at 4,266 feet (which at this Alaskan latitude is far above the tree line), goes under 18 miles of snow sheds, trundles over 300 bridges, and passes through 200 tunnels in just under seven hours. (About

Norway in a Nutshell

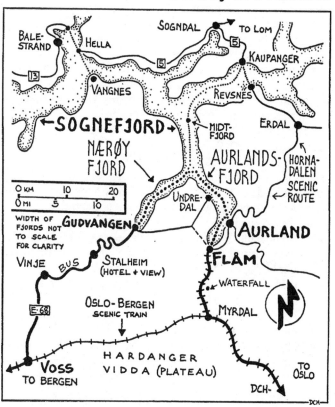

500 kr, second class one-way, 100 kr cheaper if you buy a day early and don't travel on Friday or Sunday, departures at about 7:40, 10:45, 14:45, 16:05, and 23:00 daily in both directions, reservations required.) Nutshell travelers get off the Oslo–Bergen train at Myrdal and rejoin it later.

▲▲**Myrdal–Flåm Train**—This little 12-mile spur line leaves the Oslo–Bergen line at Myrdal (2,800 feet) and winds down to Flåm (sea level) in 50 thrilling minutes (50-kr supplement for Eurail and Scanrail passholders). It's party time on board, and the conductor even stops the train for photos at the best waterfall. This line has 20 tunnels (more than 3 miles' worth) and is so steep that the train has five separate braking systems. Extra-hardy folks can hike or mountain bike the gravelly construction road down to Flåm (four hours, great mountain scenery but no fjord views) or hike the best two hours from Myrdal to Berek-vam, where you can catch the train into the valley. Myrdal is nothing but a scenic train junction.

▲**Flåm**—On the Norway in a Nutshell route, this scenic, touristy transit junction at the head of the Aurlandsfjord is little more than a train station, ferry landing, grocery store, souvenir shop, and cluster of hotels and hostels. (daily June–September 8:30–20:30, then shorter hours, TI tel. 57 63 21 06.) For accommodations, see Sleeping, below. Nightlife in Flåm is sparse. A walk on the sandy beach is fine at twilight (if it's not too windy). Pubs include the more touristy and older Furnkroa at the ferry dock and Heimly Lodge's pub, which serves pizza and beer and caters to a younger crowd.

▲▲**Aurland**—A few miles north of Flåm, Aurland is more of a town and less of a tourist depot. Nothing exciting, but it's a good, easygoing fjord-side home base (see Sleeping, below). You can hike up the valley or tour the electrical works (public tours show visitors the source of most of Oslo's electricity from July to mid-August, Monday–Friday at 12:00 and 13:30). The harborside public library is a pleasant refuge, and the 800-year-old church is worth a look.

The local *geitost* (goat's cheese) is sweet and delicious. The area has as many goats as people (1,900). The one who runs the tourist office speaks English (mid-June to August, 9:00–19:00, Saturday and Sunday 10:00–16:00, shorter hours off-season, tel. 57 63 33 13, fax 57 63 32 80). Pick up the English-language Bergen guide.

Note: Every train (except for the late-night one) arriving in Flåm connects with a bus or boat to Aurland. Fifteen buses and at least four ferries link the towns daily. The nearest bike rental is at the Flåm TI (20 kr/hour, 100 kr/day for mountain bikes).

▲▲▲**Flåm/Aurland–Gudvangen Fjord Cruise**—At Flåm, if you're doing the Nutshell Suite, follow the crowds and hop on the sightseeing boat. (Boats leave Flåm daily at 9:00, 11:05, 14:00, and 14:40, stopping at Aurland, then continuing to Gud-vangen, 120 kr one-way, 60 kr for those with an ISIC card. Couples ask for the "family" discount that lets the spouse go for half price.) The boat takes you right into the mist of the many fjord waterfalls and close to the goats, sheep, and awesome cliffs.

You'll cruise up the lovely Aurlandsfjord and hang a left at the stunning Nærøyfjord. It's a breathtaking voyage no matter what the weather does. For 90 glorious minutes, camera-clicking tourists scurry on the drool-stained deck like nervous roosters, scratching fitfully for a photo to catch the magic. Waterfalls turn the black rock cliffs into bridal veils, and you can nearly reach out and touch the Nærøyfjord's awesome sheer cliffs. The ride is the ultimate fjord experience. It's one of those fine times, like when you're high on the tip of an Alp, and a warm camaraderie spontaneously combusts between all the strangers who came together for the experience.

You can request a stopover in Undredal or Styvi (which has a farm museum, 20 kr). There's an idyllic 6-km shore along the 17th-century postal road from Styvi to Bleikindli, where a ferry connects to Gudvangen in the summer. If you do get off the boat, you can let the next boat know that you'd like to be picked up by turning on a signal light.

Gudvangen–Voss Bus—Gudvangen is little more than a boat dock and giant tourist kiosk. Norway Nutshellers get off the boat at Gudvangen and catch a bus (50 kr, about a one-hour ride, buses depart with each ferry landing) up the Nærøydalen (Narrow Valley) to Voss. Try to catch a bus taking the extra-scenic route via Stalheim.

Voss—A plain town in a lovely lake-and-mountain setting, Voss does have an interesting folk museum (open 10:00–19:00 June–August, closes earlier off-season), a 13th-century church, and a few other historic sights, but it's basically a home base for summer or winter sports. At Voss, the bus drops you at the train station (on the Oslo–Bergen train line). Drivers should zip right through. You can spend the night, but I wouldn't. **Vang Pensjonat** is in the center of town (D-480 kr, Uttragata 31, tel. 56 51 21 45), **Kringsja Pension** is nice with a lake view (D-480 kr, Db-560 kr, tel. 56 51 16 27), and the **Voss Youth Hostel** is luxurious (tel. 56 51 20 17). **Voss Camping**, on the lake, has huts, bikes, and rowboats (tel. 56 51 15 97). TI tel. 56 51 17 16.

▲▲Sognefjord Scenic Express Boat—Boats speed between Flåm and Bergen through the Sognefjord. Boats depart Bergen at 8:00 and arrive in Flåm at 13:30; depart Flåm at 15:30 and arrive in Bergen at 20:45 (455 kr, 510-kr round-trip special returning by train, couple or family discounts available, 50 percent off with ISIC card, daily in June, July, and August; all stop in Aurland).

▲Undredal—This almost impossibly remote community of 52 families was accessible only by boat until 1985, when the road from Flåm was opened. Undredal has Norway's smallest still-used church (built in the 12th century, holds up to 40 people). The 15-minute drive from Flåm is mostly through a new tunnel. There's not much in the town, which is famous for its goat cheese and church, but I'll never forget the picnic I had on the ferry wharf. If you want the ferry to stop, turn on the blinking light (though some express boats will not stop). You'll sail by Undredal on the Flåm–Gudvangen boat.

Sleeping on Sognefjord
(6 kr = about $1)
Sleep Code: **S** = Single, **D** = Double/Twin, **T** = Triple, **Q** = Quad, **b** = bathroom, **CC** = Credit Card (**V**isa, **M**asterCard, **A**mex).

Sleeping in Flåm
Heimly Lodge is doing its best to go big time in a small-time town. It's clean, efficient, and the best normal hotel in town (S-450 kr, D-650 kr, Db-960 kr with breakfast, CC:VMA, tel. 57 63 23 00, fax 57 63 23 40). Sit on the porch with new friends and watch the clouds roll down the fjord. Located 400 yards along the harbor from the station.

Flåm Youth Hostel and Camping Bungalows has the cheapest beds in the area. On the river just behind the Flåm train station, the Holand family offers dorm beds in four-bed youth hostel rooms (85 kr per bed with kitchenette, 25 kr for sheets, 25 kr if not a hostel member). They also have some doubles for 300 kr with bedding, four-bed cabins for 300 kr without sheets, and a deluxe cabin for 500 kr (tel. 57 63 21 21, fax 57 63 23 80). Note that the season is boom or bust here, and it can be very crowded in July and August.

Sleeping in Aurland
Aabelheim Pension, located right in the town center, is run by the folks at Vangen Motel next door. This is far and away Aurland's best cozy-like-a-farmhouse place. "Cozy" is *koselig*, a good Norwegian word. (Six D-350 kr, breakfast 68 kr, very traditional award-winning living room, mid-June to early September, tel. 57 63 35 80.)

Vangen Motel, nestled between Aabelheim and the fjord, is a simple old hotel that offers basic rooms (Db-425 kr, only 325 kr if you provide the sheets). There's a big self-serve kitchen and a dining and living area. Open all year. The motel has four-bed cabins right on the water for 300 kr without sheets (tel. 57 63 35 80). Astrid speaks English.

At the farmhouse **Skahjem Gård**, Aurland's deputy mayor, Nils Tore, rents out family apartments (one 300-kr hut, five newer 500-kr huts, with private bath and kitchenettes, 35 kr extra per person for sheets, tel. 57 63 33 29). It's a 20-minute walk from town, but Nils will pick up and drop off travelers at the ferry. This is best for families who are driving.

Aurland Fjord Hotel is a modern place with more comfort (sauna, steam bath, TV) and less traditional coziness. Basic restaurant, central location, friendly (Db-950 kr with breakfast, CC:VMA, tel. 57 63 35 05, fax 57 63 36 22).

GUDBRANDSDALEN VALLEY

This in-depth look at scenic Norway is best for drivers with more time. Gudbrandsdalen Valley (*dal* means "valley," so this is redundant) is the country of Peer Gynt, the Norwegian Huck Finn. This romantic valley of timeworn hills, log cabins, and velvet farms has connected northern and southern Norway since ancient times. Lillehammer, with Norway's best folk museum, provides an excellent introduction to the area. You might spend the night in a log and sod farmstead-turned-hotel, tucked in a quiet valley under Norway's highest peaks.

Next, Norway's highest mountain pass takes you on an exhilarating roller-coaster ride through the heart of Jotunheimen (the "giant's home"), which bristles with Norway's most gigantic mountains.

The road then hairpins down into fjord country, a softer world of fjords full of medieval stave churches, peely fishing boats, and brightly painted shiplap villages.

Planning Your Time

While you could enjoyably spend five or six days in this area, on a three-week Scandinavian rampage this slice of the region is worth three days. By car, I'd spend them like this:

Day 1: Leave Oslo early, spend midday at the Maihaugen Open-Air Folk Museum for a tour and picnic. Drive up Gudbrandsdalen Valley, making a short stop at the Lom church. Evening in Jotunheimen country.

Day 2: Drive out of the mountains, along Lustrafjord, over Hornadalen Pass, and into Aurlandsfjord. Sleep in Aurland.

Day 3: Cruise the Aurland and Nærøy fjords (round-trip)
before carrying on to Bergen.

Sights—Gudbrandsdalen Valley

▲**Lillehammer**—This pleasant winter and summer resort
town of 23,000 was the smallest town ever to host the winter
Olympics (1994). Any visit should include the high-tech
Olympics Experience Centre at the TI (50 kr, daily 10:00–
19:00, weekends 12:00–18:00, request an English-language
showing of the 15-minute, eight-projector slide presentation
as well as the 15-minute video on the 1994 games; exhibit
may close in 1997). At Håkon Hall, the 1994 Ice Hockey
arena, you can try a ski-jump simulator, visit a museum showcasing Olympics history, and see the "world-famous egg"
from the Lillehammer opening ceremonies (open weekdays
8:00–22:00, Saturday 9:00–18:00, closed Sunday, tel. 61 25 11
40). Lillehammer has a happy old wooden pedestrian zone
and several interesting museums, including a popular transportation museum and the Maihaugen Open-Air Folk
Museum (see below). Lillehammer's TI (9:00–19:00, less on
weekends and off-season, tel. 61 25 92 99) and the Olympic
Experience Centre are situated right in the colorful pedestrian shopping zone.

The town's best budget hotel, with a great view of the valley, is the **Gjestehuset Ersgaard** (D-490 kr, Db-590 kr–650
kr with breakfast, CC:VMA, 2 km east and above town at
Nordseterveien 201, tel. 61 25 06 84, fax 61 25 31 09). **Som-
merstuene** rents three rooms with kitchenettes (250 kr to 350
kr, 25 kr extra for sheets, Kirkegata 6, 2600 Lillehammer, tel.
61 25 79 29). For cheap beds, try the **GjesteBu** private hostel
(dorm bed-60 kr, D-250 kr and up, sheets extra, Gamleveien
110, 3 blocks from TI, reserve in advance, tel. 61 25 43 21) or
the **IYHF hostel** in the train/bus station (bed in quad-165 kr
for members, sheets extra).

▲▲▲**Maihaugen Open-Air Folk Museum**—Located in
Lillehammer, this wonderfully laid out look at the local culture
provides an excellent introduction to the Gudbrandsdalen Valley. Anders Sandvig, a "visionary dentist," started the collection
in 1887. The outdoor section has 150 old buildings from the
Gudbrandsdalen region, with plenty of free English tours,
crafts in action, and even people living there from ages ago
(Williamsburg-style, July only).

Indoors, the "We won the land" exhibit gives a look at local life during the Ice Age, the Vikings, the plague, the Industrial Revolution, etc. The indoor museum also has the original shops of 40 crafts- and tradespeople (such as a hatter, cooper, bookbinder, and Dr. Sandvig's old dental office). There's a thorough English guidebook (50 kr), English descriptions at each house, and free 45-minute guided tours daily in English (11:00, 13:00, 15:00, and sometimes on request).

The museum welcomes picnickers and has a café and an outdoor cafeteria (60 kr, 9:00–18:00 June through mid-August, 10:00–17:00 shoulder season, houses are closed in winter, tel. 61 28 89 00; call to be sure you arrive for a tour, especially off-season). Ask on arrival about special events, crafts, or music, and don't miss the indoor museum. Maihaugen is a steep 20-minute walk or short bus ride from the Lillehammer train station.

▲**Eidsvoll Manor**—During the Napoleonic period, Denmark was about to give Norway to Sweden. This ruffled the patriotic feathers of Norway's Thomas Jeffersons and Ben Franklins, and in 1814, Norway's constitution was written and signed in this stately mansion (in the town of Eidsvoll Verk, north of Oslo). It's full of elegant furnishings and stirring history (2 kr, 10:00–17:00, 12:00–15:00 in shoulder season, tel. 63 95 13 04).

Scenic Drives—Two side trips give visitors a good dose of the wild beauty of this land. Peer Gyntveien is a 30-kr toll road that leaves E-6 at Tretten, looping west for 25 miles and rejoining E-6 at Vinstra. This trip sounds romantic, but it's basically a windy, curvy dirt road over a high desolate heath and scrub brush plateau with fine mountain views: scenic, but so is E-6. The second scenic side trip, which is lesser known but more rewarding, is the Peer Gynt Seterveg.

▲**Lom**—This isn't much of a town—except for its great stave church, which causes the closest thing to a tour-bus jam this neck of the Norwegian woods will ever see. Drop by the church (you'll see its dark spire just over the bridge, 20 kr, 9:00–21:00, mid-June to mid-August, shorter off-season and during funerals, fine 5-kr leaflet, check out the little footbridge over the waterfall), and take advantage of the tourist information office (9:00–21:00, 10:00–19:00 Sunday in summer, shorter hours off-season, tel. 61 21 12 86). I'd sleep elsewhere, though Lom, about 10 miles north of Røisheim, has plenty of accommodations, such as the rustic **Strind Gard**. This 150-year-old farmhouse offers rooms in sod-roofed huts and in the main house (D-130 kr–

200 kr, T-230 kr, Quint-300 kr, great valley views, 3 km outside Lom on route 55 towards Sogndal, tel. 61 21 12 37).

Sleeping in Gudbrandsdalen Valley
(6 kr = about $1)

This is a very popular vacation valley for Norwegians, and you'll find loads of reasonable small hotels and campgrounds with huts (*hytter* means "bungalow," *rom* is "private room," and *ledig* means "vacancy") for those who aren't quite campers. These huts normally cost around 200 kr and can hold from four to six people. Although they are simple, you'll have a kitchenette and access to a good WC and shower. When available, sheets rent for an extra 40 kr per person. Local TIs can find you rooms. Only in the middle three weeks of July will finding a bed without a reservation prove difficult.

In the town of Kvam, the **Kirketeigen Ungdomssenter** (literally "Church Youth Center") welcomes travelers all year long. They have camping places (75 kr per tent or van), huts (220 kr per four-person hut), and very simple four-bed rooms (220 kr for two to four people with sheets, CC:V). Sheets and blankets (60 kr) can be rented (2650 Kvam i. Gudbrandsdalen, located behind the town church, tel. 61 29 40 82, fax 61 29 40 76, call in advance). One hundred meters away is the **Sinclair Vertshuset Motel**, which has an inexpensive pizzeria (Db-590 kr without breakfast or personality, cheaper off-season, tel. 61 29 40 24, fax 61 29 45 55). The motel was named after a Scotsman who led a band of adventurers into this valley, attempting to set up their own Scottish kingdom. They failed. (All were kilt.)

Sights—Jotunheimen Mountains

▲▲**Sognefjell**—Norway's highest mountain crossing (4,600 feet) is a thrilling drive through a cancan line of northern Europe's highest mountains. In previous centuries, the farmers of Gudbrandsdalen took their horse caravans over this difficult mountain pass on their necessary treks to Bergen. Today the road (Route 55) is still narrow, windy, and otherworldly, but it is usually closed from mid-October to May. The ten hairpin turns between Turtagrø and Fortun are white-knuckle exciting. Be sure to stop, get out, look around, and enjoy the lavish views. Treat each turn as if it were your last.

Scenic Drives and Hikes—From the main road near Bøverdal and Røisheim, you have several options springing from three toll roads. The Bøverdal youth hostel has good information and a fine 1:150,000 hiking map.

Spiterstulen: From Røisheim, this 18-km toll road (60 kr) takes you to the Spiterstulen mountain hotel/lodge (1,100 meters). This is the best destination for serious all-day hikes to Norway's two mightiest mountains: Glittertinden (2,470 meters) and Galdhopiggen (a four-hour hike up and a three-hour hike down, doable without a guide).

Juvasshytta: This toll road, starting from Bøverdal, takes you the highest you can drive and the closest you can get to Galdhopiggen by car (1,840 meters). At the end of the 50 kr toll road, there are daily guided five-hour hikes across the glacier to the summit and back (60 kr, 10:00 and 11:30 in the summer, 6 km each way, hiking shoes a good idea, easiest ascent but very dangerous without a guide). You can sleep in the Juvasshytta lodge (D-400 kr, D without sheets-350 kr, 130 sheetless beds in larger rooms, sheets 20 kr, breakfast 75 kr, dinner 140 kr, tel. 61 21 15 50).

Leirvassbu: This 18-km, 30-kr toll road is most scenic for "car hikers." It takes you to a lodge (owned by the Elvesæter Hotel people, see Sleeping, below) at 1,400 meters with great views and easy walks. A serious (four-hour round-trip) hike goes to the lone peak, Kyrkja (2,030 meters).

Besseggen: This ridge offers an incredible opportunity to hike between two lakes separated by 5 feet of land and a 1,000-foot cliff. To get to the trailhead, drivers detour down road #51 after Otta south to Maurvangen. Turn right to Gjendsheim to park your car. From Gjendesheim, catch the boat to Memurubu. The path starts at the boat dock. Hike along the ridge with a blue lake on one side and a green lake on the other, and keep your balance. The six-hour trail leads back to Gjendesheim. (This is a thrilling but potentially dangerous hike. And it's a major detour: Gjendesheim is about 55 miles from Røisheim.)

▲▲**Jostedalsbre's Nigardsbreen Glacier Hike**—Jostedalsbre is the most accessible branch of mainland Europe's largest glacier (185 square miles), and the Nigardsbreen Glacier Hike is a good chance for a hands-on glacier experience. It's an easy drive up Jostedal from Lustrafjord.

From Gaupne, drive up road #604 for 23 miles just past Gjerde, where the private toll road (20 kr) continues 2 miles to the lake. (Look for Breheimsenteret, an information center on the glacier and its history, at the entrance to the Nigard

Glacier valley, daily in summer 9:00–20:00, May and September 10:00–17:00, tel. 57 68 32 50.) From here take the special boat (15 kr round-trip, two 15-minute rides/hr, 10:00–18:00, mid-June to mid-August) to within a 20-minute walk of the glacier.

The walk is steep and slippery. Follow the red marks. There are 90-minute guided "family" walks of the glacier (60 kr, 40 kr for kids, daily from 12:00 depending on demand, minimum age 5, I'd rate them PG-13 myself, you get clamp-on crampons). Tougher glacier hikes are also offered (starting at 175 kr including boots, real crampons, and more, daily 10:30 and 13:00, four hours, but you'll need to be at the Glacier Center nearly two hours early to buy tickets and pick up your gear).

Respect the glacier. It's a powerful river of ice, and fatal accidents are not uncommon. The guided walk is the safest, and exciting enough. Use the Gaupne TI (tel. 57 68 15 88) to confirm your plans. If this is your first glacier, it's worth the time and hike even without the tour. If glaciers don't give you tingles and you're feeling pressed, it's not worth the long drive.

Sleeping in Jotunheimen
(6 kr = about $1)

Røisheim and Elvesæter are just hotel road stops in the wild. Bøverdal, 2 miles up the road, is a tiny village with a hostel.

Røisheim, in a marvelously remote mountain setting, is a storybook hotel comprised of a cluster of centuries-old, sod-roofed log farmhouses. Filled with antiques, Norwegian travelers, and the hard work of its owners, Røisheim is a cultural end in itself. Each room is rustic but elegant (Db-900 kr–1,100 kr without breakfast, CC:V). Some rooms are in old log huts with low ceilings and heavy beams. The honeymooner's special has a canopy bed. Gilded lily breakfasts are 110 kr, and a full three-course traditional dinner (one that Norway's royalty travels far to eat) is served at 19:00 (325 kr). Call ahead so they'll be prepared. (Open May to mid-October, 6 miles south of Lom on the Sognefjell Road #55 in Bøverdalen, tel. 61 21 20 31, fax 61 21 21 51.)

The **Elvesæter Hotel** is as Old World romantic as Røisheim but cheaper and less impressed with itself (Db-520 kr with breakfast, wonderful 150-kr buffet dinners, open June–September, CC:VMA, a few minutes farther up road 55, just past Bøverdal, tel. 61 21 20 00, fax 61 21 21 01). They also offer apartments with kitchens and all bedding (four to six people, 450 kr–810 kr without breakfast). The Elvesæter family has done a great job of retaining the historic character of their medieval farm, even though the place is big enough to handle large tour groups. They have the dubious distinction of being, as far as I know, the only hotel in Europe that charges for its advertising flier (3 kr). It's scenic—but not that scenic.

Bøverdalen Youth Hostel, just a couple of miles from Røisheim, is in another galaxy price-wise (four- to six-bed rooms, 75 kr per bed, D-190 kr, the usual extra for sheets and non-members, hot and self-serve meals, open mid-May through September, tel./fax 61 21 20 64). It's in the center of a little community (store, post office, campground, and toll road up to Galdhopiggen area). The hostel is a comfortable budget value. An added advantage is that you'll be encountering real hikers rather than car tourists.

Sights—Lustrafjord

This arm of the famous Sognefjord is rugged country. Only 2 percent of this land is fit to build or farm on. Lustrafjord is ringed with tiny villages where farmers sell cherries and giant raspberries. Urnes, perched on the east bank of Lustrafjord, has an ancient stave church and a less ancient ferry dock (ferries connect with sleepy Solvorn on the west bank, car crossings at the bottom of each hour 10:00– 17:50, pedestrian ferries more often, ten-minute ride, 30 kr round-trip).

▲▲**Urnes Stave Church**—A steep but pleasant 20-minute walk takes you from the town of Urnes to Norway's oldest stave church (b. 1150) and the most important artistic and historic sight in the region (25 kr, 10:30–17:30, June–August, ask for an English tour).

Sogndal—About a ten-minute drive from the Mannheller ferry, Sogndal is the only sizable town in this region. It's big enough to have a busy shopping street and a helpful tourist information office (tel. 57 67 30 83). Ten miles east of Sogndal, on the west bank of the Lustrafjord, **Solvorn** is a sleepy little Victorian town. Its tiny fjerry crosses the fjord regularly to Urnes (ten-minute ride, 32 kr round-trip). See Sleeping, below.

Honorable Mention—As you drive along Lustrafjord, check out these towns and sights. Skjolden, a village at the north tip of Lustrafjord, has a helpful tourist office (tel. 57 68 67 50) with advice on fjord ferries, glacier hikes, etc., and a cozy youth hostel on the river (75 kr per bed, D-180 kr, open mid-May through mid-September, tel. 57 68 66 15). From the little town of Nes on the west bank of the Lustrafjord, look across the fjord at the impressive Feigumfoss Waterfall. Drops and dribbles come from miles around for this 200-yard tumble. **Viki Fjord Camping**, located directly across from Feigumfoss Waterfall, has great fjord-side huts (tel. 57 68 64 20). Dale, a village on the west bank, boasts a 13th-century stone Gothic church with 14th-century frescoes. It's unique and worth a peek.

Kaupanger–Gudvangen by Car Ferry—Ferries take tourists through an arm and elbow of the Sognefjord. Marvel at the staggering Nærøyfjord. Boats leave Kaupanger daily at 9:20, 12:15, 16:00, and 18:50 (two-hour trip, ferry info: 94 50 65 20). Kaupanger is a ferry landing set on the scenic Sognefjord, and little more. The little stave-type church at the edge of Kaupanger is worth a free peek.

▲▲**Sogndal/Mannheller/Fodnes/Lærdal/Hornadalen/Aurland Scenic Drive**—This drive takes you over an incredible mountain pass, offers classic fjord aerial views, and winds into the pleasant fjord-side town of Aurland. From near Sogndal, catch the Mannheller–Fodnes ferry (20-minute ride, no reservations so arrive early in summer) and drive through the tunnel to Lærdal. While work is in progress on a 24-km long tunnel from Lærdal under Hornadalen to Aurland (open in 1998), the scenic route over the pass is worth the messy pants. Leave E-68 at Erdal (just west of Lærdal) for the breathtaking 90-minute drive to Aurland over 4,000-foot-high Hornadalen. This summer-only road passes remote mountain huts and terrifying mountain views before its 12-hairpin zig-zag descent into the Aurlandsfjord. Stop at the first fjord viewpoint as you begin your descent; it's the best.

Short-cut directly from Kaupanger to Gudvangen by ferry (4/day, 180 kr for car and driver, 51 kr per adult passenger) to get a quick taste of all this fjord scenery.

Sleeping on Lustrafjord
(6 kr = about $1)

Sleeping in Sogndal
For budget rooms, try the home of **Bjarne and Ella Skieldestad** (150 kr per person, kitchenette, on the main drag at Gravensteinsgate 10, tel. 57 67 21 83), the **Loftenes Pensjonat**

(D-550 kr, Db-600 kr with breakfast, CC:VM, near the water, tel. 57 67 15 77), or the excellent **youth hostel** (beds in three- and four-bed rooms for 90 kr, D-210 kr, sheets and guest membership extra, breakfast-50 kr, members' kitchen—bring your own pots; at fork in the road as you enter town, closed 10:00–17:00 and mid-August to mid-June, tel. 57 67 20 33).

Sleeping in Solvorn

The **Walaker Hotel**, a former inn and coach station, has been run by the Walaker family for 307 years (that's a lot of pressure on the next generation). In the main house, tradition drips like butter through the halls and living rooms. The rooms are simple but good, a warm family feeling pervades, and there are only patriotic hymns on the piano. The modern annex is comfortable and functional. The Walaker, set right on the Lustrafjord (in the perfect garden to get over a mental breakdown), is open mid-April to mid-October. Oda and Hermod Walaker are a wealth of information, and they help serve fine food (D-660 kr, Db-880 kr with breakfast, dinners are worth the 250-kr splurge, CC:VM, tel. 57 68 42 07, fax 57 68 45 44).

Transportation Connections

Cars are better, but if you're without wheels: **Oslo to Lillehammer** (11 trains/day, 2.5 hrs), **Lillehammer to Otta** (4 trains/day); a bus meets the train for travelers heading on to **Lom** (1 hr, 60 kr), **Lom to Sogndal** (2 buses/day).

Route Tips for Drivers

Oslo Across Norway to Jotunheimen: It's 2.5 hours from Oslo to Lillehammer and four hours after that to Lom. Wind out of Oslo following signs for E-6 (not to Drammen, but for a few yards to Stockholm and then to Trondheim). In a few minutes, you're in the wide-open pastoral countryside of eastern Norway. Norway's Constitution Hall is a five-minute detour off E-6, a couple of miles south of Eidsvoll in Eidsvoll Verk (follow the signs to Eidsvoll Bygningen). Then E-6 takes you along Norway's largest lake (Mjosa), through the town of Hamar, over a toll bridge (15 kr), and past more nice lake scenery into Lillehammer (site of the 1994 Winter Olympics). The old E-6 stays east of the lake, is only marginally slower, and avoids the toll bridge. Signs direct you uphill from downtown Lillehammer to the Maihaugen museum.

There's free parking near the pay lot (10 kr) above the entrance. Then E-6 enters the valley of Gudbrandsdalen. From Lillehammer, cross the bridge again and follow signs to E-6/Dombås and Trondheim. At Otta, exit for Lom.

Mountain driving tips: Use low gears and lots of patience both up (to keep it cool) and down (to save your brakes). Uphill traffic gets the right-of-way, but drivers, up or down, considerately dive for the nearest fat part whenever they meet. Ask backseat drivers not to scream until you've actually been hit or have left the road.

Ferry travel: Car ferries and express boats connect towns along the Sognefjord and Bergen. Ferries cost roughly $4 per hour for walk-ons and $14 per hour for a car, driver, and passenger. Reservations are generally not necessary (and sometimes not possible), but in summer, especially on Friday and Sunday, I'd get one to be safe (free and easy, tel. 55 32 40 15).

From Gudvangen to Bergen (85 miles): From Gudvangen, drive up the Nærøydalen (Narrow Valley) past a river bubbling excitedly about the plunge it just took. You'll see the two giant falls just before the road marked "Stalheimskleiva." Follow the sign to the little Stalheimskleiva road. This incredible road doggedly worms its way up into the ozone. My car overheated in a few minutes. Take it, but take it easy. (The main road gets you there easier—through a tunnel and 1.3 km back up a smaller road.) As you wind up, you can view the falls from several turnouts. At the top, stop for a break at the friendly but very, very touristy Stalheim Hotel. This huge eagle's-nest hotel is a stop for just about every tour group that ever saw a fjord. Here, genuine trolls sew the pewter buttons on the sweaters, and the priceless view is free.

The road continues into a mellower beauty, past lakes and farms, toward Voss. Tvindefossen, a waterfall with a handy campground/WC/kiosk picnic area right under it, is worth a stop. Unless you judge waterfalls by megatonnage, this 150-yard-long fall has nuclear charms. The grassy meadow and flat rocks at its base were made especially for your picnic lunch.

The highway takes you through Voss and into Bergen. On Monday–Friday, 6:00–22:00, drivers pay a 5-kr toll to enter Bergen. (If you plan to visit Edvard Grieg's home and the nearby Fantoft stave church, now is the ideal time since you'll be driving right by them. Both are overrated but kind of obligatory, a headache from downtown, and open until 17:30.)

BERGEN

Bergen has a rugged charm, permanently salted with robust cobbles and a rich sea-trading heritage. Norway's capital in the 12th and 13th centuries, Bergen's wealth and importance were due to its membership in the heavyweight medieval trading club of merchant cities called the Hanseatic League. Bergen still wears her rich maritime heritage proudly.

Enjoy her salty market, stroll the easy-on-foot old quarter, and treat yourself to a grand Norwegian-style smørgåsbord dinner. From downtown Bergen, a funicular zips you up a little mountain for a bird's-eye view of this sailors' town.

Planning Your Time

Bergen can be enjoyed even on the tail end of a day's scenic train ride from Oslo before returning on the overnight train. But that teasing taste will make you wish you had more time. On a three-week tour of Scandinavia, Bergen is worth a whole day. Start that day at the harborfront fish market and spend the rest of the morning in the Bryggen quarter (the tour is a must).

Bergen, a geographic dead end for most, is an efficient place to end your Scandinavian tour. Consider flying home from here. (Ask your travel agent about the economic feasibility of this "open jaws" option.)

Orientation

The action is on the waterfront. Bergen's historic "Hanseatic" quarter (Bryggen) lies on the far side of the harbor (the TI is behind the tall sailing ship). Boats from Flåm and Stavanger tie up at the left side of the harbor. Two blocks from Torget (behind Bryggen), a funicular stands ready to whisk you to the top of Mount Fløyen.

Famous for its lousy weather, Bergen gets an average of 80 inches of rain annually (compared to 30 inches in Oslo). A good year has 60 days of sunshine. With 221,000 people, Bergen has its big-city tension, parking problems, and high prices. But visitors stick mainly to the old center—easily handled on foot.

Tourist Information

On the harborfront in the old town, this TI covers Bergen and West Norway. They change money at 4 percent less than the banks (but with no 15-kr-per-check fee for traveler's checks, so they're OK for small exchanges or people who are stuck with small checks in Norway). They also have information and tickets for tours and concerts and a daily events board (open May–September 8:30–21:00, Sunday 10:00– 19:00; off-season 9:00–16:00, closed Sunday; a ten- to 15-minute walk from the train station; tel. 55 32 14 80). From mid-May through August, there's also a TI at the train station (daily 7:15–23:00). Pick up a free *Bergen Guide*, which lists all sights, hours, and special events and has a fine map. The **Bergen Card** gives you 24 hours of city buses, the Mount Fløyen funicular, and admission to many sights for 120 kr (48 hours for 190 kr). But check carefully to see if it will pay off for you, as it doesn't cover the Hanseatic Museum or Troldhaugen.

Arrival in Bergen

By Train or Bus: Bergen's train and bus stations are on Strømgaten, facing a park-rimmed lake. Walk around the lake to Ole Bulls Plass, then take a right on the wide street called Torgelmenning, which leads down to Torget (a ten- to 15-minute walk from the station), where you'll find Bergen's famous and fragrant fish market and the waterfront.

By Plane: The SAS bus runs between Bergen's Flesland Airport and downtown Bergen, stopping at the SAS hotel in Bryggen, Hotel Norge, and the bus station at platform 17 (40 kr, 40 min). Taxis take up to four people and cost about 200 kr for the 30-minute ride. SAS info tel. 55 99 76 10.

Getting Around Bergen

Most sights are walkable. Buses cost 14 kr per ride or 90 kr for a 48-hour Tourist Ticket (purchase one as you board). The best

Bergen and Harbor

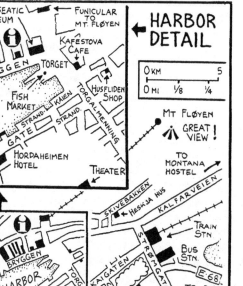

buses for a city joyride are #1 and #4. A little orange ferry chugs across the harbor every half-hour for 8 kr. This three-minute "poor man's cruise" has great harbor views. Miljøsykkelen's bike rental is a great deal: 20 kr for four hours or free with a valid city bus ticket (off King Oscar's Gate, around the corner from the YMCA hostel, summers, tel. 55 56 88 70 or 55 56 79 06).

Sights—Bergen's Hanseatic Quarter

▲▲▲**Hanseatic Quarter**—Called "the German wharf" until WWII, now just called "the wharf," or "Bryggen" (BREW-gun), this is Bergen's old German trading center. From 1370 to 1754, German merchants controlled Bergen's trade. In 1550, it was a German city of 2,000 workaholic merchants—walled and surrounded by 8,000 Norwegians. Bryggen, which has burned down several times, is now gentrified and boutiquish, but still lots of fun. Explore. You'll find plenty of sweater shops, restaurants, planky alleys, leaning old wooden warehouses, good browsing, atmospheric eating, and two worthwhile museums. The following Hanseatic sights are within a five-minute walk of each other.

▲▲▲**Walking Tour**—Every day at 11:00 and 13:00 June–August, a local historian takes visitors on an excellent 90-minute walk through the old Hanseatic town. This is a great way to get an understanding of Bergen's 900 years of history. Tours cost 60 kr and leave from the Bryggens Museum (next to the SAS Hotel). This fee includes entry tickets and tours of the Hanseatic and Bryggens Museums and the medieval assembly rooms called the Schøtstuene (very worthwhile, but only with a guide, tel. 55 31 67 10).

▲▲▲**The Hanseatic Museum**—This wonderful little museum is in an atmospheric old merchant house furnished with dried fish, old ropes, an old oxtail (used for wringing spilled cod liver oil back into the bucket), sagging steps, and cupboard beds from the early 1700s, one with a medieval pin-up. (35 kr, open daily in summer 9:00–17:00; September through May weekdays 11:00–14:00, Saturday 12:00–15:00, Sunday 12:00–16:00, tel. 55 31 41 89.) Drop in and ask when the next sporadic, but very good, English tour is scheduled.

▲▲▲**Bryggens Museum**—This modern museum on the archaeological site of the earliest Bergen (1050–1500), with interesting temporary exhibits upstairs, offers almost no English information (if you take the tour, the 20-kr English guidebook is unnecessary). You can see the actual excavation for free from the window just below St. Mary's Church (20 kr, 10:00–17:00, less off-season, tel. 55 31 67 10). The museum has a good, inexpensive cafeteria with soup-and-bread specials.

St. Mary's Church—Dating from about 1150, this is Bergen's oldest building and one of Norway's finest churches (10 kr, summer Monday–Friday 11:00–16:00).

Fish Market—This famous, bustling market has become quite touristy but still offers lots of smelly photo fun (Monday–Friday 7:00–16:00, Saturday until 15:00). Don't miss it. I believe this is the only outdoor fish market that accepts credit cards.

More Sights—Bergen

▲**Håkon's Hall/Rosenkrantz Tower**—These reminders of Bergen's medieval importance sit barren and boldly out of place on the harbor just beyond Bryggen. Håkon's Hall was a royal residence 700 years ago, when Bergen was the political center of Norway. Tours of both start in Håkon's Hall and leave on the hour (15 kr, 45 min, May–September 10:00–16:00, last tour at 15:00 daily, tel. 55 31 60 67). There's a great harbor view from the tower's rooftop.

▲▲**Fløibanen**—Just 2 blocks up from the fish market is the steep funicular ride to the top of "Mount" Fløyen (1,000 feet up), for the best view of the town, surrounding islands, and fjords all the way to the west coast. There are endless hikes on top and a pleasant walk back down into Bergen. It's a popular picnic or pizza-to-go perch (30 kr round-trip, departures each way on the half-hour and often on the quarter-hour). Peppe's Pizza is a block away from the base of the lift.

▲▲**Wandering**—Bergen is a great strolling town. The harborfront is a fine place to kick back and watch the pigeons mate. Other good areas to explore are Klostergate, Marken, Knosesmanet, Ytre Markevei, and the area behind Bryggen. The modern town also has a pleasant ambience, especially around Ole Bulls Plass.

▲▲**Aquarium**—Small but great fun if you like fish, this aquarium, wonderfully laid out and explained in English, claims to be the second-most-visited sight in Norway. A pleasant 20-minute walk from the center, it has a cheery cafeteria with fresh fish sandwiches (45 kr, daily 9:00–20:00, off-season 10:00–18:00, feeding times 11:00, 14:00, and 18:00; bus #4; tel. 55 23 85 53).

▲**Old Bergen**—Gamle Bergen is a Disney-cute gathering of 40 18th- and 19th-century shops and houses offering a cutesy, cobbled look at "the old life." The town is free, and some of the buildings are art galleries and gift shops. English tours departing on the hour (30 kr) get you into the 20-or-so museum buildings (open daily mid-May to August 11:00–18:00, with English guided tours on the hour, tel. 55 25 78 50). Take bus #1 or #9, from Bryggen (direction Lonborg) to Gamle Bergen (first stop after the second tunnel).

▲▲**Art Museums**—If you need to get out of the rain (or want to see more of Dahl, the realist Krogh, Munch, and other Norwegian painters), check out Rasmus Meyer's Collection (35 kr,

7 Rasmus Meyers Allé). The Stenersen Collection next door has some interesting modern art, including Munch and Picasso (35 kr). Both are free with the Bergen Card.

▲**Various City Tours**—The tourist information center sells tickets to several tours, including a daily 90-minute introduction at 17:00 (90 kr) and a daily two-hour tour at 14:30 (110 kr). These tours, which leave from the TI, are barely worthwhile for a quick orientation. More fun and very informative, if you're into city tours, are the harbor tours (15:30, from the fish market, aboard the *White Lady*, tel. 55 31 43 20) and the tacky tourist train with English-language headphone tours. Both cost 60 kr for 50 minutes and leave on the hour from the harborfront.

▲**Fantoft Stave Church**—The huge, preserved-in-tar, most touristy stave church in Norway burned down in 1992. It was rebuilt and reopened in 1996, but it can never be the same. Situated in a quiet forest next to a mysterious stone cross, this 12th-century wooden church is bigger, but no better, than others covered in this book. But it's worth a look if you're in the neighborhood, even after hours, for its evocative setting.

▲**Edvard Grieg's Home, Troldhaugen**—Norway's greatest composer spent his last 22 years here (1885–1907), soaking up inspirational fjord beauty and composing many of his greatest works. In a very romantic Victorian setting, the ambience of the place is pleasant, even for non-fans, and essential to anyone who knows and loves Grieg's music. The house is full of memories, and his little studio hut near the water makes you want to sit down and modulate. Unfortunately, it gets the "Worst Presentation for a Scandinavian Historical Sight" Award, since it's mobbed with tour groups, offers nothing in English, and uses no imagination in mixing Grieg's music with the house. (40 kr, daily, May–September 9:30–17:30, tel. 55 91 17 91.) Ask the tourist office about concerts in the concert hall at the site (100 kr, plus 50 kr for the shuttle bus from the TI, Wednesday and Sunday at 19:30, Saturday at 14:00 in late July and August; arrive one hour early for tickets).

The TI's free "Bergen Guide" pamphlet gives bus directions to Troldhaugen (the bus leaves you with a 30-minute walk). The daily 3-hour bus tour (10:00, 180 kr) is worthwhile for the very informative guide and the easy transportation. If you've seen other stave churches and can't whistle anything by Grieg, skip them.

Shopping—The Husfliden Shop (just off the market at 3 Vågsalmenning) is a fine place for handmade Norwegian sweaters and goodies (good variety and quality but expensive). Like most shops, it's open 9:00–16:30 Monday–Friday, Thursday until 19:00, Saturday 9:00–14:00. Major shops are closed on Sunday, but shop-'til-you-drop tourists manage to find plenty of action even on the day of rest.

Folk Evenings—The "Fana Folklore" show is Bergen's most advertised folk evening. An old farm hosts this very touristy collection of cultural clichés, with food, music, dancing, and colorful costumes. While many think it's too gimmicky, and many think it's lots of fun, *nobody* likes the meager dinner; 190 kr includes the short bus trip and the meal. (Most nights June–August 19:00–22:30, tel. 55 91 52 40.)

The **Bergen Folklore show** is a smaller, less gimmicky program, featuring a good music-and-dance look at rural and traditional Norway. Performances are downtown at the Bryggens Museum (every Tuesday and Thursday evening mid-June to August, tickets for the one-hour show are 95 kr at the TI or at the door, tel. 55 31 95 50).

Scenic Boats and Trains from Bergen—The TI has several brochures on tours of the nearby Hardanger and Sogne fjords. There are plenty of choices. For all the specifics on "Norway in a Nutshell," a scenic combination of buses, ferries, and trains, that can be done in a day from Bergen (7:30–14:30 or 9:00–20:00), see the Fjords, Mountains, and Valleys chapter.

Sleeping in Bergen
(6 kr = about $1)
Sleep Code: **S** = Single, **D** = Double/Twin, **T** = Triple, **Q** = Quad, **b** = bathroom, **CC** = Credit Card (**V**isa, **M**asterCard, **A**mex).

July through mid-August is peak season for rainy Bergen, and reservations are advisable (though off-season you can find a room just about any time without a reservation). The hotel scene is bleak (minimum 400-kr doubles), with none of the great summer discounts found in other big Nordic cities. But if you can handle showers down the hall and cook breakfast yourself in the communal kitchens, several pensions offer better rooms with a homey atmosphere and a fine central location for half the hotel prices.

The private homes I list are cheap, central, and quite pro-fessional. The cheapest dorm/hostel-style beds are not much less than the private homes, and unless the shoestring you're traveling on is really frazzled or you like to hang out with other vagabonds and hostelers, I'd stick with the private rooms. The tourist office is helpful in finding the least-expensive rooms, but if you call the hotel direct, you'll save yourself the TI fee (15 kr–20 kr).

Sleeping in Hotels and Pensions

If you must have a uniformed person behind the key desk, the prestigious old **Hotel Hordaheimen** is central, just off the harbor, and your best budget-hotel bet (Db-995 kr, or 790 kr in summer with reservations no more than 48 hours in advance, CC:VMA, C. Sundts Gate 18, tel. 55 23 23 20, fax 55 23 49 50). Run by the same alcohol-free, give-the-working-man-a-break organization that brought you Kaffistova restau-rants, their cafeteria, open late, serves traditional, basic (drab), inexpensive meals.

Mycklebust Pension is a family-run explosion of homey-ness, offering better rooms than the Hordaheimen but pension rather than hotel services. It's friendly, central (a five-minute walk to market), with your own kitchen and laundry service, and showers down the hall (D-450 kr, Db-500 kr, family room for four-600 kr, includes breakfast, Rosenberggate 19, tel. 55 90 16 70, fax 55 23 18 01).

Kloster Pension, in a funky cobbled neighborhood 4 blocks off the harbor, has basic doubles including breakfast (S-300 kr, D-450 kr, Db-600 kr, Strange Hagen 2, tel. 55 90 21 58, fax 55 23 30 22). **Fagerheim Pension** offers some of the cheapest doubles in town (S-200 kr, D-360 kr, breakfast extra; up King Oscar's Gate half a mile, Kalvedalsveien 49A; tel. 55 31 01 72). **Park Pension** is classy, nearly a hotel, and in a wonderful neighborhood—central but residential. People who have the money for a cheap hotel but want Old World lived-in elegance love this place (Sb-610 kr, Db-750 kr with breakfast, CC:VMA, Harald Hårfagres Gate 35, tel. 55 32 09 60, fax 55 31 03 34).

Sleeping in Rooms in Private Homes

Since the Bergen hotel owners don't quite understand the magic of the marketplace, there are more private homes opening up to travelers than ever. While (for a price) the TI would love to help you out, here are several you can book direct.

Alf and Elisabeth Heskja are a young couple with four doubles, one shared shower/WC, and a kitchen. This is my home in Bergen, and far better than the hostel for budget train travelers (D-270 kr, 17 Skivebakken, 5018 Bergen, reserve in advance, tel. 55 31 30 30, fax 55 31 30 90, E-mail heskja@online.no). It's located five minutes from the train station (down King Oscar's Gate, uphill on D. Krohns Gate, up the stairs at the end of the block) on Skivebakken, the steep cobbled "most painted street in Bergen." (They also have a house at Lille Øvregatan 20-C, a quiet road leading to the funicular, with similar rooms for the same price.) Also on Skivebakken is the **Olsnes' home** (S-160 kr, D-270 kr, Db-320 kr, 24 Skivebakken, tel. 55 31 20 44). These are all central and cheap, quite private, and lacking a lot of chatty interaction with your hosts.

The **Vågenes family** has six doubles in a large, comfortable house on the edge of town (D-320 kr, no breakfast, J.L. Mowinckelsvei 95, tel. 55 16 11 01). It's ten minutes from downtown on bus #60. Driving from downtown, cross the Puddefjordsbroen bridge (road #555), go through the upper tunnel on road #540, and turn left on J.L. Mowinckelsvei until Helgeplasset Street, just past the Hogesenter.

Sleeping in Hostels

Intermission offers 40 cheap bunks in one co-ed dorm and one quad for 95 kr, all-you-can-eat breakfasts for 20 kr, packed lunches for 10 kr, and free Norwegian waffles on Monday and Thursday nights (open mid-June to mid-August, 7:00–11:00, 17:00–24:00 only, kitchen, free laundry machines, Kalfarveien 8, about a five-minute walk from the train station, reservations accepted, tel. 55 31 32 75 or 55 31 06 70).

For 100 kr at the **YMCA Interrail Center**, you get a mattress on the floor in 10- to 50-person rooms (one for women, the others mixed). If you don't have a sleeping bag, you can rent sheets and blankets for 30 kr. (Open 7:00–01:00, mid-June to early September, five minutes from the station, near the center, in a pink house at Korskirke alm #4, tel. 55 31 72 52, fax 55 31 35 77.)

Montana Youth Hostel (IYHF) is one of Europe's best hostels, but its drawbacks are the remote location and relatively high price. Still, the bus connections (#4, 15 minutes from the center) and the facilities (modern five-bed rooms, classy living room, no curfew, huge parking lot, member's kitchen) are excellent. (150 kr per bed with a big breakfast, sheets 30 kr, non-members pay 25 kr extra, 30 Johan Blydts Vei, tel. 55 29 29 00.)

Eating in Bergen

The **Kaffistova Ervingen Cafeteria,** facing the fish market (in the building with the Eskimo on top), is a good basic food value. Fine atmosphere in the first-floor self-service cafeteria (open 8:00–18:00, closed earlier off-season). The **Kafe Bergen**, next door, offers similar food, prices, and hours. For similar old Norwegian fare, eat at the borderline-dreary cafeteria in the **Hordaheimen Hotel**—great prices and lots of *lefse*. Students and budget travelers carbo-load at **Pasta Sentral** (50 kr meals, open late, Vestre Strømkai 6). The **Augusta Conditori and Lunchsalon** serves good meals at a fair price in a cheery atmosphere (open 10:00–18:00, next to Hotel Hordaheimen at C. Sundts Gate 24).

Bryggestuene is actually one restaurant with one menu on two levels with two different styles, at #6 in the Bryggen harborfront, offering good (but smoky) atmosphere and seafood and traditional meals for around 150 kr. Small servings but more potatoes on request. The Dagens Menu is 69 kr (off-season only). There are plenty of classy atmospheric places along the Bryggen harborfront.

Enhjørningen ("the unicorn") offers Bergen's top seafood buffet but is quite expensive (160 kr, Monday–Saturday 12:00–16:00). And **Kjøttbørsen** (literally, "meat market"; hearty servings, Vaskerelven 6, tel. 55 23 14 59) is a splurge local carnivores enjoy.

Hotel Norge's "Koltbord" buffet—Bergen's ritziest hotel serves a daily all-you-can-eat spread in its classy Ole Bull restaurant—hot dishes, seafood, and desserts rich in both memories and calories (165 kr lunch, enter 12:00–16:00; 198 kr for dinner, from 19:00, tel. 55 21 01 00).

Bergen's "in" cafés are stylish, cozy, small, open very late, and a great place to experience the local yuppie scene. The trendy **Café Opera** is good (80-kr dinners, 35-kr soup-and-bread specials, often with live music, always with live locals, English newspapers, chess, open 'til the wee hours).

The **Zachariasbryggen** restaurant complex has a good pub (Freddie's) with piano music (open late, popular with locals), located right on the Torget, or harbor square. For a louder crowd and a younger scene, try **På Folkemunne** (light lunches for 59 kr, "cheapest dinners in town," Ole Bulls Plass 9, around the corner from the taxi station, serves food until about 22:00). A good place for a drink is **Dickens** on Ole Bulls Plass, packed on Friday and Saturday nights, and **Bryggen Tracteursted** in the atmospheric center of Bryggen.

Transportation Connections—Bergen

Bergen is conveniently connected to Oslo only by train (5/day, seven scenic hrs). Train info tel. 81 00 33 00.

To get to **Stockholm, Copenhagen**, or even **Trondheim**, you'll be going via Oslo unless you fly. Before buying any long train ticket from Bergen, look into cheap flights. **Kilroy Travels** has a handle on cheap flights for youths (Parkveien 1 in Student Sentret, tel. 55 32 64 00). **British Midland** airlines has a cheap ($139) flight between Bergen and London.

By bus to Kristiansand: If you're heading to Denmark, you'll catch the ferry from Kristiansand. Catch the Haukeliexpress bus #180B departing Bergen at 7:20. After a two-hour layover in Haukeligrend, take bus #221 at 15:20, arriving at 19:30 in Kristiansand (520 kr, cheaper for students with ISIC cards), easily in time for the overnight ferry to Denmark.

Cruising to Newcastle, England: The Color Line sails from Bergen to Newcastle, England, on Tuesday, Friday, and Sunday, June–August (tel. 55 54 86 60). The cheapest peak-season crossing for the 22-hour trip is 880 kr on Tuesday or Sunday for a reclining chair ("sleeperette"). Cars with up to four passengers cost about 2,700 kr.

Cruising to Stavanger: FlaggRuten catamarans sail to Stavanger (2–4/day in four hours, 450 kr, 50 percent discount for students or those with a ScanRail pass). From Stavanger you can take a train to Kristiansand and Oslo (overnight possible).

Cruising to the Arctic: Hurtigrute coastal steamers depart daily in summer at 22:30 for the seven-day trip north up the scenic west coast to Kirkenes on the Russian border. Cabins should be booked well in advance. Call Bergen Lines in the U.S. at 212/319-1300. Deck space and seats are usually available with short or no notice (info in Bergen, tel. 55 55 72 00, reservations 77 64 81 00).

SOUTH NORWAY'S SETESDAL VALLEY

Welcome to the remote—and therefore very traditional—Setesdal Valley. Probably Norway's most authentic cranny, the valley is a mellow montage of sod-roofed water mills, ancient churches, derelict farmhouses, yellowed recipes, and gentle scenery. The locals practice fiddles and harmonicas, rose painting, whittling, and gold- and silverwork. The famous Setesdal filigree echoes the rhythmical design of the Viking era and Middle Ages.

The Setesdal Valley joined the 20th century with the construction of the valley highway in the 1950s. All along the valley you'll see the unique two-story storage sheds called *stabburs* (the top floor stored clothes; the bottom, food) and many sod roofs. Even the bus stops have rooftops the local goats love to munch.

In the high country, just over the Sessvatn summit (3,000 feet), you'll see goat herds and summer farms. If you see an *"Ekte Geitost"* sign, that means genuine homemade goat cheese is for sale. (It's sold cheaper and in more manageable sizes in grocery stores.) To some it looks like a decade's accumulation of ear wax. I think it's delicious. Remember, *ekte* means all-goat—real strong (the more popular and easier-to-eat regular goat cheese has cow's-milk cheese mixed in).

Each town in the Setesdal Valley has a weekly rotating series of hikes and activities for the regular, stay-put-for-a-week visitor. The upper valley is dead in the summer but enjoys a bustling winter. This is easygoing sightseeing—nothing earthshaking. Let's just pretend you're on vacation.

Setesdal Valley

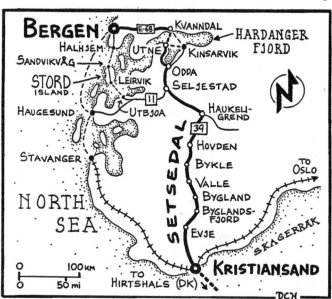

Planning Your Time

Frankly, without a car, Setesdal is not worth the trouble. There are no trains, bus schedules are as sparse as the population, and the sights are best for joyriding. If you're driving in Bergen and want to get back to Denmark, this route is more interesting than repeating Oslo. On a three-week Scandinavian trip, I'd do it in one long day, as follows:

6:00:	Leave Bergen.
8:00:	Catch the Kvanndal ferry to Utne.
9:00:	Say good-bye to the last fjord at Odda.
12:00:	Lunch in Hovden at the top of Setesdal Valley.
13:00:	Frolic south with a few short stops in the valley.
18:00:	Arrive in Kristiansand—dinner and a movie?
23:00:	Board boat for overnight crossing.

Sights—Setesdal Valley

These sights are listed from north to south.

Odda—At the end of the Hardanger fjord, just past the huge zinc and copper industrial plant, you'll hit the industrial town of Odda (well-stocked TI for whole region and beyond, tel. 53 64 12 97). Odda brags that Kaiser Wilhelm came here a lot, but he's dead, and I'd drive right through. If you want to visit the tongue of a glacier, drive to Buar and hike an hour to Buarbreen. From Odda, drive into the land of boulders, where rocks so big that trees grow on them seem to be hurled into the river and fields by the mighty waterfalls that almost line the road. Stop at the giant double fall (on the left, pull out on the right, drive slowly through it if you need a car wash).

Røldal—Continue over Røldalsfjellet and into the valley below, where the old town of Røldal is trying to develop some tourism. Drive straight through. Its old church isn't worth the time or money. Lakes like frosted mirrors make desolate huts come in pairs. Haukeliseter, a group of sod-roofed buildings filled with cultural clichés and tour groups, offers pastries, sandwiches, and reasonable (65-kr to 85-kr) hot meals in a lakeside setting. Try the traditional *rømmegrøt* porridge.

Haukeligrend—The TI is open 10:00–18:00 in summer (tel. 35 07 03 67). If you plan to stay here, **Haukelid Turistheim Pensjonat** offers quaint old rooms (in the quaint old half of the building), a feel-at-home Old World living room, a Ping-Pong table, and no breakfast but a reasonable cafeteria (D-300 kr, at the junction of roads #39 and #11 in Haukeligrend, about six hours out of Bergen, 30 minutes before Hovden, tel. 35 07 01 26). Haukeligrend is a bus/traffic junction, with daily bus service to/from Bergen and to/from Kristiansand.

Hovden—At the top of the Setesdal Valley, Hovden is a ski resort (2,500 feet high), barren in the summer and painfully in need of charm. Locals come here to walk and relax for a week. Good walks offer a chance to see reindeer, moose, Arctic fox, and wabbits—so they say. Every other day a chairlift takes summer visitors to its nearby 3,700-foot peak. The Hegni Center, on the lake at the south edge of town, rents canoes for 30 kr an hour. A new super indoor spa/pool complex, the Hovden Badeland (110 kr, daily 11:00–19:00 in summer) provides a much-needed way to spend an otherwise dreary (and very likely) drizzly early evening here. The TI is open in summer (Monday–Friday 9:00–16:00, Saturday 10:00–14:00, tel. 37 93 96 30).

If you stay in Hovden, the **Hovdehytta Hostel**, a big old ski chalet with an inviting ski lodge atmosphere (large dining room and open fire in the living room), offers clean, modern bunk-bed doubles with a large breakfast for 330 kr (40 kr extra for sheets and those without a hostel card). Good 75-kr dinners must be ordered by 15:00, dinner at 18:00 (tel. 37 93 95 22). Built in 1911, this is the oldest place in town and the only cozy and reasonable accommodations in this booming winter resort of sprawling ranch-style ski hotels.

▲**Dammar Vatnedalsvatn**—Just south of Hovden is a 2-mile side trip to a 400-foot-high rock-pile dam. Great view, impressive rockery. This is one of the highest dams in northern Europe. Read the chart. Sit out of the wind a few rows down the rock pile and ponder the vastness of Norwegian wood.

▲**Bykle**—The most interesting folk museum and church in Setesdal are in the teeny town of Bykle. The 17th-century interior has two balconies—one for men and one for women (10 kr, mid-June to mid-August 10:00–18:00, weekends 12:00–18:00).

The Huldreheimen Museum, a wonderful little open-air museum, is a typical 800-year-old seterhouse used when the cattle spent the summer high in the mountains. Follow the sign up a road to a farm high above the town, park, then hike a steep 150 yards into Norway's medieval peasant past—fine view, six houses filled with old stuff, and a good English brochure (10 kr, open mid-June to mid-August 10:00–18:00, Saturday and Sunday 12:00–18:00).

Grasbrokke—On the east side of the main road (at the "Grasbrokke" sign) you'll see an old water mill (1630). A few minutes farther south is a "Picnic and WC" sign. Exit onto that little road. You'll pass another old water mill with a fragile rotten-log sluice. At the second picnic turnout (just before this roadlet returns to the highway, you'll find a covered picnic table for rainy lunches), turn out and frolic along the river rocks.

Flateland—One mile east, off the main road, is the Setesdal museum (Rygnestadtunet), offering more of what you saw at Bykle (20 kr, two buildings, open daily mid-June to mid-August 10:00–18:00, otherwise 11:00–17:00). Unless you're a glutton for culture, I wouldn't do both.

▲**Valle**—This is Setesdal's prettiest village (but don't tell Bykle). In the center, you'll find fine silver- and goldwork at Grete and Ørnulfs Sylvsmie, traditional dinners in the cozy Bergtun Hotel (100 kr to 150 kr, summer only, daily specials), homemade crafts and old-fashioned *lefse* cooking demonstrations at the *husflid* shop, and a fine suspension bridge for little boys of any age who still like to bounce (and for anyone interested in a great view over the river of the strange mountains that look like polished, petrified mud slides). European rock climbers, tired of the over-climbed Alps, often entertain spectators with their sport. Is anyone climbing? (The TI is open mid-June to mid-August, Monday–Friday 10:00–17:00, Saturday 10:00–14:00, normally closed Sunday except in July 10:00–14:00, less off-season, tel. 37 93 73 12.)

If you stay in Valle, try the **Bergtun Hotel**. Run by Halvor Kjelleberg, it's a real folksy, sit-a-spell Setesdal lodging full of traditional furniture, paintings, and carvings in each charming room (D-500 kr to 600 kr, some rooms have bunks, some have four-poster beds, extra bed-100 kr, includes breakfast, Valle i Setesdal, tel. 37 93 72 70, fax 37 93 74 37).

Nomeland—Sylvartun, the silversmith with the valley's most aggressive publicity department, demonstrates the Setesdal specialty in a 17th-century traditional log cabin and a free little gallery/museum. He also gives a free fiddle concert weekdays in July at 13:00. On Monday and Thursday at 14:30, you can see a 30-minute folk-dancing show (40 kr).

Grendi—The Ardal Church (1827) has a runestone in its yard and 300 yards south of the church is a 900-year-old oak tree.

Evje—A huge town by Setesdal standards (3,500 people), Evje is famous for its gems and mines. Fancy stones fill the shops here. Only rockhounds would find the nearby mines fun (for a small fee you can hunt for gems). The super-for-rockhounds new Setesdal Mineral Park is on the main road, 3 km south of town. For modern, bright, functional doubles in Evje, stay with the **Haugen family** (two-bunk rooms for 180 kr, 270 kr with sheets, a pleasant garden, a kitchenette, and a huge stuffed moose in the garage) on the Arendal Road (last house on the left, look for "Rom" sign, tel. 37 93 08 88, fax 37 93 01 14).

KRISTIANSAND

This "capital of the south" has 67,000 inhabitants, a pleasant, grid-plan Renaissance layout (Posebyen), a famous zoo with Norway's biggest amusement park (10 km toward Oslo on the main road), a daily bus to Bergen, and lots of big boats going to England and Denmark. It's the closest thing to a beach resort in Norway. The Posebyen center, around the bustling pedestrian market street, is the shopping/eating/browsing/people-watching town center. Stroll along the Strand Promenaden (marina) to the Christiansholm Fortress.

The TI is at Dronningensgate 2 (daily 8:00–19:30, Sunday

12:00–19:30; off-season Monday–Friday 8:00–16:00 only, tel. 38 12 13 14). The bank at the Color Line terminal opens for each arrival and departure (even the midnight ones) and is reasonable. There are two cinema complexes (50 kr, seven screens, showing movies in English, check schedules at TI or cinemas) within 2 blocks of the Color Line docks and the TI. During summer, they usually have "green days" (Monday–Thursday), when movies cost only 40 kr.

Sleeping and Eating in Kristiansand

Your best modern, comfy, and cozy bet is **Hotel Sjøgløtt**. Friendly Helene Ranestad gives this small hotel lots of class (S-390 kr, Sb-490 kr, D-530 kr, Db-590 kr with breakfast, CC:VM, near the harbor on a quiet street at Østre Strandgt 25, tel./fax 38 02 21 20). Otherwise, Kristiansand hotels are expensive and nondescript. The cheap, musty old **Bonde-heimen** is being renovated, so its appearance and prices will probably change in 1997 (S-330 kr, D-560 kr, Db-660 kr with breakfast, CC:VMA, tel. 38 02 44 40, fax 38 02 73 21). The **Hotel Norge** is more modern and expensive but reduces its rates during the summer to roughly 700 kr for a double (Dronningensgate 5, tel. 38 02 00 00, fax 38 02 35 30).

Villa Frobusdal Hotel, outside the city center, is a 1917 villa and classy B&B run by the friendly Herigstads (S-400 kr, Sb-450 kr, Db-630 kr, includes breakfast, Frobusdalen 2, access from E-18 going east, tel. 38 07 05 15, fax 38 07 01 15). The **hostel** is cheap, but not central (tel. 38 02 83 10).

Along the marina, you'll find plenty of *kafeterias*, a **Peppe's Pizza** (open until 23:00, salad bar, on Gyldenløvesgate), and budget ethnic restaurants. For the best dinner in town, splurge at **Bak Gården** (Tollbodgaten 5, hiding in the center).

Transportation Connections—Kristiansand

Cruising to Hirtshals, Denmark: The Color Line ferry sails from Kristiansand in Norway to Hirtshals in Denmark (usually daily departures at about 8:00, 13:30, 19:00, and 00:30, mid-June to late August; 8:15, 19:15, and 20:30 the rest of the year). The trip takes just over four hours (the overnight ride is slower, to arrive at 6:30). Passengers pay 98 kr to 360 kr (July and weekends are most expensive). A car costs 180 kr to 500 kr. The "car package" lets five in a car travel for 1,390 kr (summer Monday–Thursday). There are decent smørgåsbords, music, duty-free shopping, a desk to process your Norwegian duty-free tax rebates, and a bank for small changes (no fee).

When you can commit yourself to a firm date, call Color Line to make a reservation. They accept telephone reservations to be paid when you get to the dock. Color Line's information and reservation line is open 8:00–22:00, Sunday 8:00–21:00, tel. 38 07 88 88, in Kristiansand. Or you can use their office in Oslo (tel. 22 94 44 70), Bergen (tel. 55 54 86 60), or New York (c/o Bergen Line, tel. 212/319-1300, fax 212/319-1390). Ask about specials. Round-trip fares can be lower than one-way fares.

Take the night boat to save the cost of a hotel. Enjoy an evening in Kristiansand then sleep (or vomit) as you sail to Denmark. Beds are reasonable (reclining seats euphemistically called "sleeperettes" are 40 kr; simple couchettes are 60 kr; a bed in a four-berth room is 110 kr to 130 kr; and a private double with shower ranges from 130 kr–260 kr per person). You owe yourself this comfort if you're efficient enough to spend this night traveling. I slept so well, I missed the Denmark landing and ended up crossing three times! After chewing me out, the captain said it happens a lot. Set your alarm or spend an extra day at sea.

Route Tips for Drivers

Bergen to Kristiansand (ten hours): Your first key connection is the Kvanndal–Utne ferry (a two-hour drive from Bergen, departures hourly from 6:00 to 23:00, tel. 55 23 87 80 to confirm times, reservations not possible, breakfast in cafeteria). If you make the 8:00, your day will be more relaxed. Driving comfortably, with no mistakes or traffic, it's two hours from your Bergen hotel to the ferry dock. Leaving Bergen is a bit confusing. Pretend you're going to Oslo on the road to Voss (signs for Nestune, Landas, Nattland, R-7). About a half-hour out of town, leave the Voss road, after a long tunnel on road #7, for Norheimsund. This road, as treacherous for the famed beauty of the Hardanger Fjord it hugs as for its skinniness, is faster and safer if you beat the traffic (which you will with this plan).

The ferry drops you in Utne, where a lovely thread of a road will take you to Odda and on up into the scenic mountains. From Haukeligrend, turn south and wind up to Sessvatn at 3,000 feet. You're entering Setesdal Valley. It's all downhill from here, following the Otra River for 140 miles south to the major port town of Kristiansand. Skip the smaller secondary routes. As you enter Kristiansand, follow the signs for Denmark.

SWEDEN

STOCKHOLM

If I had to call one European city home, it would be Stockholm. Surrounded by water and woods, bubbling with energy and history, Sweden's stunning capital is green, clean, and underrated.

Crawl through Europe's best-preserved old warship and relax on a canal-boat tour. Browse the cobbles and antique shops of the lantern-lit Old Town and take a spin through Skansen, Europe's first and best open-air folk museum. Marvel at Stockholm's glittering city hall, modern department stores, art museums, and futuristic suburbs.

While progressive and sleek, Stockholm respects its heritage. Throughout the summer, mounted bands parade each noontime through the heart of town, from Nybroplan to the royal palace, announcing the changing of the guard, and turning even the most dignified tourist into a scampering kid. The Gamla Stan (Old Town) celebrates the Midsummer festivities (late June) with the down-home vigor of a rural village, forgetting that it's the core of a gleaming 20th-century metropolis. All of Stockholm goes wild during its Water Festival (ten days in early August).

Planning Your Time

On a two- to three-week trip through Scandinavia, Stockholm is worth two days. Efficient train travelers sleep in and out for two days in the city with only one night in a hotel. (Copenhagen and Oslo trains arrive at about 8:00 and depart at about 23:00.) To be even more economical and efficient, you could use the luxury Stockholm–Helsinki boat as your hotel for two nights (spending a day in Helsinki) and have two days in Stockholm without a hotel (e.g., Copenhagen; night train to Stockholm, day in Stockholm; night boat to Helsinki, day in Helsinki; night boat to Stockholm, day in Stockholm; night train to Oslo). That may sound crazy, but it gives you three interesting and inexpensive days of travel fun. Spend two days in Stockholm this way:

Day 1: Arrive by train (or the night before by car), do station chores (reserve next ride, change money, pick up map, *Stockholm This Week*, and a Stockholm Card at the Hotellcentralen TI), check into hotel. At 10:00 catch one-hour bus tour from Opera; 11:00, tour *Vasa* warship, picnic; 13:00, tour Nordic Museum; 15:00, Skansen; ask for an open-air folk museum tour; 19:00, folk dancing, possible smørgåsbord and evening popular dancing. Or wander Gamla Stan in the evening.

Day 2: Do the 10:00 city hall tour, climb the city hall tower for a fine view; 12:00, catch the changing of the guard at the palace, tour royal palace, explore Gamla Stan, or picnic on one-hour city boat tour; 16:00, browse the modern city center around Kungsträdgården, Sergels Torg, Hötorget market and indoor food hall, and Drottninggatan area.

Orientation (tel. code: 08)

Greater Stockholm's 1.4 million residents live on 14 islands that are woven together by 50 bridges. Visitors need only concern themselves with five islands: **Norrmalm** (downtown, with most hotels, shopping areas, and the train station), **Gamla Stan** (the old city of winding lantern-lit streets, antique shops, and classy, glassy cafés clustered around the royal palace), **Södermalm** (aptly called Stockholm's Brooklyn—residential and untouristy), **Skeppsholmen** (the small, very central traffic-free park island with the Museum of Modern Art and two fine youth hostels), and **Djurgården** (literally "deer garden," Stockholm's wonderful green playground, with many of the city's top sights).

Tourist Information

Hotellcentralen is primarily a room-finding service (in the central train station), but its friendly staff adequately handles all your sightseeing and transportation questions. This is the place for anyone arriving by train to arrange accommodations, buy the Tourist Card, and pick up free brochures, city map, *Stockholm This Week* (which lists opening hours and directions to all the sights and special events), and brochures on whatever else you need (city walks, parking, jazz boats, excursions, bus routes, shopping, etc.). While *This Week* has a decent map, the 15-kr map covers more area and bus routes. It's worth the extra money if you'll be using the buses. (Open daily June–August 7:00–21:00; May and September 8:00–19:00, shorter hours off-season; tel. 08/240880, fax 791-8666.)

Sverige Huset (Sweden House), Stockholm's official tourist information office (a short walk from the station on Kungsträdgården), is very good but usually more crowded than the Hotellcentralen. They've got pamphlets on everything; an "excursion shop" for transportation, day-trip and bus-tour information, and tickets; and an English library and reading room upstairs with racks of 5-kr information on various aspects of Swedish culture and one state's attempt at cradle-to-grave happiness. (Open June–August, 8:00–18:00, Saturday–Sunday 9:00–17:00; off-season 9:00–18:00, Saturday–Sunday 9:00–15:00; Hamngatan 27, tel. 08/789-2490 for info, 789-2415 for tickets; T-bana: Kungsträdgården.)

Arrival in Stockholm

Stockholm's central train station is a wonderland of services, shops, and people going places. The Interrail Center kiosk in the center is for general help (especially for young travelers). The Hotellcentralen TI is as good as the city TI nearby. There is a Viking Line office, if you're sailing to Finland. The FOREX long-hours exchange counter changes traveler's checks for only a 15-kr fee (two offices, upstairs and downstairs, in the station).

Getting Around Stockholm

By Bus and Subway: Stockholm complements her many sightseeing charms with great information services, a fine bus and subway system, and special passes to take the bite out of the city's cost (or at least limit it to one vicious budgetary gash).

Buses and the subway system work on the same tickets. Ignore the zones since everything I mention (except Drottningholm and Carl Millesgården) are in Zone One. Each 13-kr ticket is valid for one hour (ten-packs cost 85 kr). The subway, called T-bana or Tunnelbana, gets you where you want to go very quickly. Ride it just for the futuristic drama of being a human mole and to check out the modern public art (transit info tel. 600-1000). The **Tourist Card**, which gives you free run of all public transport and the harbor ferry (24 hours/56 kr, 72 hours/107 kr, sold at TIs and newsstands), is not necessary if you're getting the Stockholm Card (see below). The 72-hour pass includes admission to Skansen, Gröna Lund, and the Kaknäs Tower.

It seems too good to be true, but each year I pinch myself and the **Stockholm Card** is still there. This 24-hour, 175-kr pass (sold at TIs and ship terminals) gives you free run of all public transit, free entry to virtually every sight (70 places), free parking, a handy sightseeing handbook, and the substantial pleasure of doing everything without considering the cost (many of Stockholm's sights are worth the time but not the steep individual ticket costs). This pays for itself if you do Skansen, the *Vasa*, and the Royal Palace and Treasury tour. If you enter Skansen on your 24th hour (and head right for the 45-kr aquarium), you get a few extra hours. (Parents get an added bonus: two children under 18 go along for free with each adult pass.)

By Harbor Shuttle Ferry: Throughout the summer, ferries connect Stockholm's two most interesting sightseeing districts. They sail from Nybroplan and Slussen to Djurgården, landing next to the *Vasa* and Skansen (15 kr, not covered by Stockholm Card, every 20 min).

Sights—Downtown Stockholm

▲**Kungsträdgården**—The King's Garden Square is the downtown people-watching center. Watch the life-sized game of chess and enjoy the free concerts at the bandstand. Surrounded by the Sweden House, the NK department store, the harborfront, and tour boats, it's the place to feel Stockholm's pulse (with discretion).

▲▲**Sergels Torg**—The heart of modern Stockholm, between Kungsträdgården and the station, is worth a wander. Enjoy the colorful, bustling underground mall and dip into the Gallerien mall. Visit the Kulturhuset, a center for reading, relaxing, and socializing designed for normal people (but welcoming tourists), with music, exhibits, hands-on fun, and an insight into contemporary Sweden (free, Tuesday–Sunday 11:00–17:00, often later, tel. 700-0100). From Sergels Torg, walk up the Drottninggatan pedestrian mall to Hötorget (see Eating, below).

▲▲**City Hall**—The Stadshuset is an impressive mix of 8 million bricks, 19 million chips of gilt mosaic, and lots of Stockholm pride. One of Europe's most impressive public buildings

Greater Stockholm

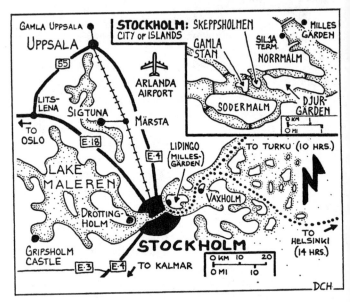

(b. 1923) and site of the annual Nobel Prize banquet, it's particularly enjoyable and worthwhile for its entertaining tours (30 kr, daily June–August at 10:00, 11:00, 12:00, and 14:00; off-season at 10:00 and 12:00; just behind the station, bus #48 or #62; tel. 785-9074). Climb the 350-foot tower for the best possible city view (10:00–16:30, May–September only, 5 kr or free with city hall ticket). The city hall also has a TI and a good cafeteria with 55-kr lunches (Monday–Friday).

▲**Orientation Views**—Try to get a bird's-eye perspective on this wonderful urban mix of water, parks, concrete, and people from the Stadshuset tower (see above), the Kaknäs Tower (at 500 feet, the tallest building in Scandinavia, 20 kr, June–August 9:00–22:00; bus #69 from Nybroplan or Sergels Torg; tel. 789-2345), the observatory in Skansen, or the top of the Katarina elevator (5 kr, near Slussen subway stop, then walk behind Katarinavagen through classy residential neighborhoods and grand views).

▲**Mini-Orientation Bus Tour**—For a quick big-bus orientation tour, consider those that leave from the Royal Opera House (120 kr, 50 min, 10:00, 12:00, 14:00, mid-April to October, tel. 411 70 23). They also organize 75-minute Old

Stockholm Center

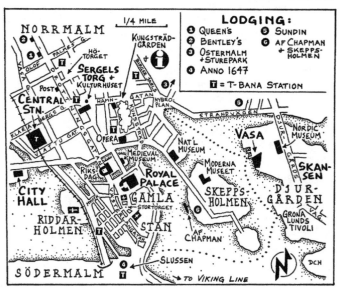

LODGING:
- ❶ QUEEN'S
- ❷ BENTLEY'S
- ❸ OSTERMALM + STUREPARK
- ❹ ANNO 1647
- ❺ SUNDIN
- ❻ AF CHAPMAN + SKEPPS- HOLMEN

🚉 = T-BANA STATION

Town walks (75 kr). For a free self-guided tour, follow the walk laid out in *Stockholm This Week*.

▲**City Boat Tour**—For a good floating look at Stockholm, and a pleasant break, consider a sightseeing cruise. Tour boats leave regularly from in front of the City Hall (tel. 23 33 75). The "Historical Stockholm" tour (70 kr, one hour, departing on the half-hour 10:00–16:00, mid-June to mid-August) offers the best informative introduction. The "Under the Bridges" tour is basically the first tour with an hour of extra territory (130 kr, 2 hours, mid-April to mid-August, departs hourly from the Grand Hotel). The "Royal Canal" tour is a scenic joyride through lots of greenery (80 kr, 1 hour, mid-May to mid-August, departs every half-hour from the Grand Hotel).

▲**National Museum**—Though mediocre by European standards, this museum is small, central, uncrowded, and very user-friendly. The highlights of the collection are several Rembrandts, Rubens, a fine group of Impressionists, and works by the popular and good-to-get-to-know local artists Carl Larsson and Anders Zorn (40 kr, free on Friday, open 11:00–17:00, Tuesday 11:00–20:00, closed Monday; some August Tuesdays until 17:00 because of special concerts, tel.

666-4250). A worthwhile audio tape (20 kr) guides you through a 50-minute tour of the collection's highlights.

Museum of Modern Art—This bright and cheery gallery is as far out as can be, with Picasso, Braque, and lots of goofy Dada art (such as the *Urinal* and the *Goat with Tire*). Normally in a pleasant park on Skeppsholmen, it's temporarily housed at 57 Birger Jarisgatan (40 kr, free Thursday, open Tuesday–Thursday 12:00–19:00, Friday–Sunday 12:00–17:00, closed Monday).

Sights—Stockholm's Gamla Stan

▲▲**Gamla Stan (Old Town)**—Stockholm's old island core is charming, fit for a film, and full of antique shops, street lanterns, painted ceilings, and surprises. Spend some time here, browse, enjoy a café, or get to know a shopkeeper. At the tip of the island is Slussen (Swedish for "locks"), where the salty Baltic meets the 1.5-foot-higher Lake Mälaren (with water so fresh that local politicians brush their teeth with it).

Military Parade—Starting at the Army Museum (daily at 12:00, Sunday at 13:00), the parade culminates at the Royal Palace for the changing of the guard.

▲▲**Royal Palace**—The stately exterior encloses 608 rooms (one more than Britain's Buckingham Palace) of glittering Baroque and rococo decor. There are eight different sights with separate admissions here. Most important are the apartments (45 kr, open daily 10:00–16:00 June–August; off-season Tuesday–Sunday 12:00–15:00, closed Monday). The Royal Treasury is another ticket (40 kr, same hours, no samples, tel. 402-6000).

Riksdaghuset—You can tour Sweden's parliament buildings if you'd like a firsthand look at its government. (Free hourly tours in English throughout the summer, usually Monday–Friday at 12:30 and 14:00, but call 786-4000 to confirm times.)

Museum of Medieval Stockholm—While grade-schoolish, this gives you the best look at medieval Stockholm (30 kr, June–September 11:00–16:00, Tuesday, Wednesday, Thursday until 18:00; September–June 11:00–17:00, closed Monday; enter from the park in front of the Parliament). The Stromparterren park, with its Carl Milles statue of the *Sun Singer* greeting the day, is a pleasant place for a sightseeing break (but an expensive place for a potty break—use the free WC in the museum).

Riddarholm Church—This final resting place for about 600 years of Sweden's royalty is pretty lifeless (20 kr, June–August 12:00–16:00, less in September, tel. 402-6000).

Sights—Stockholm's Djurgården

▲▲▲**Skansen**—Europe's original and best open-air folk museum, Skansen is a huge park gathering more than 150 historic buildings (homes, churches, schoolhouses, etc.) transplanted from all corners of Sweden. Tourists can explore this Swedish-culture-on-a-lazy-Susan, seeing folk crafts in action and wonderfully furnished old interiors. In the town quarter (top of the escalator), potters, glassblowers (especially important if you'll be missing Sweden's glass country to the south), and other craftspeople are busy doing their traditional thing in a re-created Old World Stockholm.

Spreading out from there, the sprawling park is designed to show northern Swedish culture and architecture in the northern part of the park (top of park map) and southern Sweden in the south (bottom of map). Excellent, free one-hour guided walks (from Bollnästorget info stand at top of escalator) paint a fine picture of old Swedish lifestyles (usually daily at 14:00 and 16:00 June–August). There's fiddling many nights at 18:15, folk dancing demonstrations daily in summer at 19:00, Sunday at 14:30 and 16:00, and public dancing to live bands weeknights (20:30–23:30, call for evening theme—jazz, folk, rock, or disco). Admission to the aquarium is the only thing not covered on your entry ticket (45 kr, 10:00–20:00).

Kids love Skansen, especially its zoo (ride a life-size wooden Dala-horse and stare down a hedgehog) and Lill' Skansen (Punch 'n' Judy, mini-train, and pony ride fun daily from 11:00 till at least 16:00). There are lots of special events and several restaurants. The main restaurant serves a grand smørgåsbord (180 kr). The Ekorren café offers the least expensive self-service lunches with a view. Tre Byttor (next to Ekorren) serves 18th-century–style food in a candlelit setting. Another cozy inn, the Stora Gungan Krog, at the top of the escalator, has better food (60-kr indoor or outdoor lunches with a salad bar).

Skansen is great for people-watching and picnicking, with open and covered benches all over (especially at Torslunden and Bollnästorget, where peacenik local toddlers don't bump on the bumper cars). Get the map or the 30-kr museum guidebook that has the same map, and check the live crafts schedule at the information stand at Bollnästorget to confirm your Skansen plans.

Use the west entrance (Hazeliusporten) if you're heading to or from the Nordic Museum. (50 kr entry, 45 kr in winter;

open May–August 9:00–22:00, buildings 11:00–17:00; winter 9:00–17:00, buildings 11:00–15:00; take bus #47 from the station; call 442-8000 for the day's tour, music, and dance schedule.) You can miss Gröna Lund, the second-rate amusement park across the street.

▲▲▲*Vasa*—Stockholm turned a titanic flop into one of Europe's great sightseeing attractions. This glamorous but unseaworthy warship—top-heavy with a tacked-on extra cannon deck—sank 20 minutes into her 1628 maiden voyage when a breeze caught the sails and blew her over in the Stockholm harbor. After 333 years, she rose again from the deep (with the help of marine archaeologists) and today is the best-preserved ship anywhere, housed in a state-of-the-art museum. The masts on the roof are placed to show their actual height.

Catch the 25-minute English-subtitled movie (at the top of each hour, dubbed versions often play at 11:30 and 13:30), and for more information, take the free 25-minute English tours (at the bottom of each hour from 10:30, every other hour off-season) to best enjoy and understand the ship. Learn about ship's rules (bread can't be older than eight years), why it sank (heavy bread?), how it's preserved, and so on. Private tours are easy to freeload on, but the displays are so well described that a tour is hardly necessary. (45 kr, open daily mid-June to mid-August 9:30–19:00; off-season 10:00–17:00, winter on Wednesday until 20:00, tel. 666-4800.) Take bus #47 to the big brick Nordic Museum and catch the boat from Nybroplan or Slussen, or walk from Skansen.

▲▲**Nordic Museum**—This museum, built to look like a Danish palace, offers a look at how Sweden lived over the last 500 years. Highlights include the Food and Drink section, with its stunning china and crystal table settings; the Nordic folk art (second and third floors); the huge statue of Gustav Vasa, father of modern Sweden, by Carl Milles (top of second flight of stairs); and the Sami (Lapp) exhibit in the basement. (Open 11:00–17:00, Thursday until 20:00, closed Monday, tel. 666-4600.) Worth your time if you have the Stockholm Card, but it's overpriced at 50-kr admission. The 30-kr guidebook isn't necessary, but pick up the English brochure at the entrance.

▲**Thielska Galleriet**—If you liked the Larsson and Zorn art in the National Gallery and/or if you're a Munch fan, this charming mansion on the water at the far end of the Djurgården park is worth the trip. (40 kr, Monday–Saturday 12:00–16:00, Sunday

13:00–16:00; bus #69 from the central station, tel. 662-5884.)
▲**Sauna**—Sometime while you're in Sweden or Finland, you'll
have to treat yourself to Scandinavia's answer to support hose
and a face lift. (A sauna is actually more Finnish than Swedish.)
Simmer down with the local students, retired folks, and busy
executives. Try to cook as calmly as the Swedes. Just before
bursting, go into the shower room. There's no luke-cold, and
the trickle-down theory doesn't apply—only one button,
bringing a Niagara of liquid ice. Suddenly your shower stall
becomes a Cape Canaveral launch pad, as your body scatters to
every corner of the universe. A moment later you're back
together. Rejoin the Swedes in the cooker, this time with their
relaxed confidence; you now know that exhilaration is just
around the corner. Only very rarely will you feel so good.

Any tourist office can point you toward the nearest birch
twigs. Good opportunities include a Stockholm–Helsinki cruise,
any major hotel you stay in, some hostels, or least expensively, a
public swimming pool. In Stockholm, consider the Eriksdals-
badet (Hammarby Slussvag 8, near Skanstull T-bana, tel. 643-
0673). Use of its 50-meter pool and first-rate sauna costs 30 kr.

The newly refurbished Centralbadet lets you enjoy an
extensive gym, "bubblepool," sauna, steam room, and an elegant Art Nouveau pool from 1904 (79 kr, long hours, Drott-
ningsgatan 88, five minutes up from Sergels Torg, tel. 24 24
03). Bring your towel into the sauna; the steam room is mixed,
the sauna is not. Massage and solarium cost extra, and the pool
is more for floating than for jumping and splashing. The leafy
courtyard is an appropriately relaxing place to enjoy their
restaurant (reasonable and healthy light meals).

Sights—Outer Stockholm
▲▲**Carl Millesgården**—Here is the home housing the major
work of Sweden's greatest sculptor, situated on a cliff overlooking Stockholm. Milles' entertaining, unique, and provocative art
was influenced by Rodin. There's a classy café and a great picnic
spot. (50 kr, open daily 10:00–17:00, May–September; off-season
Tuesday–Sunday 11:00–16:00, tel. 731-5060.) Catch the T-bana
to Ropsten, then take any bus to the first stop (Torsvik). It's a
five-minute walk from there (follow the signs).
▲▲**Drottningholm**—The queen's 17th-century summer castle
and present royal residence has been called, not surprisingly,
Sweden's Versailles. The adjacent, uncannily well-preserved

Baroque theater is the real highlight here, especially with its 40-kr guided tours (English theater tours twice an hour, May–August 12:00–16:30; in September 13:00–15:30). Get there by a pleasant but overpriced boat ride (70 kr round-trip, two hours) or take the subway to Brommaplan and bus #301 or #323 to Drottningholm. (40-kr entry, palace open daily 11:00–16:30 May–August; in September daily 13:00–15:30, Saturday and Sunday 12:00–15:30, tel. 402-6280 for palace tours in English, scheduled often at 11:00.)

The 18th-century Drottningholm court theater performs perfectly authentic operas (about 30 performances each summer). Tickets to these very popular and unique shows go on sale each March. Prices for this time-tunnel musical and theatrical experience are 95 kr–450 kr. For information, write to Drottningholm's Theater Museum, Box 27050, 10251 Stockholm, or phone 08/660-8281, fax 665-1473.

▲▲**Archipelago**—The world's most scenic islands (24,000 of them!) surround Stockholm. Europeans who spend entire vacations in and around Stockholm rave about them. If you cruise to Finland, you'll get a good dose of this island beauty. Otherwise, consider the pleasant hour-long cruise (90 kr each way) from Nybroplan downtown to the quiet town of Vaxholm. The tourist office has a free archipelago guide booklet.

Shopping

Modern design, glass, clogs, and wooden goods are popular targets for shoppers. Browsing is a free, delightful way to enjoy Sweden's brisk pulse. Cop a feel at the Nordiska Kompaniet (NK, also meaning "no Kroner left") just across from the Sweden House or in the nearby Gallerian mall. The nearby Åhlens is less expensive. Swedish stores are open 9:30–18:00, until 14:00 on Saturday, and closed Sunday. Some of the bigger stores (like Åhlens and NK) are open later on Saturday and on Sunday afternoon. Take a short walk to Norrmalms Torg to the new bank branch of Scandia Insurance, for its ATMs, clean design, Internet access, and free coffee, tea, or chocolate.

For a smørgåsbord of Scanjunk, visit the Loppmarknaden (northern Europe's biggest flea market) at the planned suburb of Skarholmen (10 kr on weekends, Monday–Friday 11:00–18:00, Saturday 9:00–15:00, Sunday 10:00–15:00, busiest on weekends, tel. 710-0060).

Sleeping in Stockholm
(6 kr = about $1, tel. code: 08)
Sleep Code: **S** = Single, **D** = Double/Twin, **T** = Triple, **Q** = Quad, **b** = bathroom, **CC** = Credit Card (**V**isa, **M**asterCard, **A**mex). "Summer rates" means mid-June to mid-August, and Friday and Saturday (sometimes Sunday) the rest of the year. Prices include breakfast unless otherwise noted.

Stockholm has plenty of money-saving deals for the savvy visitor. Its youth hostels are among Europe's best ($15 a bed), and plenty of people offer private accommodations ($50 doubles). Peak season for Stockholm's expensive hotels is business time—workdays outside of summer. Rates drop by 30 to 50 percent in the summer or on weekends, and if business is slow, occasionally any night—ask. To sort through all of this, the city has helpful, English-speaking room-finding services with handy locations and long hours. (See Hotellcentralen and Sweden House, above.)

The **Stockholm Package** offers business-class doubles with buffet breakfasts for 790 kr, includes two free Stockholm Cards, and lets two children up to 18 years old sleep for free. This is limited to mid-June to mid-August, and Friday and Saturday throughout the year. Assuming you'll be getting two Stockholm Cards anyway (350 kr), this gives you a $200 hotel room for about $50. This is for real (summertime is that dead for business hotels). The procedure (through either tourist office) is easy: a 100-kr advance booking fee (you can arrange by fax, pay when you arrive) or a 40-kr in-person booking fee if you just drop in. Arriving without reservations in July is never a problem. It gets tight during the Water Festival (ten days in early August) and during a convention stretch for a few days in late June.

My listings are a good value only outside of Stockholm Package time, or if the 790 kr for a double and two cards is out of your range and you're hosteling. Every place listed here has staff who speak English and will explain their special deals to you on the phone. If money is limited, ask if they have cheaper rooms. It's not often that a hotel will push their odd misfit room that's 100 kr below all the others. And at any time of year, prices can be soft.

About the only laundromat in central Stockholm is Tvätto-maten, at Vøastmannagatan 61 on Odenplan, bus route #53 from Upplandsgaten to Central Station (across from Gustav Vasa church, 60 kr, helpful manager).

Sleeping in Hotels

Queen's Hotel is cheery, clean, and just a ten-minute walk from the station, in a great pedestrian area across the street from the Centralbadet (city baths, listed on all maps). With a fine TV and piano lounge, coffee in the evenings, and a staff that enjoys its guests, this is probably the best cheap hotel in town (summer rates: S-440 kr, D-540 kr, Ds-570 kr, Db-695 kr, 660 kr–995 kr in winter, CC:VMA, Drottninggatan 71A, tel. 24 94 60, fax 21 76 20).

Bentley's Hotel is an interesting option with an old English flair and renovated rooms (summer rates include winter Sundays: small Db-590 kr, Db-690 kr, suite Db-750 kr–850 kr, CC:VMA, a block up the street from Queen's at Drottninggatan 77, 11160 Stockholm, tel. 14 13 95, fax 21 24 92). Klas and Agi Kallstrom are attempting to mix elegance, comfort, and simplicity into an affordable package. Each room is tastefully decorated with antique furniture but has a modern full bathroom. All rooms are nonsmoking.

Hotel Östermalm is in a simple stately building a block from the T-bana: Stadion. Narrow yellow halls connect its generally huge (formerly elegant but now a tad musty) rooms. A funkiness rare in Stockholm, and for the right traveler, a ripe deal (summer rates: no sink D-350 kr, Db-420 kr–540 kr, Db suite/family room-490 kr, 120 kr–150 kr for extra beds, 30 kr per person less without breakfast, pricing here seems arbitrary and banana-firm, elevator, Karlavägen 57, tel. 660-6996, tel./fax 661-0471). Nearby, the proud little **Stureparkens Gästvåning** is a carefully run, traditional-feeling place with lots of class and ten tastefully decorated rooms. It's a better value during the high season (summer rates: S-395 kr, D-550 kr, Db-595 kr; high season: S-425 kr, D-650 kr, Db-725 kr, two-night minimum, elevator, CC:VM, Sturegatan 58, tel. 662-7230, fax 661-5713).

Hotel Anno 1647, a typical old Swedish hotel with a few showerless rooms, just off the Old Town near Slussen (under the Katarina elevator), is a good splurge (rates vary with season and day of week: D-495 kr, Db-890 kr–1,190 kr; CC:VMA, Mariagrand 3, tel. 644-0480, fax 643-3700).

Sleeping in Rooms in Private Homes

Stockholm's centrally located private rooms are as expensive as cheap hotels—a deal only in the high season. More reasonable rooms are a few T-bana minutes from the center. Stockholm's tourist offices refer those in search of a room in a private house to Hoteljanst (near the station, at Vasagatan 15, tel. 10 44 67, fax 21 37 16). They can set you up for about 330 kr per double, minimum two nights. Go direct—you'll save your host the listing service's fee. Be sure to get the front door security code when you call, as there's no intercom connection with front doors.

Else Mari Sundin is an effervescent retired actress who rents two rooms in her very homey place, beautifully located just 2 blocks from the bridge to Djurgården (D-500 kr with breakfast, bus #47 or #69 to Torstenssonsgatan 7, go through courtyard to "garden house" and up to second floor, tel. 665-3348).

Mrs. Lichtsteiner offer rooms with kitchenettes and has a family room with a loft (Db-400 kr without breakfast, a block from T-bana: Rådhuset, exit T-bana direction Polishuset, at Bergsgatan 45, inside go through door on left and up elevator to second floor, tel. 746-9166, call ahead).

Sleeping in Hostels

Stockholm has Europe's best selection of big-city hostels offering good beds in simple but interesting places for 100 kr. If your budget is tight, these are right. Each has a helpful English-speaking staff, pleasant family rooms, good facilities, and good leads on budget survival in Stockholm. All will hold rooms for a phone call. Hosteling is cheap only if you're a member (guest membership: 35 kr a night necessary only in IYHF places); bring your own sheet (paper sheets rent for 30 kr), and picnic for breakfast (breakfasts cost 40 kr). Several of the hostels are often booked up well in advance but hold a few beds for those who are left in the lurch.

Af Chapman (IYHF), Europe's most famous youth hostel, is a permanently moored cutter ship. Just a five-minute walk from downtown, this floating hostel has 140 beds—two to eight per stateroom. A popular but compassionate place, it's often booked far in advance, but saves some beds each morning for unreserved arrivals and gives away unclaimed rooms each evening at 18:00. If you call at breakfast time and show up before 12:00, you may land a bed, even in summer. A warm, youthful atmosphere prevails. Study the warden's personal scrapbook of budget Stockholm information (100 kr/bed, April to mid-December, 7:00–12:00, 15:00–02:00, sleeping bags allowed, with a lounge and cafeteria that welcomes non-hostelers, 11:30–18:00, STF Vandrarhem *Af Chapman*, Skeppsholmen, 11149 Stockholm, tel. 679-5015).

Skeppsholmen Hostel (IYHF), just ashore from the *Af Chapman*, is open all year. It has better facilities and smaller rooms (100 kr per bed in doubles, triples, and quads, only 70 kr in dorms, non-members pay 35 kr extra, tel. 679-5017), but it isn't as romantic as its seagoing sister.

Zinken Hostel (IYHF) is a big, basic hostel in a busy suburb, with 100-kr dorm beds (40 kr extra for sheets and non-members), plenty of 275-kr doubles, a laundromat, and the best hostel kitchen facilities in town. (STF Vandrarhem Zinken, Zinkens Väg 20, T-bana: Zinkensdamm, tel. 616-8100 or 616-8188, open 24 hours all year.) A great no-nonsense, user-friendly value.

Vandrarhemmet Brygghuset, in a former brewery near Odenplan, is small (57 beds in 12 rooms), spacious, bright and clean, quiet, with a laundromat and a kitchen. Since this is a private hostel, its two- to six-bed rooms are open to all for 125 kr per bed (no sleeping bags allowed, sheets rent for 35 kr). Doubles are 310 kr. (Open June–August 7:00–12:00, 15:00–23:00, no curfew, Norrtullsgatan 12 N, tel. 312424.)

Café Bed and Breakfast is Stockholm's newest cozy hostel with only 30 beds (125 kr per bed in eight- to 12-bed rooms, 30 kr for breakfast, 30 kr for sheets, near Radmansgatan T-bana stop, Rehnsgatan 21, tel. 15 28 38). They have three 320-kr doubles. Note: used sheets are rented for 10 kr ("locals don't mind").

Stockholm has 12 **campgrounds** (located south of town) that are a wonderful solution to your parking and budget problems. The TI's "Camping Stockholm" brochure has specifics.

Eating in Stockholm

Stockholm's elegant department stores (notably NK and Åhlens, near Sergels Torg) have cafeterias for the kroner-pinching local shopper. Look for the 50-kr "rodent of the day" (dagens rett) specials. Most museums have handy cafés. The café at the *Af Chapman* **youth hostel** (open to the public in summer daily 11:30–18:00) serves a good salad/roll/coffee lunch in an unbeatable deck-of-a-ship atmosphere (if the weather's good).

The Old Town (Gamla Stan) has lots of restaurants. Try the wonderfully atmospheric **Kristina Restaurang** (Västerlånggatan 68, Gamla Stan, tel. 200529). In this 1632 building, under a leather ceiling steeped in a turn-of-the-century interior, you'll find good dinners from 135 kr, including a salad and cracker bar. (The delicious Swedish meatballs with lingonberries is one of the least expensive meals.) They serve a great 50-kr lunch (11:00–15:00)—entrée, salad bar, bread, and drink. The place is best Wednesday–Saturday 20:00–23:00, when live jazz accompanies your meal (silent in July and August). You can enjoy the music over just a beer or coffee, too. **Hermans** has great vegetarian food and daily specials (Stora Nygatan 11, also in Gamla Stan).

Picnics

With higher taxes almost every year, Sweden's restaurant industry is suffering. You'll notice many fine places almost empty. Swedes joke that the "local" cuisine is now Chinese, Italian, and hamburgers. Here more than anywhere, budget travelers should picnic.

Stockholm's major department stores and the many small corner groceries are fine places to assemble a picnic. Åhlens department store (near Sergels Torg, open until 21:00) has a great food section. The late-hours supermarket downstairs in the central train station is picnic-friendly, with fresh, ready-made sandwiches (Monday–Friday 7:00–23:00, Saturday and Sunday 9:00–23:00).

The market at **Hötorget** is a fun place to picnic shop, especially in the indoor, exotic ethnic Hötorgshallen. The outdoor market closes at 18:00, and many merchants put their unsold produce on the push list (earlier closing and more desperate merchants on Saturday).

For a classy vegetarian buffet lunch (70 kr, Monday–Friday until 17:00), often with a piano serenade, or dinner (85 kr, evenings and weekends), eat at **Örtagården** (literally, "the herb garden," Nybrogatan 31, tel. 662-1728), above the colorful old Østermalms food market at Østermalmstorg.

Transportation Connections—Stockholm

By train to: Uppsala (30/day, 45 min), **Kalmar** (12/day, 6 hrs), **Copenhagen** (6/day, 8 hrs), **Oslo** (3/day, 7 hrs). For train information, call 020/757575 (toll-free in Sweden) for domestic trains, 227940 for international trains.

By boat to: Helsinki (daily/nightly boats, 14 hrs; see Helsinki chapter), **Turku** (daily/nightly boats, 10 hrs).

Estline runs a regular ferry from Stockholm to **Tallinn, Estonia** (every other night at 17:30, arriving at 9:00 the next morning, 385 kr each way). It offers a 36-hour tour (no visa necessary, round-trip, simple two-bed cabins, two breakfasts, two dinners) for 1,170 kr per person (tel. 08/667-0001).

Parking in Stockholm: Only a Swedish meatball would drive his car in Stockholm. Park it and use the public transit. But parking is confusing, a major hassle, and expensive. Unguarded lots generally aren't safe. Take everything into your hotel or hostel, or pay for a garage. The tourist office has a "Parking in Stockholm" brochure. Those hosteling on Skeppsholmen feel privileged with their 25 kr-a-day island parking passes. Those with the Stockholm Card can park free in a big central garage or at any meter for the duration of the ticket. Ask for your parking card and specifics when you get your Stockholm Card. There's a safe and reasonable (10 kr per day) lot at Ropsten—the last subway station (near the Silja Line terminal). Those sailing to Finland can solve all parking worries by long-term parking on arrival in Stockholm at either terminal's safe and reasonable parking lot (60 kr per day).

NEAR STOCKHOLM: UPPSALA AND SIGTUNA

Uppsala

Uppsala is a compact and bustling little city with a cathedral and university that win "Sweden's oldest/largest/tallest" awards. While not of great touristic importance, Uppsala has a lot of history, and if you want a look at smaller-town Sweden, this is a handy place to start. Uppsala could absorb the better part of a day, including the frequent train connection from Stockholm.

The sights of historic Uppsala, along with its 30,000 university students, cluster around the university and cathedral. Just over the river is the bustling shopping center and pedestrian zone.

Tourist Information: The Uppsala TI has a branch near the cathedral (Monday–Friday 10:00–18:00, Saturday 10:00–15:00, Sunday 12:00–16:00; closed Sundays off-season) and one in the castle (daily in summer, tel. 018/27 48 00). Pick up their free, entertaining, and helpful *Uppsala Guide*.

Sights—Uppsala

▲▲**Uppsala Cathedral**—One of Scandinavia's largest and most historic cathedrals, it has a breathtaking interior, the tomb of King Gustavus Vasa, and twin 400-foot spires. Ask about a guided tour. Otherwise, push the English button, sit down, and listen to the tape-recorded introduction in the narthex opposite the tourist information table (daily June–August 8:00–18:00).

The University—Scandinavia's first university was founded here in 1477. Linnaeus and Celsius are two famous grads. Several of the old buildings are open to guests. A very historic (but not much to see) silver-bound Gothic Bible is on display with many other rare medieval books in the Carolina Rediviva (library). The anatomy theater in the Gustavianum is thought-provoking. This strange theater's only show was a human dissection.

Gamla Uppsala—Old Uppsala is rooted deeply in history but now almost entirely lost in the sod of centuries. Look at the postcards of Gamla Uppsala's 15 grassy burial mounds from downtown. That's all you'll see if you go out there. Easy by car, not worth the headache by bus (#20, #24, or #54).

Other Uppsala Sights—The free (and cute) little **Uppland Museum** is on the river by the waterfall (daily 12:00–17:00). Nearby is the **Carl Linnaeus Garden and Museum** and the 16th-century **castle** (with its slice-of-castle-life exhibits) on the hilltop overlooking the town.

Eating in Uppsala

Browse through the lively **Saluhallen,** the riverside indoor market in the shadow of the cathedral. You'll find great picnic stuff and pleasant cafés. This entire university district abounds with inexpensive eateries. Try **Kung Kral** for great food; ask about a special five-shot sampler of Scandinavian schnapps for the brave (St. Persgata 4, tel. 018/12 50 90).

Sigtuna

Between Stockholm and Uppsala you'll pass Sigtuna. Possibly Sweden's cutest town, Sigtuna is basically fluff. You'll see a medieval lane lined with colorful wooden tourist shops, a very pleasant tourist office with a reading room, a café, a romantic park, a promenade along the lake, an old church, and some rune stones. The TI organizes walking tours in English (call 08/59 25 00 20 for info). If it's sunny, Sigtuna is worth a browse and an ice-cream cone, but little more.

Route Tips for Drivers

Stockholm to Oslo: From downtown, follow Sveavegen west and signs to Nortull/Gottberg/E-3/E-4 south. Take the second E-18 you see (immediately after the first). From Uppsala to Oslo, it's about 325 miles. That's seven hours of mostly clear freeway motoring. Leaving Uppsala, follow signs for Route 55 and Nörrköping. When you hit E-18, just follow the Oslo signs past forests, lakes, and prettily painted wooden houses. It's pleasant, but I'd stop only to fill and empty the tanks. (Or maybe to browse through one of the many *Loppmarkets*, flea markets, you may see advertised, or at Ester's Café, on the right just before Arjang.)

You'll also pass several youth hostel signs (the house and tree indicates 90-kr dorm beds). The town of **Arjang,** just before the Norwegian border, is a good place to stop if you don't make it to Oslo. The Arjang TI (open 9:00–20:00, less on weekends and off-season, tel. 0573/14136) books private rooms (D-220 kr plus a 50-kr fee). **Hotel Karl XII** offers the cheapest hotel beds (all year D-300 kr without breakfast, Sveavägen #22, near marketplace, tel. 0573/10156, fax 71 14 26).

There are no border formalities. At the border, change money at the bank desk at the little TI kiosk (left side of road under flags, daily summer 10:00–19:00, fair rates, standard 20-kr-per-traveler's-check or cash fee). If you change a traveler's check, you can convert your extra Swedish paper and coins for no extra fee. Call to reconfirm your Oslo hotel, and pick up the free Oslo map and *What's On* publication.

The ride from the border to Oslo is particularly scenic. The freeway dumps you right into downtown Oslo. Just follow the E-18 signs to Sentrum, then Sentral Stasjon (the main train station) and Paleet P (a central parking garage). If you're going directly to a room on the west end, keep left, following signs to Oslo V, veering right toward the palace immediately after passing the harborfront and twin brick towers of the city hall. If your hotel is in the center near the station, don't take the Sentrum O exit; instead, follow the sign for Paleet P. (At the Paleet P parking garage, turn right on Fred Olsens Gate, 1.5 blocks for the Sjømannshjem.)

For driving from Kalmar and the south into Stockholm, see Route Tips for Drivers in the next chapter, South Sweden.

SOUTH SWEDEN: VÄXJÖ AND KALMAR

Outside of Stockholm, the most interesting region in Sweden is Småland. This Swedish province is famous for its forests, lakes, great glass, and the many immigrants it sent to the U.S.A. More Americans came from this area than any other part of Scandinavia, and the immigration center in Växjö tells the story well. Between Växjö and Kalmar is Glass Country, a 70-mile stretch of forest sparkling with glassworks. Of the prestigious glassworks that welcome curious visitors, Kosta's is best. Historic Kalmar has a rare Old World ambience and the most magnificent medieval castle in Scandinavia. From Kalmar, you can cross Europe's longest bridge to hike through the Stonehenge-type mysteries of the strange island of Öland.

Planning Your Time

By train, on a three-week Scandinavian trip, I'd skip this area in favor of the slick night train from Copenhagen to Stockholm (and a side trip to Estonia). If you're driving, the sights described below make that same trip an interesting way to spend a couple of days. You'll gather that—and this has only a little to do with my Norwegian heritage—I'm not so hot on the Swedish countryside. Still, you can't see only Stockholm and say you've seen Sweden. Växjö and Kalmar give you the best possible dose of small-town and countryside Sweden. (I find Lund and Malmö, both popular side trips from Copenhagen, really dull. And I'm not old or sedate enough to find a sleepy trip along the much-loved Göta Canal appealing.) Drivers spend three days getting from Copenhagen to Stockholm this way:

South Sweden: Växjö and Kalmar

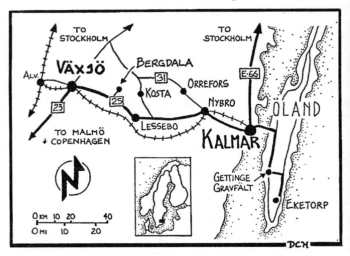

Day 1: Leave Copenhagen after breakfast, tour the Frederiksborg Castle, picnic under the Kronborg Castle; take the 14:00 ferry to Sweden then drive northeast; 18:00, set up in Växjö.

Day 2: Tour Växjö's Småland folk museum and Emigrants Center, drive into Glass Country, tour the Kosta glassworks (or the smaller, more traditional Bergdala works); 14:30, set up in Kalmar in time to tour the castle and its provincial museum; evening in Kalmar.

Day 3: 8:00, begin five-hour drive north along the coast to Stockholm; 10:30, break in Västervik; 12:00, stop in Söderköping for a picnic lunch and a walk along the Göta Canal; 13:30, continue drive north; 16:00, arrive in Stockholm and possibly catch the night boat to Helsinki.

Thinking ahead to your Helsinki cruise: boat tickets may be cheaper (off-weekend) and your drive to Oslo more reasonable (earlier start) if you do the Helsinki excursion immediately after Kalmar, before seeing Stockholm.

VÄXJÖ

A pleasant but rather dull town of 70,000, Växjö (veh-quah, the Swedish "xj" is like our "qu") is in the center of Småland. A stroll through downtown Växjö is perhaps the purest Swedish experience you can have.

The town is compact, with the train station, town square, two important museums, and the tourist office all within 2 blocks of each other. Växjö has an easy-to-enjoy pedestrian center, and the nearby lake is encircled by a pleasant 3-mile path.

Tourist Information: The busy TI is off the main square (open mid-June through August Monday–Friday 9:00–18:00, Saturday 10:00–14:00, Sunday 11:00–15:00; September to mid-June Monday–Friday 9:00–16:30, Kungsgatan 11, tel. 0470/41410 or 41000).

Helpful Hints: A farmers' market bustles on the main square on Wednesday and Saturday mornings. The bank across from the train station opens at 9:00. ATMs are everywhere.

Sights—Växjö

▲**House of Emigrants**—A large part of the 1,300,000 Swedes who moved to the U.S.A. came from this neck of the Swedish woods. If you have Swedish roots, this place is really exciting. If not, its small exhibit is mildly interesting. The "Dream of America" exhibit tells the story of the 1850s–1920s "American Fever." The emigration festival, three days around the second Sunday in August, is a real hoot, as thousands of Minnesotans storm Växjö.

Upstairs is an excellent library and research center. You're welcome to take a peek. Root-seekers (10,000 a year from the U.S.) are very welcome. Advance notice is urged (write well in advance to Box 201, S-351 04, Växjö, for research form and information) and bring what information you have—such as ship names and birthdays. (25 kr, open June–August Monday–Friday 9:00–18:00, Saturday 11:00–15:00, Sunday 13:00–17:00, shorter hours off-season, tel. 0470/20120. The research center is open Monday–Friday 9:00–16:00, shorter hours off-season, 50 kr per half-day.) The Liv Ullman movie about the emigration, *The Immigrants*, and its sequel, *The New Land*, are great pre-trip viewing.

▲**Småland and Swedish Glass Museum**—This recently renovated, cute small-townish museum (one of Sweden's oldest) offers a good look at local forestry, a prehistoric exhibit, a wonderful traditional costume display (top floor), and most important, an introduction to the area's glass industry with the best glass collection around. There's a free, helpful English brochure. (30 kr, Monday–Friday 11:00–18:00, weekends 11:00–16:00, just next to the House of Emigrants and worth more time.)

Domkyrka—Växjö's fine church (dedicated to the 11th-century English missionary, Saint Sigfrid) offers free summer concerts many Thursday evenings at 20:00.

Linneparken—This lovely park, behind the cathedral, is dedicated to the great Swedish botanist Carl von Linne (a.k.a. Carolus Linnaeus). It has an arboretum, lots of well-categorized perennials, and a big children's playground.

Swimming pool—From the House of Emigrants you can see the town's super-modern lakeside swimming hall (Simhall) a five-minute walk away (25 kr including the sauna, plus a little more if you want to tan or use the exercise room, towels 5 kr, open Tuesday morning and weekday afternoons except Tuesday, tel. 41204).

Sleeping in Växjö
(6 kr = about $1, tel. code: 0470)
Sleep Code: **S** = Single, **D** = Double/Twin, **T** = Triple, **Q** = Quad, **b** = bathroom, **CC** = Credit Card (Visa, MasterCard, Amex). Rates include breakfast.

Sleeping in Hotels and Motels
Hotel Esplanad is your best central hotel value. This quiet, comfortable old hotel, run by Birgit, is just three blocks from the town center (summer rates: D-350 kr, Db-440 kr; high-season rates: D-520 kr, Db-690 kr, CC:VM, N. Esplanaden 21A, 35231 Växjö, tel. 22580, fax 26226). From the freeway, follow "Centrum" signs into town. At the Royal Corner Hotel, turn left; 200 yards later, at the first light, turn right onto N. Esplanaden. The yellow hotel is on the right.

    Best Western Hotel Statt, in the town center, is more traditional and borderline-luxurious (Db-1125 kr; summer rate: Db-750 kr, CC:VMA, 6 Kungsgatan, tel. 13400, fax 44837).

    Hotell Teaterparken, in the Konserthus complex, has sleekly designed rooms that are a good value in the summer and on winter weekends (Sb-500 kr, Db-690 kr, includes breakfast, CC:VMA, V. Esplanaden 10-12, tel. 39900, fax 47577).

Sleeping in Rooms in Private Homes
For a 25-kr fee, the tourist office can always find private rooms for 140 kr per person, 115 kr if you have sheets. Breakfast is usually 35 kr extra. To save money and be assured of a good value, go or call direct to the following places.

Eva and Håkan Edfeldt are a young professional couple with one boy who live in a woodsy 80-year-old house in a folksy old neighborhood (130 kr per person, includes sheets, one double and one triple, kitchenette; eight-minute walk from the station, take the bridge over the tracks, follow Värendsgatan to the lake, at Skånegatan turn right, Skånegatan ends at the Edfeldt's driveway, Telestadsgatan 6, 35235 Växjö, tel. 0470/19242, or during the day at their workplace, tel. 88279). The whole family speaks great English. If interested, ask about their rentable cabin on the lake (with boat).

Siv Kidvik, a more comfortable, newer home run by an older couple, is fine for families with a car and has a great garden (four rooms only, May–August, kitchenette, children half-price). Drive north from the center on Linnegatan, which becomes Sandsbrovägen. At the end of the cemetery before the Shell Tankomat station, go right on Lillestadsvägen, take the first left onto Gamla Norrvägen, then the first left onto Kastanjevägen to #70 Kastanjevägen (125 kr without sheets, sheets-25 kr, breakfast-35 kr, tel. 17053, speak slowly and clearly).

Sleeping in the Youth Hostel
Växjö has a fine **youth hostel** on a lake 2 miles out of town (open 8:00–10:00, 17:00–20:00, two- to four-bed rooms, 100-kr beds, 40-kr breakfast, 35 kr extra for non-members; STF Vandrarhem Evedal—IYHF, 35590 Växjö, tel. 63070, telephone reservations required in summer). Take bus #1C from the TI to the last stop (summer only, last ride 16:15, first ride 9:15, so hitch a ride into Växjö with a fellow hosteler).

Eating in Växjö
For reasonable eating in downtown Växjö, try **La Gondola** (corner of Storgatan and Liedbergsgatan, open nightly until midnight, plenty of 50-kr Italian-style meals [great lasagna] with a salad bar, tel. 27632), **McDonald's** (on Storgatan), **Åhlens Department Store** (on Storgatan, open Monday–Friday until 19:00, smørrebrød your way into a classy dinner picnic), **Spisen** (more expensive Swedish food, across from the station), or the **hot dog and burger kiosk** next to the train station. If you're staying at the hostel, you can find everything you need for a picnic dinner at the neighboring campground's little store.

Transportation Connections—Växjö

By train to: Copenhagen (6/day, 5 hrs, change in Alvesta), **Kalmar** (11/day, 1.5 hrs). While there are **buses** from Växjö to Kosta and **bus tours** of the Glass Country from Växjö, the glassworks aren't worth the time and trouble unless you have a car. Instead, take a careful look at the glass exhibit in the Växjö museum and train straight to Kalmar.

Sights—Between Växjö and Kalmar

Lessebo Paper Mill—The town of Lessebo has a 300-year-old paper mill that's kept working for visitors to see. If you've never seen handmade paper produced, this mill is worth a visit. Get the English brochure. (7:00–17:00 Monday–Friday, tours in English at 9:30, 10:30, 13:00, and 14:15 in summer; the mill makes paper 7:00–11:15, 12:30– 15:30; otherwise it's open but dead, tel. 0478/10600.) By car, Lessebo is an easy stop between Växjö and Kosta. Just after the Kosta turnoff, you'll see a black-and-white "Handpapersbruk" sign.

▲▲The Kingdom of Crystal—This is Sweden's Glass Country. Frankly, these glassworks cause so much excitement because of the relative rarity of anything else thrilling in Sweden, outside of greater Stockholm. Pick up the Glasriket "Kingdom of Crystal" brochure in Växjö or Kalmar. The following three glassworks give tours and welcome visitors. Bergdala is cutest; Kosta treats its tourists best; Orrefors is the most famous.

Bergdala has a glassworks that offers a fine close-up look at actual craftsmen blowing and working the red-hot glass, a good shop (with Bergdala's tempting blue-ringed cereal bowls), and a fine picnic area with covered tables in case it's wet. (30 minutes east of Växjö, exit road 25 at Bergdala sign, drive 3 miles north; open 9:00–14:30, Saturday 10:00–15:00, Sunday 12:00–16:00, no action 12:00–12:30, tel. 0478/31650).

Kosta is your best major glassworks stop. This town boasts the oldest of the *glasbruks*, dating back to 1742. Today the glassworks is a thriving tourist and shopping center (open year-round 9:00–18:00, Saturday 9:00–16:00, Sunday 11:00–16:00; tours leave on the hour 11:00–14:00; actual glassblowing is seen only on workdays but not from 10:00–11:00, tel. 0478/50705, Diana Fredriksson is a great guide). On arrival, report to the information desk to get your English tour. Tours start in the historic and glass display rooms, then go to the actual blowing room, where guides are constantly narrating the ongoing work.

Kosta is making great strides toward lead-free crystal; their crystal is already 80 percent lead-free. Visitors show the most enthusiasm in the shopping hall, where crystal "seconds" and discontinued models are sold at very good prices. This is duty-free shopping, and they'll happily mail your purchases home. Kosta's best picnic tables (rainproof) are at the Gamla Kosta museum. Kosta is a well-signposted 15-minute drive from Lessebo. In town, follow signs for "Glasbruk."

Orrefors has the most famous of the several renowned glassworks in Glass Country, but its glassworks are quite a tourist racket and offer lousy tours (tel. 0481/34000 to confirm tour times). Most visitors just observe the work from platforms. Like Kosta, their shop sells nearly perfect crystal seconds at deep discounts. (Open June to mid-July Monday–Friday 9:00–18:00, Saturday 9:00–16:00, Sunday 11:00–16:00; off-season closes an hour earlier.) Don't miss the dazzling "museum" (open same hours as shop).

KALMAR

Kalmar feels formerly strategic and important. In its day, the town was called "the gateway to Sweden." Today it's just a sleepy has-been, and gateway only to the holiday island of Öland. Kalmar's salty old center, fine castle, and busy waterfront give it a wistful sailor's charm. The town is wonderfully walkable. Kalmar's summer is from about mid-June to mid-August.

Tourist Information: The TI is central and helpful (open mid-June to mid-August Monday–Friday 9:00–21:00, Saturday 9:00–17:00, Sunday 12:00–18:00; closing at 17:00 other months and closed on winter weekends, Larmgatan 6, tel. 0480/15350). Get the handy town map and confirm your sightseeing plans.

Sights—Kalmar

▲▲**Kalmar Castle**—This moated castle is one of Europe's great medieval experiences. The stark exterior, cuddled by a lush park, houses a fine Renaissance palace interior, which is the work of King Gustavus Vasa. The castle will be remodeled for 1997, its 600-year anniversary. The elaborately furnished rooms are entertainingly explained in English (40 kr, open mid-June to mid-August 10:00–18:00, Sunday 12:00–18:00; shoulder season 12:00–18:00; November–March much shorter hours, tel. 56351). Ask about English tours.

Kalmar

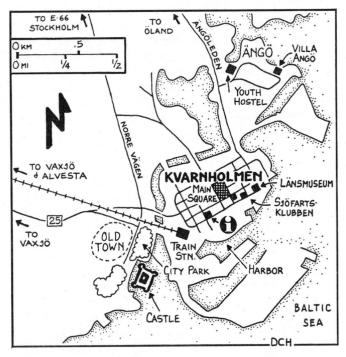

▲▲**Kalmar Provincial (Lans) Museum**—This museum displays the impressive salvaged wreck of the royal ship *Kronan*, which sank nearby in 1676. Lots of interesting soggy bits and old pieces with a here's-the-buried-treasure thrill, but unfortunately no information in English. (You can borrow the *Kronan* English brochure exhibit). See the excellent 12-minute film (request an English showing as you enter). It's right downtown on the waterfront. (40 kr, open daily mid-June to mid-August, 10:00–18:00, off-season closes at 16:00, tel. 56300.)

▲**The Island of Öland**—Europe's longest bridge (free, 4 miles) connects Öland with Kalmar and the mainland. The island, 90 miles long and only 8 miles wide, is a pleasant local resort known for its birds, windmills, flowers, beaches, and prehistoric sights. Public transportation is miserable, and the island is worthwhile only if you have a car and three extra hours. A 60-mile circle south of the bridge will give you a good dose of the island's windy rural charm.

The **Gettlinge Gravfalt** (just off the road about 10 miles up from the south tip) is a wonderfully situated boat-shaped Iron Age gravesite littered with monoliths and overseen by a couple of creaky old windmills. It offers a commanding view of the windy and mostly treeless island.

Farther south is the **Eketorp Prehistoric Fort**, a very reconstructed fifth-century stone fort that, as iron age forst go, is fairly interesting. Several evocative huts and buildings are filled with what someone inagines may have been the style back then, and the huge rock fort is surrounded by strange, runty, pig-like creatures that were common 1,500 years ago. A sign reads: "For your convenience and pleasure, don't leave your children alone with the animals." (45 kr, open daily May to mid-September 10:00–17:00, free English tours usually at 13:00 in summer, tel. 0485/62023.)

Sleeping in Kalmar
(6 kr = about $1, tel. code: 0480)
Sleep Code: **S** = Single, **D** = Double/Twin, **T** = Triple, **Q** = Quad, **b** = bathroom, **CC** = Credit Card (Visa, MasterCard, Amex).

The tourist office can always find you a room in a private home (220 kr per double, 40 kr per person for sheets, and a 40-kr-per-booking fee, no breakfast). They can also get you special last-minute discounts on fancy hotels.

A 15-minute walk from the center, you'll find a wonderful **IYHF hostel** and hotel annex run by Torsten Knutsson and family. The hostel has two- or seven-bed rooms, laundry, TV, and sauna (40 kr/hour per couple, 100 kr per bed, 45 kr for sheets, 35 kr without hostel card, 40-kr breakfast, closed 10:00–16:30, reservations recommended). Try the hotel annex, the **Kalmar Lagprishotell Svanen** (S-295 kr, D-410 kr including sheets and breakfast, STF Vandrarhem, Rappegatan 1, 39230 Kalmar, tel. 25560, fax 88293). You'll see a blue-and-white hotel sign and hostel symbol at the edge of town on Angoleden Street, less than a mile from the train station.

The **Sjöfartsklubben (Seaman's Club)** is run by Mr. Persson, who speaks only a little English and opens this clean, salty dorm to tourists June through August. (It's the home of student sailors during the school year.) He has one- to five-bed rooms with kitchen privileges and a lively common room. At 100 kr per person plus 40 kr for sheets, with a garden facing the harbor, this has by far the best cheap beds in Kalmar (Olandsgatan 45, tel. 10810).

Söderportsgärden is a university dorm that opens mid-June to mid-August for tourists (S-300 kr, D-450 kr including sheets and breakfast, Slottsvägen 1, tel. 12501). It's beautifully located next to a park, directly in front of the castle.

Hotel Villa Ängö, a big old house on the water, has a price that fluctuates with its erratic management (S-195 kr, D-300 kr, Db-350 kr to 500 kr with breakfast in summer, a 15-minute walk out of town, Bagensgatan 20, tel. 85415).

Best Western Stadts Hotel is a 1,400-kr place with an affordable summer price (summer rate: Db-650 kr, CC:VMA, very central at Stortorget 14, tel. 15180, fax 15847).

Eating in Kalmar
Bistro Matisse (1 Kaggensgatan) offers a delicious, inexpensive lunch on weekdays. The **Domus Department Store** (2 blocks off the town square on the pedestrian street) has a ground-floor café with cheap sandwich-type meals. Upstairs, its **4 Kok** cafeteria serves reasonable meals. This is the place for evening picnic-dinner shopping (open daily until 20:00, café and cafeteria until 19:00). Pizza, Chinese food, salad bars, **Kalmar Hamkrog** for fish on the harbor, or the café in the Strøget mall (just off Storgatan) are also good budget bets.

For a splurge in a venerable old restaurant with music on many summer evenings, head out to the castle and enjoy **Slottsparken Restaurant**'s great waterfront terrace, a 120-kr meal, or a memorable cup of coffee.

Transportation Connections—Kalmar
By train to: Växjö (9/day, 1.5 hrs), **Stockholm** (12/day, 6 hrs, possible transfer in Alvesta; direct night train available, sleeper only, nightly except Saturday).

Route Tips for Drivers
Copenhagen to Sweden: See Route Tips for Drivers at the end of Copenhagen chapter.

Helsingborg to Växjö to Kalmar: In Helsingborg, follow signs for E-4 and Stockholm. The road's good, traffic's light, and towns are clearly signposted. At Ljungby, road 25 takes you to Växjö. Entering Växjö, skip the first Växjö exit and follow the freeway into "Centrum," where it ends.

The 70-mile drive from Växjö to Kalmar is a joy—light traffic with endless forest and lake scenery punctuated by numerous glassworks (*glasbruk*). The TI's free "Kingdom of Crystal" map lists them all and is your best navigational tool. Leave Växjö on road 25 to Kalmar. The driving time between Växjö and Kosta is 45 minutes; between Kosta and Kalmar, 45 minutes.

Kalmar to Stockholm: Leaving Kalmar, follow E-22 Lindsdal and Norrköping signs. The Kalmar–Stockholm drive is 240 miles and takes 5.5 hours. Sweden did a cheap widening job, paving the shoulders of the old two-lane road to get 3.8 lanes. Still, traffic is polite and sparse. There's little to see, so stock the pantry, set the compass on north, and home in on Stockholm.

Make two pleasant stops along the way. Ninety miles north is Vastervik, with a pleasant 18th-century core of wooden houses (3 miles off the highway, "Centrum" signs lead you to the harbor. Park at the little salty, six-days-a-week-and-great-smoked-fish market on the waterfront next to the seven-days-a-week, picnic-perfect Exet supermarket and a public WC).

Söderköping is just right for a lunch on the Göta Canal stop. Stay on E-22 past the town center, turn right at the TI/Kanalbåtarna/Slussen/Kanal P signs. Park by the canal, 1 block toward the hill from the town square and TI.

Sweden's famous Göta Canal is 110 miles of canals cutting Sweden in half, with 58 locks (*slussen*) working up to a summit of 300 feet. It was built 150 years ago, with more than 7 million 12-hour man-days (60,000 men working about 22 years) at a low ebb in the country's self-esteem—to show her industrial oats. Today it's a lazy three- or four-day tour. Take just a peek at the Göta Canal over lunch, in the medieval town of Söderköping.

The TI on Söderköping's Rådhustorget (a square about a block off the canal) has good town maps, canal information, and Stockholm maps. From there go to the canal. The Toalett sign points to the Kanulbatiquen, a yachters' laundry (40 kr, wash and dry, open daily), shower, shop, and WC, with idyllic canal-side picnic tables just over the lock. From the lock, stairs lead up to the Utsiktsplats pavilion (a nice view but not quite worth the hike).

Leaving Söderköping, E-22 takes you to Norrköping. Follow E-4 signs through Norrköping, then past a handy over-the-freeway rest stop into Stockholm. The centrum is clearly marked. (Viking's ferry terminal for Helsinki is in Södermalm, while Silja's terminal is northeast of town in Ropsten.)

FINLAND

HELSINKI

Finland is the odd duck in this book, and as such, it deserves special comment. First, a brief history lesson. As far as the sightseer is concerned, Finland's history breaks into three parts:

Swedish—Finland was dominated by Sweden before the 1809 Russian takeover. Because of city fires, very little remains of this era.

Russian—From 1809–1917, under Russian control, most of Helsinki's great buildings were built.

Independent—From 1918 on, Finland's bold, trend-setting modern design and architecture blossomed.

After World War II, Finland teetered between independence and the U.S.S.R., treading very lightly on matters concerning her fragile autonomy and relations with her giant neighbor to the east. The recent collapse of the U.S.S.R. has done to Finland what a good long sauna might do to you.

Lately, unemployment and a high cost of living have been Finland's main problems. The average income is about $30,000—with about 35 percent going to taxes. About 70 percent of the people rent apartments that can be had in Helsinki for about $800 a month including heat.

Money
There are about 4.5 Finnish *markka* (mk) in a U.S. dollar. One markka is about 20 cents.

Weather in Finland
They say the people of Finland spend nine months in winter and the other three months waiting for summer. The

weather dictates a brief (June–August) tourist season. February in Finland is not my idea of a good time. During particularly cold winters, Helsinki's bus #19 extends its route over the frozen bay to a suburban island! When summer arrives, the entire population jumps in with street singing and beach-blanket vigor.

Finnish

Finnish is a difficult-to-learn Finno-Ugric language originating east of Russia's Ural Mountains and related in Europe only to Estonian and Hungarian. Finland is officially bilingual; 6 percent of the country's population speaks Swedish as a first language. You'll notice that Helsinki is called Helsingfors in Swedish. Many street signs list places in both Finnish and Swedish. Since English is Finland's third language, you'll find that Finns speak less English than their Scandinavian neighbors. Still, nearly every educated young person will speak effortless English.

The only essential word needed for a quick visit is "*Kiitos*" (key-toes)—that's "thank you," and locals love to hear it. "*Kippis*" ("Keep peace") is what you say before you down a shot of Finnish vodka or some cloudberry liqueur.

And now, on to Helsinki—via a cruise ship.

SAILING FROM STOCKHOLM TO HELSINKI

The next best thing to being in Helsinki is getting there. Europe's most enjoyable cruise starts with lovely archipelago scenery, a setting sun, and a royal smørgåsbord dinner. Dance 'til you drop and sauna 'til you drip. Budget travel rarely feels this hedonistic. Then it's "Hello, Helsinki."

Planning Your Time

When planning your cruise, consider how much time you'd like to spend in Helsinki (one day is normally enough) and the day you'd like to depart (Friday and Saturday are more crowded and expensive). Also consider the efficient arrangement of schedule ripples caused by the ship. Assuming you sleep into and out of Stockholm by train and take two night boats, you'll have two days in Stockholm with no nights. Stockholm is worth two days on a three-week Scandinavian trip, but four in-transit nights in a row is pretty intense. Doable, but intense.

Sailing from Stockholm to Helsinki

Orientation

Two fine and fiercely competitive lines, Viking and Silja, connect the capitals of Sweden and Finland daily and nightly. The
scenic 14-hour cruise passes through three hours of the countless islands that buffer Stockholm from the open sea. Each line
offers state-of-the-art ships with luxurious smørgåsbord meals,
reasonable cabins, plenty of entertainment (discos, saunas,
gambling), and enough duty-free shopping to sink a ship.

The Cruise Lines: Viking and Silja

The Pepsi and Coke of the Scandinavian cruise industry vie to
outdo each other with bigger and fancier boats. The ships are
big—at 56,000 tons, nearly 200 yards long, and with 2,700
beds, they're the largest (and some of the cheapest) luxury
hotels in Scandinavia. Many other shipping lines buy their
boats used from Viking and Silja.

Which line is best? You could count showers and compare
smørgåsbords, but each line goes overboard to win the loyalty
of the 9 million duty-free-crazy Swedes and Finns who make
the trip each year. Viking, with an older, less luxurious fleet, is
cheaper by about 100 kr per round-trip. While both lines offer

Eurail travelers free passage, Silja requires passengers to rent a bed (about 195 kr each way), and Viking lets stowaways (or those who find the boat booked up) sleep for free on chairs, sofas, and under the stars or stairs. Silja offers those with a Scanrail pass free crossings to Turku.

Cruise Schedules

Both lines sail daily from Stockholm and Helsinki, usually leaving at 18:00 and arriving the next morning between 8:00 and 9:00. There are morning departures, too, but overnight crossings are more fun and efficient. Both lines also sail daily between Stockholm and Turku, Finland.

Time Change: Finland is one hour ahead of Sweden. Sailing from Stockholm to Helsinki, operate on Swedish time until you go to bed, then reset your watch. Morning schedules are Finnish time (and vice versa when you return).

Cost

Fares vary with the season and are inconsistent. Fridays throughout the year and mid-June to mid-August are most expensive (and crowded). Even in high season, a round-trip with the cheapest bed (in a below-sea-level, under-car-deck quad) is remarkably cheap: about $100 (700 kr on Viking, 900 kr to 1,000 kr on Silja). Each ship offers a whale of a smørgåsbord.

Beds cost the same throughout the year, starting at around 120 kr (on Viking, under the car deck, quads) and going up with the elevator. Viking also lets vagabonds sail without a bed (600 kr round-trip, deck class, peak season except Fridays).

The fares are so cheap because the boats operate tax-free and the hordes of locals who sail to shop and drink duty- and tax-free spend a fortune on board. It's a very large operation— mostly for locals. The boats are filled with about 60 percent Finns, 35 percent Swedes, and 5 percent cruisers from other countries. Last year, the average passenger spent nearly as much on booze and duty-free items as for the boat fare (about 600 kr).

Sleeping Free

Most new boats lack cheap "slum" beds, but some older boats may have a few free dorm beds for vagabonds. To get one (on Viking only), get to the boat as soon as it opens (usually 16:00) and head straight for the bottom of the boat. There may be eight to ten bunks with no closing doors.

If you end up on a boat without a cabin (allowed on Viking, and necessary if everything's booked up), you can dance, drink, or gamble until the wee hours with the Finns and Swedes, knowing your bag is locked safely from port to port in the luggage checkroom.

Reservations

Making reservations is easy in Copenhagen or Stockholm, or even from the U.S.A. Call and compare deals (Silja, 800/323-7436; Viking, 800/688-3876). For best prices, book in Scandinavia, but if you want a bed and are traveling in summer or on a Friday, make a reservation as soon as you can commit. Pick up your reserved ticket at the terminal an hour before sailing. (Viking Line, tel. 08/452-4000 in Stockholm, 33 32 60 36 in Copenhagen; Silja Line tel. 08/22 21 40 in Stockholm, 33 14 40 80 in Copenhagen.) You can also get a ticket through any travel agent in Scandinavia (same price plus booking fee, if any).

Terminals

Locations: In Stockholm, the Viking terminal is more central. Take the bus (15 kr) from Central Station's gate #24 or take bus #53 to "London Viaducten." The ship is parked just past the Gamla Stan. For Silja, take the bus (15 kr) from Central Station's gate #35. In Helsinki, both lines are perfectly central, each on opposite sides of the harbor, a ten-minute walk from the market, Senate Square, and shopping district.

Terminal Buildings: These are well organized with cafés, lockers, tourist information desks, lounges, and phones. Remember, 2,000 passengers come and go with each boat. Customs is a snap. Boats open two hours before departure.

Parking: Both lines offer safe and handy 50 kr/day parking in Stockholm. Viking's ticket machine takes 5- and 10-kr coins (come with 90 kr for 46 hours or credit cards). Keep inserting money until you see the date and time of your return on the meter, then hit the red button and leave the ticket on your dashboard. Park your car here on arrival in Stockholm, and leave it while you sightsee Stockholm, take the cruise, and tour Helsinki.

Services On Board

Meals: The cruise is famous for its smørgåsbords, and understandably so. Board the ship hungry. Dinner is self-serve in two sittings, one immediately upon departure, the other two hours later. The scenery is worth being on deck for, but if you call in advance, you can reserve a window seat. If you board without a reservation, go to the headwaiter and make one. Breakfast buffets are 50 kr; dinner buffets, 115 kr. Pick up the "How to Eat a Smørgåsbord" brochure. The key is to take small portions and pace yourself. Drinks (25 kr) or free water can be ordered from the waiters. There are also several reasonable or classy à la carte restaurants on board for lighter eaters or those on a budget.

Sauna: Each ship has a sauna. This costs about 45 kr extra. Reserve a time upon boarding. Saunas on Silja are half-price or even free in the morning (for those with a cabin towel).

Banking: The change desk on board has bad rates but no fee, which means it's actually a better deal than a Helsinki bank for those changing less than $100. There are about 4.5 Finnish markka (mk) in a U.S. dollar. Helsinki banks charge 15 mk for cash and 20 mk for traveler's checks, while the change desk in the boat changes cash for no fee and charges 30 mk for checks. FOREX has an office at N. Esplanaden 27 in Helsinki and gives the best rates for small exchanges. For a quick visit to Helsinki, just change some of your Swedish kroner. While city sightseeing tours can be paid for in kroner, you'll need local currency for public transport, shops, and museums.

Day Privileges: If you're spending two nights in a row on the Stockholm–Helsinki boat, you have access to your stateroom all day long. If you like, you can sleep in and linger over breakfast long after the boat has docked. But there's really way too much to do in Helsinki to take advantage of these privileges (unless you take the round-trip passage twice, on four successive nights—a reasonable option given the high cost of hotels and meals on shore and the frustration of trying to see Helsinki in a day).

Options
Staying Overnight in Helsinki: If you're staying in Helsinki, your boat line can get you a $100 double in a $200 hotel when you book your tickets, but you can find a cheaper room by telephoning my budget listings (see below).

Open Jaws: Consider an "open jaws" plan, sailing from Stockholm into Helsinki and returning to Stockholm from Turku. The cheaper round-trip boat fare saves enough to pay for the two-hour train ride from Helsinki to Turku. Turku

Helsinki Center

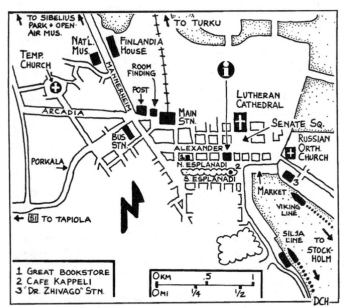

1 GREAT BOOKSTORE
2 CAFE KAPPELI
3 "DR. ZHIVAGO" STN.

boats may have free airplane seats or couchettes in the bilge, but the boats are usually smaller and lack cruise-ship excitement. However, Silja's addition of the 3,000-bed *Europa* to its Turku lineup will liven up the crossing. Passengers are rushed on and off, since the boat stays only one hour in the port.

HELSINKI

Helsinki feels close to Russia. It is. Much of it reminds me of St. Petersburg. It's no wonder Hollywood chose to film *Dr. Zhivago*, *Reds*, and *Gorky Park* here. (They filmed the Moscow Railway Station scenes in *Dr. Zhivago* in the low red-brick building near the Viking Terminal.) There is a huge and impressive Russian Orthodox church overlooking the harbor, a large Russian community, and several fine Russian restaurants.

In the early 1800s, the Russians took Finland from Sweden, and moved the capital eastward from Turku, making Helsinki the capital of their "autonomous duchy." I asked a woman in the T.I. if a particular café was made for Russian officers. In a rare spasm of candor (this was during the Cold War), she said, "All of 19th-century Helsinki was made for Russian officers."

Today Helsinki is gray and green. A little windy and cold, it looks like it's stuck somewhere in the north near the Russian border. But it makes the best of its difficult situation and will leave you impressed and glad to have dropped in. Start with the two-hour "Hello, Helsinki" bus tour that meets the boat at the dock. Enjoy Helsinki's ruddy harborfront market, count goosebumps in her churches, and dive into Finnish culture in the open-air folk museum.

Europe's most neoclassical city has many architectural overleafs, and it tends to turn guests into fans of town planning and architecture. Its buildings, designs, fashions, and people fit sensitively into their surroundings. Dissimilar elements are fused into a complex but comfortable whole. It's a very intimate and human place.

Planning Your Time

On a three-week trip through Scandinavia, Helsinki is worth the time between two successive nights on the cruise ship—about nine hours. Take the orientation bus tour upon arrival, mingle through the market, buy and eat a picnic, and drop by the TI. People-watch and browse through downtown to the National Museum. For the afternoon, choose between the National Museum, the Open-Air Folk Museum, the 15:30 English walking tour (from the TI, if scheduled), or a harbor boat tour. Enjoy a cup of coffee in the Café Kappeli before boarding time. Sail away while sampling another smørgåsbord dinner.

Orientation

(tel. code to Helsinki from outside Finland: 358-9)

Helsinki is a colorful shopping town of 500,000 people. The compact city center is great for roaming and brisk walking.

Tourist Information: Helsinki has TIs at the boat terminals, inside the train station, and (closest to the ferries) on Market Square (market square office open 9:00–19:00, weekends 9:00–15:00, shorter hours off-season, tel. 169-3757 or 174-088, fax 169-3839). The TIs are uniformly friendly, helpful, well stocked in brochures, and blond(e). Pick up the city map; the "Route Map" (public transit); "Helsinki on Foot" (six well-described and -mapped walking tours); the monthly *Helsinki This Week* magazine that lists sights, hours, and events; and *City* magazine, geared for the younger crowd. Ask about the 3T tourist tram and go over your sightseeing plans.

Telephoning: Helsinki's area code is 09, and Finland's country code is 358. When calling Helsinki from outside Finland, add the country code and drop the 0 (358-9-local number).

Ferries: If you're returning to Stockholm, the boat departs Helsinki at Finnish time. Remember, Finland is one hour ahead of Sweden. Ferry info: Viking Line, tel. 12351; Silja Line, tel. 9800-74552.

Getting Around Helsinki

By Bus and Tram: With the public transit route map and a little mental elbow grease, the buses and trams are easy, giving you the city by the tail. Tickets (9 mk) are good for an hour of travel and are purchased from the driver. The tourist tram, 3T, makes the rounds of most of the town's major sights, letting you stop and go for 9 mk an hour. The TI has a helpful explanatory brochure (not available on the bus).

The Tourist Ticket (25 mk for 24 hours of unlimited travel) pays if you take three or more rides. The Helsinki Card (105 mk) gives you free entry to city sights and use of all buses and trams for 24 hours. In summer the red "Pub Tram" makes a 40-minute loop through the city while its passengers get looped on the (one) beer that comes with the 25-mk ticket (hourly from 11:00 to 15:00, from Mikaelsgata near the train station).

By Bike: Greenbike rents bikes (at Mannerheimtie 13, across from the Parliament House).

Do-It-Yourself "Welcome to Helsinki" Walk

Start at the harbor. The colorful **produce market** on Market Square thrives daily 7:00–14:00 and 15:30–20:00 (closed Saturday afternoon and sometimes on Sunday). At the head of the harbor, facing the cruise ships, this is Helsinki's center. Don't miss the busy two-tone red-brick indoor market hall adjacent. Across the street you'll see the **Tourist Office**. Drop in to ask questions. The round door next to the TI leads into the delightful **Jugendsalen.** Designed, apparently, by a guy named Art Nouveau, this free and pleasant information center for locals offers interesting historical exhibits and a public WC. The art deco interior is a knockout (Monday–Friday 9:00–18:00, Sunday 12:00–18:00, closed Saturday, Pohjoisesplanadi 19).

One block inland behind the tourist office are the fine neoclassical **Senate Square** and the **Lutheran Cathedral.**

You'll pass the Schroder Sport Shop on Unioninkatu, with a great selection of popular Finnish-made Rapula fishing lures—ideal for the fisherfolk on your gift list.

Across the street from the TI, in the park facing the square, is my favorite café in northern Europe, **Café Kappeli.** When you've got some time, dip into this turn-of-the-century gazebo-like oasis of coffee, pastry, and relaxation. Built in the 19th century, it was a popular hangout for local intellectuals and artists. Today the café closest to the market offers the romantic tourist waiting for his ship to sail a great 8-mk-cup-of-coffee memory (unguarded WC just inside the door).

Behind the café runs the entertaining park, sandwiched between the north and south **Esplanadi**—Helsinki's top shopping boulevard. Walk it. The north (tourist office) side is interesting for window shopping, people-watching, and sun-worshiping. You'll pass several stores specializing in Finnish design. The huge Academic Bookstore, designed by Alvar Aalto (nearby at 1 Keskuskatu), has a great map and travel guide section and café. Finally you'll come to the prestigious Stockman's department store—Finland's Harrod's. This biggest, best, and oldest store in town has fine displays of local design. Just beyond is the main intersection in town, Esplanadi and Mannerheimintie. Nearby you'll see the famous *Three Blacksmiths* statue. (Locals say, "If a virgin walks by, they'll strike the anvil." It doesn't work. I tried.)

A block to the right, through a busy shopping center, is the harsh (in a serene way) architecture of the central **train station,** designed by Eliel Saarinen in 1916. The four people on the facade symbolize the peasant farmers with lamps coming into the Finnish capital. Wander around inside. Continuing past the Posti and the statue, return to Mannerheimintie, which leads to the large white **Finlandia Hall,** another Aalto masterpiece. While it's not normally open, there are often two tours a day in the summer (ask at the TI). Across the street is the excellent little Finnish **National Museum** (looks like a church, designed by Finland's first three great architects), and a few blocks behind that is the sit-down-and-wipe-a-tear beautiful rock church, **Temppeliaukio.** Sit. Enjoy the music. It's a wonderful place to end this Welcome to Helsinki walk.

From nearby Arkadiankatu Street, bus #24 will take you to the **Sibelius Monument** in a lovely park. The same ticket is good on a later #24. Ride to the end of the line—the bridge to

the Seurasaari island and Finland's open-air folk museum.
From here, bus #24 returns to the Esplanadi.

Sights—Helsinki

▲▲▲**Orientation Bus Tour**—A fast, very good two-hour
introductory tour leaves daily from both terminals immediately
after the ships dock (unless there are two arrivals, in which case
some travelers will have an hour to walk down and see the
market in action). The rapid-fire two- or three-language tour
costs 90 mk (120 Swedish kroner) and gives a good historic
overview—a look at all the important buildings from the newly
remodeled Olympic Stadium to embassy row, with too-fast
ten-minute stops at the Lutheran Cathedral, the Sibelius monument, and the Church in the Rock (Temppeliaukio). You'll
learn strange facts, such as how they took down the highest
steeple in town during World War II so the Soviet bombers
flying in from Estonia couldn't see their target.

If you're on a tight budget and don't care to get the general
overview of Helsinki, you can do the essence of this tour on
your own, as explained in my city walk (above). But I thoroughly
enjoyed listening to the guide. He sounded like an audio shred-
der that was occasionally turned off so English could come out.
The tour drops you off at Market Square, near the National
Museum (if you ask), or at your hotel by 11:30.

If you'd like more time in the Church of the Rock, leave
the tour there and consider walking 3 blocks to the National
Museum and the Finlandia Hall. Architects will prefer the
2.5-hour, 95-mk tours that leave from the Silja terminal at
10:00 and 11:00; they're basically the same, with a trip
through the Aalto-designed Technical University at Otaniemi
and out to the planned "garden city" suburb of Tapiola.
There is a shorter, cheaper tour that's nearly as good (70 mk
and included on the Helsinki Card, daily in summer at 11:30
and 13:30 from the train station or near the TI at 10:30,
12:30, or 14:30, tel. 5885 166, no stop at the Lutheran Cathedral), but I like the "pick you up at the boat and drop you at
your hotel or back on Market Square" efficiency of the 9:30
tour. Buy your ticket on board or at the tourist desk in the
terminal (availability no problem).

▲▲**Lutheran Cathedral**—With its prominent green dome
overlooking the city and harbor, this church is Carl Ludwig
Engel's masterpiece. Open the pew gate and sit to savor neo-

classical nirvana. Finished in 1852, the interior is pure architectural truth. (Open 9:00–18:00, Sunday 12:00–20:00, shorter hours off-season.)

Senate Square—From the top of the steps of the Lutheran Cathedral, study Europe's finest neoclassical square. The Senate building is on your left. The small blue stone building with the slanted mansard roof in the far left corner is from 1757, one of just two pre–Russian conquest buildings remaining in Helsinki. On the right is the university building. Czar Alexander II, a friend of Finland's, is honored by the statue in the square. The huge staircase leading up to the cathedral is a popular meeting and tanning point in Helsinki.

▲▲**Uspensky Russian Orthodox Cathedral**—Hovering above Market Square and facing the Lutheran Cathedral as Russian culture faces Europe's, is a fine icon experience and western Europe's largest Russian Orthodox church (daily 9:30–16:00, except Tuesday 9:30–18:00 and Sunday 12:00–15:00).

▲▲▲**Temppeliaukio Church**—Another great piece of church architecture, this was blasted out of solid rock and capped with a copper-and-skylight dome. It's normally filled with live or recorded music and awestruck visitors. I almost cried. Another form of simple truth, it's impossible to describe. Grab a pew. Gawk upward at a 14-mile-long coil of copper wire. Look at the bull's-eye and ponder God. Forget your camera. Just sit in the middle, ignore the crowds, and be thankful for peace—under your feet is an air-raid shelter that can accommodate 6,000 people. (Open Monday–Saturday 10:00–20:00, Sunday 12:00–13:45 and 15:15–17:45.) To experience the church in action, attend the Lutheran English service (Sunday at 14:00, tel. 494698) or one of the many concerts. You can buy individual slides or the picture book.

▲**Sibelius Monument**—Six hundred stainless steel pipes shimmer over a rock in a park to honor Finland's greatest composer. Notice the face of Sibelius (which the artist was forced to add to silence the critics of this abstract work). Bus #24 stops here (or catch a quick glimpse on the left from the bus) on its way to the open-air folk museum. The 3T tram, which runs more frequently, stops a few blocks away. By the way, music lovers enjoy the English-language tours of the slick new Finnish National Opera (closed in July).

▲**Seurasaari Open-Air Folk Museum**—Inspired by Stockholm's Skansen, also on a lovely island on the edge of town, this is a collection of 100 historic buildings from every corner of Finland. It's wonderfully furnished and gives rushed visitors an opportunity to sample the far reaches of Finland without leaving the capital city. Buy the 10-mk guidebook.

Off-season it's quiet. Just you, log cabins, and birch trees—almost not worth a look. (The park is free, 15 mk to enter the buildings, daily June–August 11:00–17:00; May and September Monday–Friday 9:00–15:00, Saturday and Sunday 11:00–17:00.) In winter, the park is open but the buildings are closed. Ride bus #24 to the end and walk across the quaint footbridge. Call or check the TI for English tour (usually at 11:30 and 15:30) and evening folk-dance schedules (usually Tuesday, Thursday, and Sunday at 19:00, tel. 484712).

For a 10-mk bottomless cup of coffee in a cozy-like-someone's-home setting, stop by the café near the Seurasaari bridge, up the road at Tamminiementie 1 (June–August 11:00–23:00). Great bagels—and Chopin, too.

▲▲**National Museum**—This is a pleasant, easy-to-handle collection (covering Finland's story from A to Z with good English descriptions) in a grand building designed by three of Finland's greatest early architects. While the neoclassical furniture, portraits of Russia's last czars around an impressive throne, and the folk costumes are interesting, the highlight is the Finno-Ugric exhibit downstairs, with a 20-page English guide to help explain the Finns, Estonians, Lapps, Hungarians, and their more obscure Finno-Ugric cousins (15 mk, Tuesday 11:00–20:00, Wednesday–Sunday 11:00–17:00, closed Monday; closes one hour earlier off-season, across the street from the Finlandia Hall, tel. 40501). The museum café has light meals and Finnish treats such as lingonberry juice and reindeer quiche.

Finlandia Hall—Alvar Aalto's most famous building in his native Finland means little to the non-architect without a tour (20 mk, summer only, noon and 14:00, tel. 40241).

▲**Harbor tours**—Several boat companies line Market Square, offering 90-minute, 50-mk cruises around the waterfront nearly every hour 10:00–17:30. The narration is slow-moving and in three languages, but if the weather's good and you're looking for something one step above a snooze in the park, it's a nice break. If they're still in business, try the IHA-Lines Cruises at Market Square—if you eat the equivalent of your fare's worth on board, the ride is free.

▲**Flea Market**—Lately, Hietalahti Market, Finland's biggest flea market, is particularly interesting, with the many Russian and Baltic people hawking whatever they can—from bearskin hats to Soviet wing medals—for a little hard currency (Monday–Saturday 8:00–14:00, summer evenings Monday–Friday 15:30–21:00). If you brake for garage sales, it's well worth the 15-minute walk from the harbor.

Suomenlinna—This "fortified island" is a 20-minute ferry or water-bus ride (18 mk–22 mk round-trip, on the half-hour) from Market Square. The old fort is now a popular park with several museums.

Sauna—Finland's vaporized fountain of youth is the sauna. Public saunas are a dying breed these days, since saunas are standard equipment in nearly every Finnish apartment and home. Your boat or hotel has a sauna. Your youth hostel probably even has one. For a real experience, ask about the Finnish Sauna Society (70 mk, bus #20 for 20 minutes in a park on the waterfront, men-only most nights, Thursday is women's night). For a cheap and easy public sauna, go to the Olympic swimming pool at the Olympic Stadium (10 mk, pool and sauna open 7:00–20:00 except Sunday 9:00–20:00).

Nightlife—Remember that Finland was the first country to give women the vote. The sexes are equal in the bars and on the dance floor. Finns are easily approachable, and tourists are not a headache to the locals (as they are in places like Paris and Munich). While it's easy to make friends, anything alcoholic is very expensive. For the latest on hot night-spots, read the English insert of the *City* magazine that lists the "best" of everything in Helsinki. For very cheap fun, Hietaranta beach is where the local kids hang out (and even skinny-dip) at 22:00 or 23:00. This city is one of Europe's safest after dark.

Sleeping in Helsinki
(4.5 mk = about $1, tel. code from outside of Finland: 358-9)
Sleep Code: **S** = Single, **D** = Double/Twin, **T** = Triple, **Q** = Quad, **b** = bathroom, **CC** = Credit Card (Visa, Master-Card, Amex).

Standard budget hotel doubles start at $100. But there are many special deals, and dorm and hostel alternatives. You have four basic budget options—cheap youth hostels, student dorms turned "summer hotels," plain and basic low-class hotels, or expensive business-class hotels at special summer or weekend clearance sale rates.

Summer (mid-June to mid-August) is "off-season" in Helsinki, as are Friday, Saturday, and Sunday nights the rest of the year. You can arrive in the morning and expect to find a budget room. In the train station next to Track 4 (a pleasant 20-minute walk from your boat, or tram 3B from Silja, bus #13 from Viking, on arrival only) is the **Hotellikeskus** room-finding service (June–August 9:00–19:00, Sunday 10:00–18:00; off-season 10:00–17:00 Monday–Friday only). For 12 mk, they'll book you a bed in the price range of your choice. They know what wild bargains are available. Consider a luxury-hotel clearance deal, which may cost $20 more than the cheapies. Ask about any Helsinki card "specials," which lower prices mid-June to early September and on weekends. Their 12-mk fee is reasonable, but they're happy to do the job over the phone for free. Call from the harbor or Stockholm (tel. 09/171133).

Sleeping in Classy "Real" Hotels

Hotel Anna, plush and very central, is one of the best values in town (Sb-330 mk, Db-430 mk in summer with breakfast and private showers; near Mannerheimintie and Esplanadi, a 15-minute walk from the boat; 1 Annankatu, tel. 616 621, fax 602 664).

Hotel Cumulus Olympia is often about the least-expensive hotel in town (D-365 mk in summer with private showers and breakfast; not so central but on the 3B or #1 tram line at the Sport Hall stop, 2 Lantinen Brahenkatu, tel. 69151, fax 691-5219). Hotels Anna and Olympia both charge 600 mk during business season.

Hotel Arthur, a five-minute walk from the train station and Senate Square, has spacious rooms (Sb-330 mk–395 mk, Db-400 mk–495 mk, CC:VMA, Vuorikatu 19, 00100 Helsinki, tel. 173 441, fax 626 880).

Sleeping in Hostels

Eurohostel is a modern hostel located a block from the Viking terminal or a ten-minute walk from Market Square (S-175 mk, D-230 mk, T-345 mk, including sheets, private lockable closets, and morning sauna; less 15 mk per person with hostel cards, breakfast 25 kr, doubles and triples can be shared with a stranger of the same sex for 115 mk per bed; Linnankatu 9, 00160 Helsinki, tel. 622-0470, fax 655 044). It's packed with facilities including a TV room, laundry room, a members' kitchen with a refrigerator that lets you lock up your caviar and beer, a cheap cafeteria, and plenty of good budget information on travel to Russia or the Baltics.

Kallio Retkeilymaja is cozy, cheery, central, well run, and very cheap (only 35 beds; 50 mk for dorm bed for boys, or a bed in five-bed rooms for girls, sheets-10 mk, lockers, kitchen facilities, closed 10:00–15:00, open June–August; Porthaniankatu 2, tel. 90/7099-2590). From Market Square, take the metro or tram 3T, #1 or #2 to Hakaniemi Square Market.

Olympic Stadium Hostel (Stadionin Retkeilymaja, IYHF) is big, crowded, impersonal, and a last resort. (54 mk per bed in eight- to 12-bed rooms, D-150 mk, sheets-15 mk, 15 mk extra per person with no youth hostel card; open all year, dorm closed daily 10:00–16:00 off-season, tel. 496 071.) Take tram 7A to the Olympic Stadium.

Eating in Helsinki

In Helsinki, Russian food is an interesting option. Most popular, with meals for around 100 mk, are the **Troikka** (good Russian food in a tsarific setting, Caloniukesenkatu 3, tel. 445 229 for reservations), and **Kasakka** (old Russian style, Meritullinkatu 13, tel. 1356-288). Seafood is another local specialty. Many restaurants serve daily lunch specials for around 30 mk to 40 mk.

The **Palace Café**, overlooking the harbor and Market Square above the Palace Hotel, is a good (if a little pricey) place for lunch. **Holvari** serves tasty Finnish food in an art-filled setting (Yrjonkatu 15, tel. 642 394).

Könstan Mölja features an all-you-can-eat lunch for 45 mk on weekdays. This family-run restaurant, decorated with old photos and farming tools, serves Finnish cooking and hearty home-baked Karelian bread (Hietalahdenkatu 14, just a couple blocks from the flea market at the end of Bulevardi).

The Lutheran Cathedral, National Museum, and Academic bookstore all have handy cafés. For a meal with folk music, ask at the tourist office about the dinner show at the **Seurasaari Open-Air Folk Museum.**

The best food values are, of course, the department store cafeterias and a picnic assembled from the colorful stalls on the harbor and nearby bakery. Take advantage of the red-brick indoor market on the edge of the square. At the harbor you'll also find several local fast-food stalls and delicious fresh fish (cooked if you like), explosive little red berries, and sweet carrots. While the open-air market is the most fun, produce is cheaper in large grocery stores. Each open-air market has a popular-with-local-shoppers "tent café."

In the train station, the **Eliel Self-Service** restaurant offers reasonable midday specials in a splendid architectural setting.

Transportation Connections—Helsinki
For train info, call 010-0121 (costs 2 mk plus 4 mk/minute).

Cruising to Stockholm: The Silja and Viking lines sail between Helsinki and Stockholm daily/nightly. (See the beginning of this chapter for details.)

Cruising to Tallinn, Estonia: There are several crossings daily between Helsinki's West Terminal and Tallinn. One-way fares for regular ferries cost $20 (4-hr trip) and the hydrofoil costs $45 (2-hr trip). Specials can be half-price for same-day return trips. Tallink has the most frequent departures (tel. 358/9/228-2177 in Helsinki). The best local information source is the Eurohostel (358/9/622-0470).

NEAR HELSINKI: TURKU, NAANTALI, AND PORVOO
Turku and Naantali get good publicity, but I found these towns a little disappointing. The train ride is nothing special, Turku is a pale shadow of Helsinki, and Naantali is cute, commercial, and offers little (if you've seen or will see Sigtuna, near Stockholm). Porvoo may be for you.

Turku, the historic, old capital of Finland, is a two-hour train ride from Helsinki (10/day, 80 mk, free with Eurail or save 50 percent by getting RR connection with an "open jaws" boat ticket). Turku has a handicraft museum in a cluster of wooden houses (the only part of town to survive a devastating fire in the early 1800s), an old cathedral, and a market square. Viking and Silja boats sail from Turku to Stockholm at 21:30, or 20:00 off-season (the cheap fare saves enough to pay for the train from Helsinki to Turku). Train info tel. 101-0115.

Naantali, a well-preserved medieval town with a quaint harbor, is an easy bus ride from Turku (4/hr, 20 min, 16 mk).

Porvoo, the second-oldest town in Finland, has wooden architecture that dates from the Swedish colonial period. This coastal town can be reached from Helsinki by boat from Market Square or by train (4/hr, 60 min, 74 mk round-trip).

APPENDIX

Let's Talk Telephones

In Europe, card-operated public phones are speedily replacing coin-operated phones. Each country sells telephone cards good for use in its country. In Scandinavia, get a phone card at a post office, newsstand, or tobacco shop. To make a call, pick up the receiver, insert your card in the slot in the phone, dial your number, make your call, then retrieve your card. The price of your call is automatically deducted from your card as you use it. If you have a phone-card phobia, you'll usually find easy-to-use "talk now–pay later" metered phones in post offices. Avoid using hotel-room phones, which are major rip-offs for anything other than local and calling card calls (see below). Incidentally, using directory assistance in Scandinavia costs about the same as telephone sex. Really.

Calling-Card Operators

Calling home from Europe is easy from any type of phone if you have a calling card. From a private phone, just dial the toll-free number to reach the operator. If you're using a public phone, first insert a coin or a Scandinavian phone card. Then dial the operator, who will ask you for your calling-card number and place your call. You'll save money on calls of three minutes or more. When you finish, your coin should be returned (or if using a card, no money should have been deducted). Your bill awaits you at home (one more reason to prolong your vacation). For more information, see the Introduction chapter, Telephones and Mail.

USA Direct Services

Country	AT&T	MCI	Sprint
Denmark	800 100 10	800 100 22	800 108 77
Finland	9800 100 10	9800 102 80	9800 102 84
Norway	800 190 11	800 199 12	800 198 77
Sweden	020 795 611	020 795 922	020 799 011

Dialing Direct

Calling Between Countries: First dial the international access code, then the country code, followed by the area code (if it starts with zero, drop the zero), then the local number.

Calling Long Distance Within a Country: First dial the area code (including its zero), then the local number.

Some of Europe's Exceptions: A few countries lack area codes, such as Denmark, Norway, and France; you still use the same sequence and codes to dial, just skip the area code. In Spain, area codes start with nine instead of zero (just drop or add the nine as you would a zero when calling in other countries).

International Access Codes

When dialing direct, first dial the international access code of the country you're calling from.

Austria:	00	France:	00	Norway:	00
Belgium:	00	Germany:	00	Portugal:	00
Britain:	00	Ireland:	00	Russia:	810
Czech Rep:	00	Italy:	00	Spain:	07
Denmark:	00	Latvia:	00	Sweden:	009
Estonia:	800	Lithuania:	810	Switzerland:	00
Finland:	990	Netherlands:	09	U.S.A./Canada:	011

Country Codes

After you've dialed the international access code, then dial the code of the country you're calling.

Austria:	43	France:	33	Norway:	47
Belgium:	32	Germany:	49	Portugal:	351
Britain:	44	Ireland:	353	Russia:	7
Czech Rep:	42	Italy:	39	Spain:	34
Denmark:	45	Latvia:	371	Sweden:	46
Estonia:	372	Lithuania:	370	Switzerland:	41
Finland:	358	Netherlands:	31	U.S.A./Canada:	1

Public Transportation

You can tour Scandinavia efficiently and enjoyably by train and bus. You even have a few options that drivers don't. If you sleep on the very comfortable Nordic trains, destinations not worth driving to on a short trip become feasible. Add your own Scandinavian highlights. Consider a swing through Finland's eastern lakes district or the scenic ride to Trondheim. I'd go overnight whenever possible on any ride six or more hours long.

Scandinavia: Main Train Lines

The Norway chapter is heavy on fjord scenery (my kind of problem). Fjord country buses, boats, and trains connect, but not without one- to three-hour layovers. "Norway in a Nutshell" is an exception. The Flåm–Bergen boat is a great fjord finale.

Train, Bus, and Boat Connections

Pick up exact schedules as you travel, available free at any tourist office. Some lines make fewer runs or even close in the off-season.

Departures	Daily	Hours
Copenhagen to:		
Amsterdam	2	11
Berlin via Gedser	2	9
Frankfurt/Rhine castles	4	10
Helsingør (ferry to Sweden)	40	.5
Hillerød (Frederiksborg)	40	.5
Louisiana (Helsingør train to Humlebæk)	40	.5
Odense	16	.5
Oslo	4	10
Roskilde	16	.5
Stockholm	6–8	8
Växjö via Alvesta	6	5
Stockholm to:		
Helsinki	2	14
Helsinki to Turku	7	2.5
Kalmar	6	8
		(1-night train)
Oslo	3	7
Turku	2	10
Uppsala	30	1
Växjö to glassworks	TI tour or side trip by bus	
Växjö to Kalmar	9	1.5
Oslo to:		
Åndalsnes	3	6.5
Bergen	4	7–8
Lillehammer	12	2.5
Trondheim	3	7–8

Norway's Mountain and Fjord Country

Lillehammer to Åndalsnes	4	4
Åndalsnes over Trollstigvege to Geiranger Fjord	early each morning	4
Åndalsnes to Ålesund by bus (with each arriving train)	2	.5
Lillehammer to Lom (change at Otta)	3	4
Lom to Sogndal	2	
(bus departures 8:50 and 15:50, summer only)		

Departures	Daily	Hours
Bergen to:		
Ålesund	1	10
Kristiansand	1 (bus)	12
Stavanger	3 (boat)	4
South Norway		
Setesdal Valley, Hovden to:		
Kristiansand	2	5
Kristiansand to:		
Hirtshals, Denmark (by ferry)	4	4
Oslo	6	4–5
Denmark		
Ærø to Copenhagen	5	5
Århus to Odense	16	2
Halsskov–Knudshoved	26	1
Hirtshals to Århus	16	2.5
Odense to Svendborg	16	1
Svendborg to Ærø, (by ferry)	5	1

Numbers and Stumblers

- Europeans write a few of their numbers differently than we do: $1 = 1$, $4 = 4$, $7 = 7$. Learn the difference or miss your train.
- In Europe, dates appear as day/month/year, so Christmas is 25-12-97.
- Commas are decimal points and decimals commas. A dollar and a half is 1,50 and there are 5.280 feet in a mile.
- When pointing, use your whole hand, palm downward.
- When counting with fingers, start with your thumb. If you hold up your first finger to request one item, you'll probably get two.
- What we Americans call the second floor of a building is the first floor in Europe.
- Europeans keep the left "lane" open for passing on escalators and moving sidewalks. Keep to the right.

Metric Conversion (approximate)

1 inch = 25 millimeters   32 degrees F = 0 degrees C
1 foot = 0.3 meter   82 degrees F = about 28 degrees C
1 yard = 0.9 meter   1 ounce = 28 grams
1 mile = 1.6 kilometers   1 kilogram = 2.2 pounds
1 centimeter = 0.4 inch   1 quart = 0.95 liter
1 meter = 39.4 inches   1 square yard = 0.8 square meter
1 kilometer = .62 mile   1 acre = 0.4 hectare

Climate

First line, average daily low temperature; second line, average daily high; third line, days of no rain

	J	F	M	A	M	J	J	A	S	O	N	D
Copenhagen,	28	31	37	44	51	55	54	49	42	35	32	29
DENMARK	36	41	50	61	67	72	69	63	53	43	38	36
	21	23	21	23	22	22	19	22	22	20	20	22
Helsinki,	15	22	31	41	49	58	55	46	37	30	22	17
FINLAND	26	32	43	55	63	71	66	57	45	37	31	27
	20	23	22	23	21	23	19	19	19	19	20	20
Oslo,	20	25	34	43	51	56	53	45	37	29	24	20
NORWAY	32	40	50	62	69	73	69	60	49	37	31	30
	21	24	23	24	22	21	20	22	21	21	21	23
Stockholm,	22	26	32	41	49	55	53	46	39	31	26	23
SWEDEN	31	37	45	57	65	70	66	58	48	38	33	31
	21	24	24	23	23	22	21	22	22	21	22	23

Road Scholar Feedback for
SCANDINAVIA 1997

We're all in the same travelers' school of hard knocks. Your feedback helps us improve this guidebook for future travelers. Please fill this out (attach more info or any tips/favorite discoveries if you like) and send it to us. As thanks for your help, we'll send you our quarterly travel newsletter free for one year. Thanks! **Rick**

I traveled mainly by: ___ Car ___ Train/bus tickets
___ Railpass Other (please list _____)

Number of people traveling together:
___ Solo ___ 2 ___ 3 ___ 4 ___ Over 4 ___ Tour

Ages of traveler/s (including children):

_____

I visited _____countries in _____weeks.

I traveled in: ___ Spring ___ Summer ___ Fall ___ Winter

My daily budget per person (excluding transportation):
___ Under $40 ___ $40–$60 ___ $60–$80 ___ $80–$120
___ over $120 ___ Don't know

Average cost of hotel rooms: Single room $_____
Double room $_____ Other (type _____) $_____

Favorite tip from this book:

_____

Biggest waste of time or money caused by this book:

_____

Other Rick Steves books used for this trip:

_____

Hotel listings from this book should be geared toward places that are:
___Cheaper ___More expensive ___About the same

Of the recommended accommodations/restaurants used, which was:

Best _____

    Why? _____

Worst _____

    Why? _____

I reserved rooms:

___from USA   ___in advance as I traveled

___same day by phone   ___just showed up

Getting rooms in recommended hotels was:

___easy   ___mixed   ___frustrating

Of the sights/experiences/destinations recommended by this book, which was:

Most overrated _____

    Why? _____

Most underrated _____

    Why? _____

Best ways to improve this book:

_____

I'd like a free newsletter subscription:

___ Yes   ___ No   ___ Already on list

_____

Name

_____

Address

_____

City, State, Zip

Please send to:
Europe Through the Back Door,
Box 2009, Edmonds, WA 98020

Faxing Your Hotel Reservation

Most hotel managers know basic "hotel English." Faxing is the preferred method for reserving a room. It's more accurate and cheaper than telephoning and much faster than writing a letter. Use this handy form for your fax. Photocopy and fax away.

One-Page Fax

To: _____ @ _____
          hotel   *fax*

From: _____ @ _____
          name   *fax*

Today's date: ____ /_____ /____
                  day *month* *year*

Dear Hotel _____,

Please make this reservation for me:

Name: _____

Total # of people: _____   # of rooms: _____   # of nights: _____

Arriving: ____ /_____ /____ My time of arrival (24-hr clock): _____
              day *month* *year*   (I will telephone if I will be late)

Departing: ____ /_____ /____
                day *month* *year*

Room(s): Single___ Double___ Twin___ Triple___ Quad___

With: Toilet___ Shower___ Bath___ Sink only___

Special needs: View___ Quiet___ Cheapest Room___

Credit card: Visa___ MasterCard___ American Express___

Card #: _____

Expiration date:_____

Name on card: _____

You may charge me for the first night as a deposit. Please fax or mail me confirmation of my reservation, along with the type of room reserved, the price, and whether the price includes breakfast. Thank you.

_____
Signature

_____
Name

_____
Address

_____
City   *State*   *Zip Code*   *Country*

INDEX

Accommodations, 15–19; *See also* Lodging and restaurants
Ærø, Island of, 53–60
Andersen Hus, Hans Christian, 60–61
Århus, 66–69

Banking, 5–6, 8
Bed and breakfast, 19
Bergen, 105–115
Bog Man of Århus, 67

Camping, 19
Car, rental, 13
Car, vs. train, 11
Copenhagen, 26–52
Costs, trip, 2–3
Crystal, Kingdom of, 148

Demographics, Scandinavia, 22
Denmark, 25–69; Ærø, Island, 53–60; Århus, 66–69; Copenhagen, 26–52; Dragør, 40; Frederiksborg Castle, 50; Helsingør, 51–52; Jutland, 63–69; Kronborg Castle, 51–52; Legoland, 63–66; Louisiana, 50–51; Odense, 60–62; Roskilde, 48–50; Viking Ship Museum, Roskilde, 49–50
Driving in Scandinavia, 13–14

Eating, 19–21
Emigrants, House of, Växjö, 145
Europe Through the Back Door, 9
Exchange rates, 3–4

Ferries: Denmark–Sweden, 52; Norway–Denmark, 47–48, 69, 87, 121–122; Norway–England, 115; Sweden–Finland, 158–162
Finland, 155–172; Helsinki, 156–172; Naantali, 173; Porvoo, 173; Turku, 173
Frederiksborg Castle, 50

Glacier Hike, 99–100
Gota Canal, 153
Grieg's home, Troldhaugen, 110
Gudbrandsdalen, 95–98
Guidebooks, 9–10

Helsingor, 51–52
Helsinki, 156–172
Hillerød, 50
Hostels, 17
Hotels, 17; *See also* Lodging and restaurants

Jelling, 64
Jotunheim country, 98–101
Jutland, 63–69

Kalmar, 149–153
Kronborg Castle, Hamlet, 51–52

Language Barrier, 21–22
Legoland, 63–66
Legolamb, 63
Lodging and restaurants, in Denmark: Ærøskøbing, 58–60; Århus, 68–69; Copenhagen, 41–47; Legoland, 64–66; Odense, 61–62; in Finland: Helsinki, 169–171; in Norway:

Bergen, 111–115; Gud-
brandsdalen, 98; Jotun-
heimen, 100–101;
Kristiansand, 121; Lus-
trafjord, 102; Oslo, 82–87;
Sognefjord, 94–95; in Sweden: Kalmar, 151–152;
Stockholm, 135–139; Växjö,
146–147
Louisiana Museum, modern
art, 50–51

Maps, 10

Norway, 70–122: Aurland, 92,
94–95; Bergen, 105–115;
Eidsvoll, 97; Flåm, 92–93;
Galdhopiggen, Norway's
highest mountain, 99;
Greig's home, Troldhaugen,
110; Gudbrandsdalen, 95–98;
Gudvangen, 92–93; Hardan-
ger Fjord, 117; Jotunheim
country, 98–101; Kris-
tiansand, 120–122; Lillehammer, 95–96; Lom, 97–98;
Lustrafjord, 101–103; Maihaugen Folk Museum,
96–97; Myrdal–Flam train,
91–92; Nigard Glacier Valley, 99–100; Norway in a
Nutshell," 88–95; Oslo,
72–87; Oslo–Bergen train,
87; Roisheim, 100; Setesdal
Valley, 116–122; Sognefjell,
98–99; Sognefjord, 87–94;
Undredal, 93; Urnes Stave
Church, 101; Voss, 93
Norwegian geology, 89

Odense, 60–62
Oland, island of, 150–151
Oslo, 72–87

Philosophy, Back Door, 24

Reservations, hotel, 18; fax
form, 179
Ribe, 64

Setesdal Valley, 116–122
Sightseeing Priorities, 5
Sigtuna, 141
Silja Line, 158–162
Sleep Code, 16–17
Sweden, 123–153: Stockholm,
124–142; Kalmar, 149–153;
Kingdom of Crystal,
148–149; Sigtuna, 141; Upp-
sala, 140–142; Växjö,
144–149

Telephoning, 14–15, 174–176
Tivoli Gardens, 36
Tourist information, 8–9
Transportation, 11–14,
174–177

Uppsala, 140–141

Växjö, 144–148
Viking Line, 158–162
Viking ships, 49–50, 79

Weather, when to go, 4–5,
178

Youth hostels, 17

Rick Steves' Phrase Books

Unlike other phrase books and dictionaries on the market, my well-tested phrases and key words cover every situation a traveler is likely to encounter. With these books you'll laugh with your cabby, disarm street thieves with insults, and charm new European friends.

Each book in the series is 4" x 6", with maps.

RICK STEVES' FRENCH PHRASE BOOK & DICTIONARY
U.S. $5.95/Canada $8.50

RICK STEVES' GERMAN PHRASE BOOK & DICTIONARY
U.S. $5.95/Canada $8.50

RICK STEVES' ITALIAN PHRASE BOOK & DICTIONARY
U.S. $5.95/Canada $8.50

RICK STEVES' SPANISH & PORTUGUESE PHRASE BOOK & DICTIONARY
U.S. $7.95/Canada $11.25

RICK STEVES' FRENCH, ITALIAN & GERMAN PHRASE BOOK & DICTIONARY
U.S. $7.95/Canada $11.25

Other Books from John Muir Publications

Rick Steves' Books

Asia Through the Back Door, $17.95
Europe 101: History and Art for the Traveler, $17.95
Mona Winks: Self-Guided Tours of Europe's Top Museums, $18.95
Rick Steves' Baltics & Russia, $9.95
Rick Steves' Europe, $18.95
Rick Steves' France, Belgium & the Netherlands, $15.95
Rick Steves' Germany, Austria & Switzerland, $14.95
Rick Steves' Great Britain & Ireland, $15.95
Rick Steves' Italy, $13.95
Rick Steves' Scandinavia, $13.95
Rick Steves' Spain & Portugal, $13.95
Rick Steves' Europe Through the Back Door, $19.95
Rick Steves' French Phrase Book, $5.95
Rick Steves' German Phrase Book, $5.95
Rick Steves' Italian Phrase Book, $5.95
Rick Steves' Spanish & Portugese Phrase Book, $7.95
Rick Steves' French/German/Italian Phrase Book, $7.95

A Natural Destination Series

Belize: A Natural Destination, $16.95
Costa Rica: A Natural Destination, $18.95
Guatemala: A Natural Destination, $16.95

City•Smart™ Guidebook Series

City•Smart Guidebook: Cleveland, $14.95
City•Smart Guidebook: Denver, $14.95
City•Smart Guidebook: Minneapolis/St. Paul, $14.95
City•Smart Guidebook: Nashville, $14.95
City•Smart Guidebook: Portland, $14.95
City•Smart Guidebook: Tampa/St. Petersburg, $14.95

Travel+Smart™ Trip Planners

American Southwest Travel+Smart Trip Planner, $14.95
Colorado Travel+Smart Trip Planner, $14.95
Eastern Canada Travel+Smart Trip Planner, $15.95
Florida Gulf Coast Travel+Smart Trip Planner, $14.95
Hawaii Travel+Smart Trip Planner, $14.95
Kentucky/Tennessee Travel+Smart Trip Planner, $14.95
Minnesota/Wisconsin Travel+Smart Trip Planner, $14.95
New England Travel+Smart Trip Planner, $14.95
Northern California Travel+Smart Trip Planner, $15.95
Pacific Northwest Travel+Smart Trip Planner, $14.95

Other Terrific Travel Titles

The 100 Best Small Art Towns in America, $15.95
The Big Book of Adventure Travel, $17.95

Indian America: A Traveler's Companion, $18.95
The People's Guide to Mexico, $19.95
Ranch Vacations: The Complete Guide to Guest and Resort, Fly-Fishing, and Cross-Country Skiing Ranches, $22.95
Understanding Europeans, $14.95
Undiscovered Islands of the Caribbean, $16.95
Watch It Made in the U.S.A.: A Visitor's Guide to the Companies that Make Your Favorite Products, $16.95
The World Awaits, $16.95
The Birder's Guide to Bed and Breakfasts: U.S. and Canada, $17.95

Automotive Titles

The Greaseless Guide to Car Care, $19.95
How to Keep Your Subaru Alive, $21.95
How to Keep Your Toyota Pickup Alive, $21.95
How to Keep Your VW Alive, $25

Ordering Information

Please check your local bookstore for our books, or call **1-800-888-7504** to order direct and to receive a complete catalog. A shipping charge will be added to your order total.

Send all inquiries to:
John Muir Publications
P.O. Box 613
Santa Fe, NM 87504